THE POLITICS OF INNOCENCE

The Politics of Innocence

How Wrongful Convictions Shape Public Opinion

Robert J. Norris,
William D. Hicks, *and*
Kevin J. Mullinix

NEW YORK UNIVERSITY PRESS
New York

NEW YORK UNIVERSITY PRESS
New York
www.nyupress.org

Please contact the Library of Congress for Cataloging-in-Publication data.

ISBN: 9781479815951 (hardback)
ISBN: 9781479815968 (paperback)
ISBN: 9781479816033 (library ebook)
ISBN: 9781479815982 (consumer ebook)

New York University Press books are printed on acid-free paper, and their binding materials are chosen for strength and durability. We strive to use environmentally responsible suppliers and materials to the greatest extent possible in publishing our books.

Manufactured in the United States of America

10 9 8 7 6 5 4 3 2 1

Also available as an ebook

For the many victims of criminal injustice—exonerees, crime victims, families, and the many others who are harmed by wrongful convictions
May this work be a resource in the fight for change

CONTENTS

AUTHORS' NOTE AND SENSITIVE MATERIAL WARNING

This book is not about wrongful convictions per se but about the political dimensions of the advocacy movement that revolves around them. In part, we analyze various ways of communicating information about wrongful convictions and how they might influence state policy adoption and public opinion. Such information is common in public discourse—in the news media and in all forms of popular culture, from books to film to podcasts (and everything in between). We suspect that many readers have heard this discourse, whether it came in the form of factual information about how many innocent people are unjustly imprisoned or a single tragic story about an innocent person erroneously convicted for a crime they did not commit. We believe it is important to engage in authentic discussions about these matters and empirically analyze what effects they might have on our policies, practices, and beliefs. As such, throughout the book, we describe both real and hypothetical criminal cases that involve material that might be upsetting and/or traumatic for some readers, including homicide, sexual violence, and violence against children.

We also want to emphasize at the outset that we recognize the immense and widespread damage caused by wrongful convictions. In our discussions throughout this book, we tend to emphasize the harms for exonerees themselves. However, a wrongful conviction creates an immeasurable number of ripples. Exonerees are at the forefront, of course, as the most obvious victims, but they are not alone. Their families, communities, and social networks are harmed; the original crime victim(s) and members of their network(s) are harmed; lawyers, judges, and juries might be harmed; actual offenders may remain loose to commit additional crimes and claim new victims. Despite our specific focus, we encourage readers to consider broadly the effects of wrongful convictions and consult the many wonderful resources—scholarly and otherwise—that help us understand the various dimensions of errors in the criminal legal system.

Introduction

The Politics of Innocence

On September 25, 1983, Ronnie Buie contacted the police in Red Springs, North Carolina, a town of about thirty-five hundred people. His eleven-year-old daughter, Sabrina, had gone missing. Her body was found the next day in a nearby soybean field. She had been raped and suffocated with her own underwear.[1]

Some of Sabrina's clothing was found in a field near her body. Other pieces of evidence, including more clothing, a cigarette butt, beer cans, and a bloody piece of plywood, were found in another soybean field near a local grocery store. Police believed that Sabrina was attacked in the second field before her body was dragged to the first one where she was found.

Police searched for anyone from out of town who might have had contact with Sabrina, and nineteen-year-old Henry McCollum fit the bill. In town from New Jersey to visit his mother, McCollum was interviewed by police just two days later. He said that he had seen Sabrina near the grocery store on September 24, the day before she was reported missing, but denied being involved in the attack.

Police soon learned of a rumor at the local high school that McCollum was involved in the crime. They took him into custody and questioned him for more than four hours, during which they fed him information about the crime. McCollum—who was intellectually challenged, with an IQ that tested as low as 51—eventually confessed to the crime.[2] He said that on September 23, he and four other teenagers took Sabrina to a field where they took turns raping her before they killed her.

One of the others implicated by McCollum's confession was his fifteen-year-old half brother, Leon Brown, who arrived at the station while McCollum was still being interrogated. Shortly after McCollum

1

signed his confession, Brown—also intellectually challenged, with an IQ as low as 49—offered his own confession.

On September 29, 1983, McCollum and Brown were formally arrested on rape and capital murder charges.[3] They went to trial a year later, in October 1984. Their confessions were the crux of the state's case against them, but the prosecution also had a seventeen-year-old informant who claimed to have heard the young men brag about having sex with Sabrina and admit to killing her. Interestingly, on cross-examination, the informant admitted that he had been interviewed by police three times before the arrests and never implicated either McCollum or Brown. There was no other physical evidence linking them to the crime, and fingerprints from the beer cans did not match either of them.

Despite the limited evidence, both McCollum and Brown were convicted on October 25, 1984, and sentenced to death. Their convictions were vacated in 1988, but both were convicted a second time. McCollum was again sentenced to death in 1991, while Brown was convicted only of rape (but not murder) and sentenced to life in prison in 1992.

For years, both men maintained their innocence. Upon reinvestigation, their lawyers discovered that prior to their original trial, police had asked the North Carolina State Bureau of Investigation to compare the fingerprints from the beer cans to those of a man named Roscoe Artis. Artis had been convicted and sentenced to death in 1984 for raping and strangling a woman in Red Springs just weeks after Sabrina Buie was attacked. The attorneys found no records that the comparison was ever done, and there was no indication that the police request to do so was ever disclosed to McCollum's and Brown's lawyers. Then, in 2004, McCollum requested that DNA from the cigarette butt be tested. It was, and results showed that it matched neither McCollum nor Brown.

In 2010, Brown's attorneys requested that the case be investigated by the North Carolina Innocence Inquiry Commission, a legislatively established agency that investigates and evaluates post-conviction claims of factual innocence.[4] The DNA profile from the cigarette was run through the state database, and the results matched Roscoe Artis.

The defense also uncovered Artis's history of violent sexual assaults, including at least one in which the victim was suffocated with an object shoved down her throat. Additionally, they discovered that while on death row, Artis told another inmate about the Sabrina Buie case. He reportedly knew many details about the incident and said that McCollum and Brown were innocent. Lastly, they discovered that the prosecution's original informant was given a polygraph before the original trial, and his statements about knowing nothing of the crime were deemed truthful; this information was never disclosed to the defense.

Finally, in August 2014, lawyers requested that McCollum's and Brown's convictions be vacated and their charges dismissed. The motion was granted, and they were released on September 2, 2014, after more than thirty years of incarceration. They were pardoned by Governor Pat McCrory of North Carolina in June 2015 and were each compensated $750,000 by the state in September 2015. McCollum and Brown also pursued a civil rights lawsuit, and in May 2021, a federal jury awarded them $31 million each in compensatory damages—$1 million for each year they were incarcerated—and $13 million in punitive damages. Others named in the lawsuit—the town of Red Springs and the Robeson County Sheriff's Office—settled their parts of the cases for $1 million and $9 million, respectively.[5]

A Growing Reform Movement

The McCollum-Brown case is captivating—a heartbreaking tragedy followed by a gross miscarriage of justice. For three decades, two innocent men languished in prison, one under threat of a state-sanctioned execution, while the victim's loved ones believed justice had been served for those who were responsible. But it is not an isolated event; stories like this one are now common, though how common, exactly, is a matter of debate. It is difficult, perhaps impossible, to accurately estimate the rate at which wrongful convictions occur. That precise rate is, as the law professor and leading innocence scholar Samuel Gross has written, "not merely unknown but unknowable."[6] Still, a number of scholars have tried to estimate the rate of wrongful convictions, and, although estimates vary by measurement strategy, the most empirically sound suggest a wrongful conviction rate of about 3 to 6 percent among subsets of felonies.[7]

While exact numbers are elusive, we know with certainty that legal systems can and do convict the innocent with some regularity. In the United States, since 1989, more than three thousand people have been exonerated after being wrongly convicted of crimes they did not commit. This figure is not representative of all exonerations, let alone all (or even most) wrongful convictions.[8] Rather, it represents merely the "tip of the iceberg of a much more deeply flawed justice system," one in which factual errors may well number in the tens of thousands each year.[9]

Exact figures notwithstanding, every wrongful conviction represents a tragic injustice. Like the McCollum-Brown case, each one tells a story of lives upended by a criminal legal system gone awry. It is critical to recognize that the damage is not restricted only to the wrongly convicted individuals but encompasses the many others who become entangled in what the sociologists Saundra Westervelt and Kimberly Cook have called the "web of impact."[10] As Westervelt said during a 2014 panel, "When someone is wrongfully convicted, that does not just impact one person. It impacts the victims in the case. It impacts the families of all involved. It impacts the attorneys."[11] In short, the harms generated by wrongful convictions are vast, generating widespread "circles of harm."[12]

The growing number of exonerations, our increasing knowledge of what can derail the criminal legal process (and how we might improve it to reduce such issues), and our understanding of the harms caused by wrongful convictions convey a troubling message about the risk of factual errors in the criminal legal system. In recent decades, both research and advocacy revolving around wrongful convictions have grown, leading to the emergence of a widespread *innocence movement*.[13] Dozens of nonprofit organizations now exist across the United States (and globally) that work to overturn wrongful convictions, advocate for policy reforms, and educate policy makers and the public about systemic fallacies and failures. News media and popular culture increasingly feature stories that concern inaccuracies and associated problems in the justice system. For example, several scholars have documented the rise in media coverage dedicated to wrongful convictions and the emergence of an "innocence frame" in criminal justice rhetoric, particularly around the death penalty.[14] In addition, wrongful and other questionable convictions have been the subject of fiction and nonfiction bestsellers and the topic of highly popular films, shows, and podcasts.[15] The innocence movement has also stretched beyond casework and public discourse, and made its way onto the policy agenda. A variety of reforms have been enacted nationwide to address wrongful convictions both before and after they occur. All fifty states have enacted some type of innocence-related policy reform, and changes also have been implemented at the federal and local levels.[16]

The long-term implications of the innocence movement are yet unknown, but it has undoubtedly influenced how we think about, discuss, and practice criminal justice in the United States. In fact, legal commentators have referred to the movement as a "revolution" and "the most dramatic development in the criminal justice world since the Warren Court's due process revolution of the 1960s."[17] Some have gone so far as to refer to innocence as the "new civil rights movement."[18] While such claims may involve overstatements—one of the authors of this book has suggested that the movement is more *revelation* than *revolution*[19]— the innocence movement has, at the very least, involved the spread of "innocence consciousness" in the United States, and the effects have been real.[20]

One particularly interesting element of the innocence movement is its seemingly broad appeal. On the surface, it might appear to be a bipartisan issue. This is an intuitive notion; preventing the wrongful conviction of the innocent and ensuring the apprehension of guilty offenders seems neither controversial nor ideological. Further, the movement is widespread, with exonerations and policy reforms having occurred in every state. Wrongful convictions represent all-around errors—an innocent civilian is arrested, charged, convicted, and punished; the actual offender often escapes apprehension and remains free to potentially commit more crimes and claim additional victims; and the victim(s), their survivors, and community members go about their lives as best they can believing that their offender was captured (and then relive their trauma if and when the error is discovered).[21] As such, the law professor and cofounder of the Wisconsin Innocence Project Keith Findley has argued that the innocence movement merges both the crime control and due process perspectives, stating "that those goals are not inherently contradictory, but rather are quite complementary."[22]

Findley is right, of course, insofar as no reasonable person would advocate for the conviction of the innocent at the expense of capturing the guilty. There is, however, a political dimension to the innocence movement that remains largely underappreciated. In this book, we explore what we call the *politics of innocence*. Using a variety of data and analyses, we show that politics and ideology play a critical role in how state lawmakers and the public respond to wrongful convictions.

Overview of the Book

Elements of the innocence movement's agenda may very well appeal to people across a wide spectrum of ideological preferences; yet there are political mechanisms underlying the movement's successes and failures, and these issues have rarely been examined with empirical rigor. In the following chapters, we explore the political and ideological dimensions of wrongful convictions in two domains: state policy reform and public opinion.[23]

First, in chapter 1, we provide an overview of the innocence movement. We briefly discuss the history of wrongful convictions and related advocacy efforts, with a particular focus on the modern era. We summarize what we know and what we do not know—what exonerations look like, how often wrongful convictions may occur, and the state of the innocence advocacy network—to provide important context for the analyses presented in later chapters.

In chapter 2, we shift our focus to state policy reforms. We describe the key areas of reform that are included in our analysis, which are five priority areas widely advocated by the innocence movement and tracked by the Innocence Project: (1) eyewitness identification reform, (2) recording of custodial interrogations, (3) preservation of biological evidence, (4) access to post-conviction DNA testing, and (5) exoneree compensation statutes. We then ask why some states are seemingly more responsive to wrongful convictions vis-à-vis policy changes. Using an original data set that combines various sources of criminal justice and political data, we analyze the adoption of state-level policies over time from 1989 through 2018, or the first "thirty years of innocence."[24] Our arguments are grounded in the theory of *dynamic representation*, which suggests, in part, that lawmakers may adapt their policy positions in response to changing public opinion. Consistent with this theory, we find that the mass public's liberalism—an ideological dimension of opinion—influences policy adoption but that the effect of public opinion is contingent on the electoral vulnerability of state lawmakers. We also find that the presence of innocence advocacy organizations and the number of exonerations affect the adoption of such laws at the state level.

Expanding on our finding that public opinion matters for state policy adoption—and keeping in mind the increasing attention to wrongful convictions in news media and popular culture—the next chapters shift our focus to the political dynamics that shape public opinion in this space.

In chapter 3, we use original survey data to examine the public's level of awareness of wrongful convictions, its sources of information about them, and its beliefs about the rate and types of errors that occur in the criminal legal system. We also analyze the characteristics of people who are most and least aware of the issue, finding that people's levels of awareness and beliefs about errors differ dramatically by their ideology and interest in politics.

In chapter 4, we use both observational and experimental survey data to explore the effects of wrongful conviction information on public opinion. Here, we focus on the importance of political communication. We draw on *framing theory*, which examines the ways in which information is communicated and how different presentations of information shape how people conceptualize and think about issues. We then test the effects of two different approaches to framing information about wrongful convictions: factual information about numbers of exonerations (a *thematic frame*) and a narrative about a single wrongful conviction case (an *episodic frame*). We analyze the effects of these frames on the public's support for the death penalty, trust in the justice system, and trust in police. Our findings show that information about wrongful convictions has the power to substantially change people's attitudes about criminal justice issues but that the effects depend on how that information is framed. Further, we examine whether the effects of wrongful conviction information are contingent on people's political ideology. In doing so, we identify communication strategies that effectively alter attitudes for different audiences, which has implications for policy reform and political mobilization.

Chapter 5 includes our final set of analyses, in which we explore people's support for policy reforms, including police investigatory reforms and exoneree compensation, and highlight the influence of political ideology on support for such policies. Beyond ideology, we isolate specific political communication strategies that shift attitudes toward policy reform. In addition to framing theory, we draw on research on *priming* to examine what types of considerations need to be activated (or *primed*) to most effectively garner support for such reforms. We find not only that a wrongful conviction narrative is effective at increasing policy support but also that priming people to think about their trust in police and the financial costs associated with wrongful convictions also heightens their support for reform.

Finally, we conclude the book with a discussion of our work and its potential implications for the innocence movement going forward. The movement is evolving as it continues to grow and expand into new territory; we are entering what one innocence advocate has described as "Innocence 2.0."[25] We consider the importance of strategic political messaging for advocates and policy makers and offer some thoughts on what may be the future of the innocence movement.

Ultimately, our key argument throughout the book is a simple yet important one: despite the popularity and broad appeal of the innocence movement, politics matter. The research we present in the following chapters shows that state governments are more responsive to wrongful conviction reform efforts when public opinion trends in a liberal direction. Further, we show that relative to conservatives, liberals believe that wrongful convictions occur more frequently, are more aware of the problems surrounding them, and are more supportive of policy reforms designed to reduce them. However, these divisions hardly make this issue stagnant; the wrongful conviction issue is not *strictly* a political one. Yes, ideology matters, but it is not insurmountable. Rather, we present what we find to be compelling evidence regarding the power of information about wrongful convictions to shift public opinion. Importantly, we demonstrate the effectiveness of political communication to garner support for policy reforms and show that it is often influential for liberals and conservatives alike. These findings regarding the capacity of various communication strategies to alter citizens' attitudes toward the criminal legal system in meaningful ways is vital, both for other scholars and for advocates working in the trenches to advance reforms and pursue justice.

1

The Innocence Movement in the United States

Two crimes, unrelated in every way—separated, in fact, by more than seven years and seven hundred miles—together became foundational pieces of a twenty-first-century movement to reform the criminal legal system.

On July 9, 1977, Cathleen Crowell was on the side of the road in a Chicago suburb when a police officer found her.[1] The sixteen-year-old Crowell wore dirty clothes and was crying. She told the officer that when she left her job at a nearby mall, she was approached by a car with three men. According to her report, two of the men jumped out and threw her in the backseat. One of them got in next to her, stripped her clothes off, raped her, and carved letters into her stomach with a broken beer bottle.

Crowell was taken to a hospital, where medical staff performed a rape examination. Her underwear contained what appeared to be a seminal stain and was preserved as evidence, along with several pubic hairs and a vaginal swab. She had scratches on her stomach, but the letters were not legible.

Days later, Crowell worked with police to develop a sketch of the rapist. Several days after that, she identified Gary Dotson in a photographic lineup, or photo array. Police arrested Dotson the next morning, and Crowell picked him out of a live, in-person lineup.

Dotson went to trial in May 1979. Crowell testified and identified him in court as her attacker. The prosecution also called Timothy Dixon, a forensic analyst for the state police, who made a series of false or misleading statements regarding the biological evidence. The prosecutor, Raymond Garza, also made several misleading statements that were challenged by Dotson's public defender, Paul Foxgrover. The objections were overruled. Despite a series of inconsistencies, Dotson was convicted of rape and aggravated kidnapping and sentenced to twenty-five to fifty years.

Several years later, the now-married Cathleen Crowell Webb confessed to her pastor that she had concocted the story out of fear that she was pregnant from her then-boyfriend, David Bierne. They contacted a lawyer, and Dotson filed a motion for a new trial. The motion was denied, and the Prisoner Review Board denied clemency, but Governor James Thompson of Illinois commuted Dotson's sentence to time served. He was rearrested twice in 1987 and 1988 for other incidents unrelated to the Webb case.[2] Despite Dotson's other troubles, tests of a semen sample from Webb's underwear revealed that the sperm could not have come from Dotson but could have come from Bierne, her old boyfriend. Dotson was ordered a new trial, but the prosecution decided not to prosecute based on the new evidence. His conviction was overturned on August 14, 1989.

Gary Dotson is often referenced as the first DNA-based exoneration in the United States. He was, however, the second person to be exonerated that year with the assistance of DNA testing.

In the midst of Dotson's horrific ordeal in Illinois, David Vasquez was subjected to wrongful conviction and incarceration in Virginia.[3] On January 23, 1984, Carolyn Jean Hamm was raped and murdered in her Arlington home. She was found days later, nude, her hands bound with a blind cord. She had been hanged.

A neighbor reported seeing Vasquez in the neighborhood on the night of the crime. She described him as "creepy" and said she had previously seen him watching Hamm sunbathing in her yard. Another neighbor later reported seeing Vasquez in the neighborhood and said he was acting strange.

Police found Vasquez at the fast-food restaurant where he worked in Manassas, Virginia, about thirty miles west of Arlington. He was thirty-eight years old and had an IQ below 70. Police interrogated Vasquez for several hours. He first denied being in Arlington on the night of crime. When investigators told him that his fingerprints were found in Hamm's home, he said he may have been there. He did not know how he would have gotten there, as he did not drive.

Vasquez then said he had sex with Hamm and was asked what he used to tie her hands.

"The ropes," he said.

Investigators told him that was not it.

He then said he used his belt. Police again denied him.

"A coat hanger?" he asked.

"No, it wasn't a coat hanger," one officer said. "Remember cutting the venetian blind cord?"

Vasquez agreed it was a thin rope and proceeded to say that he stabbed Hamm. The officer told him that was incorrect and that she was hanged. Vasquez again agreed.

Because police had not given Vasquez his *Miranda* warnings, they interrogated him again. He again denied involvement but eventually said that he had "horrible dreams" about participating in the crime. He was charged with murder, rape, and burglary. The next day, he signed a *Miranda* waiver and gave another description of the dreams he had; this time, the statement was tape-recorded.

A forensic test of the semen recovered from the victim revealed that Vasquez had the wrong blood type and could not have been its source. Still, the prosecution pressed forward, assuming that Vasquez had an accomplice. On the day before the trial, Vasquez agreed to an *Alford* plea, which allowed him to maintain his innocence but accept that a jury might find him guilty and thus accept the conviction.[4] He was sentenced to twenty years in prison.

Three years later, while Vasquez was incarcerated, a series of three very similar crimes occurred, including one in the same Arlington neighborhood where Hamm was murdered. Police initially assumed that the crime was committed by Vasquez's accomplice. Vasquez was offered leniency if he would name the other attacker, but he refused and maintained his innocence.

Detective Joe Horgas wondered if Vasquez might be innocent and began checking criminal records for men who may have been incarcerated during the three-year period when no crimes occurred. He discovered a man named Timothy Spencer, who had been arrested in 1984, was released to a halfway house in 1987, and was signed out of the house during the times of all three murders. Spencer provided DNA samples, which matched the three 1987 crimes, and he was convicted and sentenced to death in July 1988.

The "overwhelming circumstantial evidence [suggested] that Spencer had killed [Hamm]" in 1984.[5] But there was not enough DNA from that case to test, so Vasquez could not pursue exoneration through the courts. He did, however, apply for a pardon, which was granted by Governor Gerald Baliles of Virginia on January 4, 1989, and Vasquez's case is typically considered a DNA exoneration by the leading organizations in the field, making it the first DNA-based exoneration in the United States.

Although there was no way to know it at the time, Vasquez's and Dotson's cases would be key pieces in what would ultimately become the innocence movement. In this chapter, we provide a brief history of the movement and an overview of what it currently entails. We then discuss the political dimensions of the innocence movement, setting the stage for the detailed analyses in the chapters that follow.

The Beginning of an Era

David Vasquez and Gary Dotson certainly were not the first individuals in the United States to be wrongly convicted and exonerated. That distinction is usually given to Stephen and Jesse Boorn, whose case predates the discovery of the "DNA fingerprint" by almost two centuries.[6] The Boorn brothers were convicted of killing their brother-in-law, Russell Colvin, in Vermont in 1819. Colvin had gone missing seven years earlier, and after a strange series of events—the supposed appearance of a ghost in their uncle's dreams, a mysterious barn fire, and a dog digging up bones that were initially said to be human but later determined to be of animal origin—the Boorns were arrested. Jesse's cellmate became an informant, claiming that Jesse admitted to the crime. Faced with possible death sentences, both brothers confessed and were convicted. Through good fortune, a traveler in New York heard about the convictions and knew a man named Russell Colvin who was very much alive. Colvin returned to Vermont, and the return of this "murder victim" ultimately led to the Boorns' exoneration.

Many other miscarriages of justice occurred during the nineteenth and early twentieth centuries, some of which were documented in the first scholarly treatise on wrongful convictions, *Convicting the Innocent*, penned by the Yale law professor Edwin Borchard in 1932.[7] In the ensuing decades, a number of other jurists and popular writers followed Borchard's model. Indeed, throughout the twentieth century, while many cases of questionable conviction certainly remained hidden, a number of others were covered widely. For instance, the case of Nicola Sacco and Bartolomeo Vanzetti, while not typically considered a wrongful conviction in the traditional sense, captured the public imagination in the United States and abroad. Their executions sparked outcry in the media and among celebrities and the general public alike. Decades later, Erle Stanley Gardner, a lawyer and popular author who created the well-known fictional detective Perry Mason assembled a team of investigators to examine real-life cases. His *Court of Last Resort* was credited with exonerating at least eighteen people and was popularized in an award-winning book and television series in the 1950s. And the wrongful conviction of the rising boxing star Rubin "Hurricane" Carter became a cause célèbre in the 1960s, including the involvement of pop-culture icons such as Muhammad Ali and Bob Dylan.[8]

Yet, despite the regular occurrence of wrongful convictions and the coverage they generated, momentum was never sustained until the 1980s and 1990s. There are a number of reasons for this, including the establishment of organizational foundations for an advocacy movement, the involvement of zealous advocates and cause lawyers, and the development of research and scholarship on wrongful convictions. But perhaps the most crucial element was the development of DNA technology and its proliferation in the legal system.[9]

DNA and Wrongful Convictions

In many early exoneration cases, like that of Rubin Carter, reasonable and sound analyses support the conclusion of grave miscarriages of justice. Yet doubt always lingered; room remained for skepticism about whether a wrongful conviction had occurred. Was the person *actually innocent*?

Such doubts were probably indicative of generally high levels of institutional confidence in the criminal legal system and its actors. Even in the 1980s, high-ranking officials questioned the very existence of wrongful convictions. Perhaps most tellingly, Edwin Meese, the United States attorney general under President Ronald Reagan, thought the notion of an innocent *suspect* was "contradictory," let alone a wrongful *conviction*. "If a person is innocent of a crime," Meese said in an interview about the importance of *Miranda*, "then he is not a suspect."[10]

To a degree, some skepticism about wrongful convictions is understandable. Short of an alleged murder victim turning up alive, how could we ever truly know that anyone is actually innocent? Thus was the potential power of DNA.

Although the first use of forensic DNA testing in a criminal case in England led to the release of an innocent suspect and the capture of the guilty party, in the United States, it was initially marketed almost exclusively to law enforcement as a pre-conviction tool to ensure the capture and punishment of guilty offenders.[11] However, the Vasquez and Dotson exonerations highlighted the benefits of DNA for the discovery and remediation of errors after the fact. Post-conviction DNA testing received another boost in 1993 when Kirk Bloodsworth, convicted and initially sent to death row for the rape and murder of a nine-year-old girl in Maryland, became the first person in the United States to be exonerated through DNA after receiving a death sentence.[12]

For innocence advocates, these early DNA exonerations helped overcome some of the skepticism around wrongful convictions. This is not to say that there was no uncertainty in reaction to DNA exonerations. Bloodsworth, for example, faced stigma from his community that rivaled what others returning from incarceration face, including those on probation, parole, and supervised release.[13] However, DNA exonerations provided a scientific basis for the argument that the criminal legal system does, with little doubt, make factual errors and wrongfully punish the innocent.

This shift in the framing of DNA—from a pre-conviction tool for law enforcement to catch the guilty to a post-conviction one to uncover prior injustices—expanded our understanding of the immense power of DNA evidence in the legal system and ushered in a new era of forensic analysis.[14] Techniques related to the collection, handling, testing, and interpretation of DNA evidence developed throughout the 1990s. Forensics were thrust into the media and public spotlight during the murder trial of O. J. Simpson in 1995, a case that had implications for the handling of biological evidence.[15] Around that same time, DNA exonerations caught the attention of US Attorney General Janet Reno, who tasked the National Institute of Justice with producing a report on the topic in 1996.[16]

As exonerations piled up and coverage spread, the network of advocates grew, culminating in the establishment of the Innocence Network in 2004. The first members were officially admitted in 2005, and as of this writing, there are more than sixty-five member organizations in the United States and abroad.[17]

The Innocence Movement

Since the inception of the Innocence Network, the innocence movement arguably has grown into a social movement. At the very least, it is undoubtedly a widespread legal reform movement aimed at improving criminal legal systems in the United States and abroad.[18] The movement comprises people and organizations formally associated with the Innocence Network, as well as other non-Network organizations, lawyers, students, journalists, scholars, criminal justice professionals, policy makers, and more.[19] Generally speaking, this movement has three broad goals: exonerating the innocent, reforming the system, and educating policy makers and the public.

Exonerations

The main goal for many innocence advocates is to help free the innocent from their unjust punishments. This is no easy task. While legal systems in the United States are designed, in theory, to promote fair procedures, factual outcomes remain probabilistic under the best of circumstances. That is, convictions at trial do not require *absolute certainty* but rather proof *beyond a reasonable doubt*, so even if the adversarial criminal process were to function exactly as intended, there would probably be factual errors made (though, hopefully, kept to a minimum). And, importantly, that full adversarial process rarely plays out. Despite the drama and suspense of criminal trials in films and on television, the overwhelming majority of criminal convictions in the United States are not secured through trials but via pleas. Indeed, although the Sixth Amendment includes a defendant's right to a trial, few criminal defendants reach that phase. In most states, pleas account for 90 percent or more of convictions; in recent years, approximately 98 percent of convictions in federal court were the result of pleas rather than trials.[20]

Regardless of the mechanism that generates convictions (plea or trial), appellate and post-conviction review systems are designed mostly to catch procedural flaws rather than factual ones.[21] For those who are unfortunate enough to be on the wrong end of a wrongful conviction, this often means limited opportunities to establish their innocence after conviction. In a review of post-conviction new-evidence statutes, the law professor and director of the California Innocence Project, Justin Brooks, and colleagues summarized the issue well when they wrote, "The constitution only requires fair trials, not ones that get the right result."[22]

Despite the many challenges in securing exonerations, innocence advocates have had an impressive degree of success. There is no complete catalog of known wrongful convictions maintained by any official agency or governmental entity. Instead, most scholars now rely on the National Registry of Exonerations (NRE), which attempts to track known exonerations in the United States since 1989. Established as a joint project between the University of Michigan Law School and Northwestern University School of Law's Center on Wrongful Convictions, the NRE launched in May 2012 with nine hundred cases. As of this writing, its database includes more than three thousand exonerations.[23]

Mapping the NRE cases shows the rise in exonerations over time. In 1989, the start of the modern era of wrongful conviction work as marked by the first DNA exonerations, there were 24 exonerations; in 2019 alone, there were 147. The number of exonerations per year is presented in figure 1.1. As the figure makes clear, the pattern has generally been toward an increasing number of exonerations, although the number has flattened as of late. Still, since 2014, there have been an average of approximately 162 exonerations per year, or more than three per week.[24]

Of the first 3,180 exonerees captured in the NRE database, approximately half are Black, 33 percent are white, and about 12 percent are Hispanic.[25] The overwhelming majority—more than 90 percent—are men. Exonerations have occurred in every state and the District of Columbia, although the four leading states—Illinois, Texas, New York, and California—account for almost half of all exonerations in the US.[26]

The NRE is the best available data set on exonerations and provides useful insights into errors in the criminal legal system, but it comes with several caveats. The NRE utilizes a definition of exoneration that relies on an official ruling or other authoritative action that is based on evidence of innocence and relieved the individual of consequences

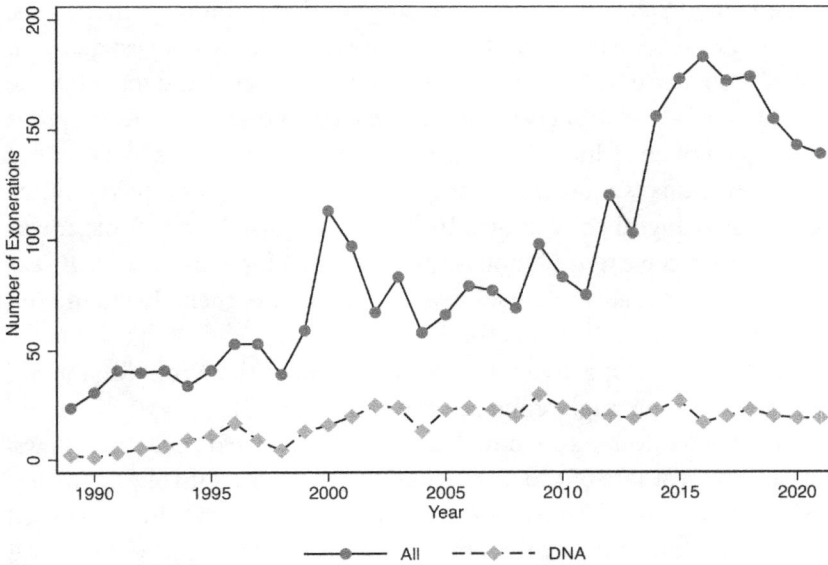

Figure 1.1. Exonerations in the United States per year, 1989–2021
Note: Figures drawn from the National Registry of Exonerations, current as of January 24, 2022.

of the conviction, but it is not necessarily an exact proxy for actual innocence.[27] However, given its definition and the challenges associated with overturning a conviction based on innocence, it is highly likely that a large majority of those who are in the NRE database are actually innocent.

It is also worth noting that the NRE is not fully comprehensive but includes only those exonerations of which the research team is aware. There are certainly untold numbers of exonerations that flew under the radar, did not receive media coverage, or for some other reason are not captured. Furthermore, there are undoubtedly exonerees who are not included for various reasons.[28] Thus, the numbers are regularly in flux as both new and old cases are added to the database.

Finally, as the name suggests, the NRE is a database of *exonerations*, not of *wrongful convictions*. This is a critical distinction. The more than three thousand cases currently captured in the NRE should not be misconstrued as the number of wrongful convictions that have occurred in the United States or even as the authoritative count of exonerations. Rather, they represent the relatively few cases that were reinvestigated, in which probative evidence was found (if even available) and in which the defendant was able to successfully secure an exoneration, which requires winning an often arduous legal and/or political battle. Thus, the number of exonerations is almost certainly minuscule compared to the number of all wrongful convictions. Indeed, Innocence Network organizations alone receive tens of thousands of requests for assistance each year and simply are unable to pursue the vast majority of them due to limited resources and organizational foci.

To put into perspective the *potential* scope of the wrongful conviction problem, we might consider the existing rate estimates discussed in the introduction. As we noted, the best estimates, despite their flaws, suggest an error rate of 3 to 6 percent (at least, in cases involving subsets of felonies and often those of the most serious variety). In the United States, a nation that incarcerates nearly two million individuals and keeps another four million under community supervision, these estimates would suggest that as many as 360,000 innocents are currently under the supervision of correctional systems across the country, with tens or hundreds of thousands of individuals wrongly convicted anew each year. Thus, despite the rate of wrongful conviction remaining a "dark figure," it is easy to understand the potential for widespread harms.[29]

Even without knowing the full extent of wrongful convictions, what we know from the cases in the NRE is staggering. On average, exonerees lost nine years of their lives, and there are almost two hundred individual exonerees who each spent more than twenty-five years incarcerated. The longest-serving exoneree, Anthony Mazza, spent more than forty-seven years incarcerated in Massachusetts for a murder and robbery he did not commit, before he was exonerated in 2021.[30] Perhaps most shockingly, the exonerees in the NRE cases to date collectively lost more than 28,150 years.[31]

We realize that this barrage of numbers may be overwhelming, but we encourage readers to pause and reflect on them. Although such figures may seem impersonal, bear in mind that every one of them represents a real case in which the lives of real people—the individuals who were wrongly convicted and those around them, victims and victim-survivors, legal actors, and more—were upended and forever changed. Families lost loved ones for years or even decades; victims and victim-survivors spent years thinking that the person responsible for their harm was being punished, only to learn that an error was made, and then were forced to relive their trauma; actual offenders went unpunished and often engaged in additional crimes. The numbers we have presented here can help us understand the scope of harm generated by wrongful convictions, but they are only meaningful when coupled with the appreciation for the human toll they represent. We also must temper this discussion with the awareness that the numbers we have offered here represent merely a fraction of the true cost, as the NRE captures only a subset of the total number of wrongful convictions. These statistics are meaningful and provide a picture of the magnitude of injustice, but, in focusing on numbers, it is easy to overlook the toll that wrongful convictions take on the many people affected by them.

Although the NRE cases do not represent all wrongful convictions, we have learned from them a number of important lessons about the many dimensions of such errors in the United States. For example, under 20 percent of exonerations involved the use of DNA evidence in some fashion, and about 25 percent of the exonerees pled guilty, rather than having been convicted at trial. Interestingly, more than 40 percent of exonerees in the NRE database were victims of "no-crime" wrongful convictions; that is, they were convicted of crimes that never actually occurred in the first place.[32]

There is a wide variety of factors that may influence the criminal legal system to run astray. From racial discrimination and stereotyping to procedural errors to media and public outcry, the mechanisms that ultimately lead to wrongful convictions are varied and complex. And while known exonerations cannot tell us everything there is to know about the factors that contribute of wrongful convictions, they do reveal some basic patterns that help us understand how and why the system errs in some cases.

The NRE tracks five contributing factors: mistaken witness identification, perjury or false accusation, false confession, false or misleading forensic evidence, and official misconduct. The prevalence of these factors in known exonerations is presented in figure 1.2.[33] As shown in

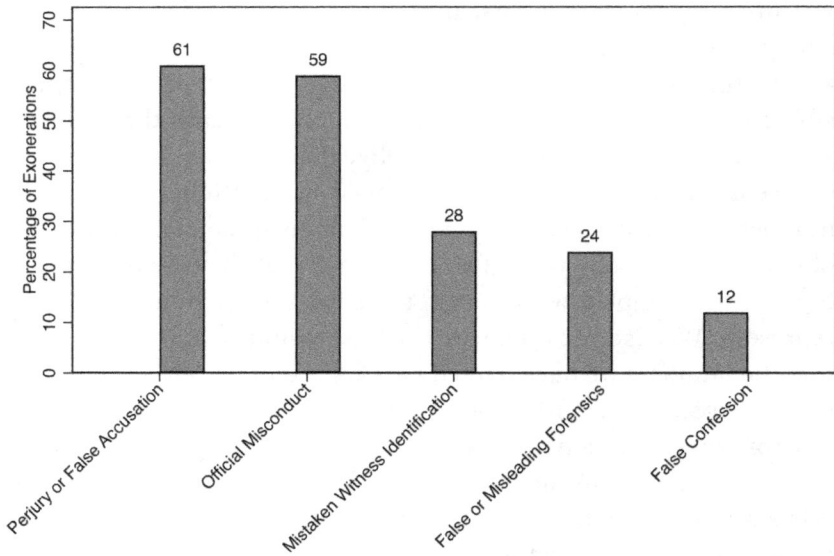

Figure 1.2. Contributing factors in National Registry of Exoneration cases
Note: Based on the first 2,939 exonerations in the NRE, as of January 24, 2022.
Percentages add up to more than 100 percent because many cases involve multiple
factors.

the figure, the leading (known) contributing factor is "perjury or false
accusation," found in 61 percent of exonerations, followed closely by "official misconduct," identified in 56 percent of cases. Interestingly, these
contributing factors shift based on crime type. For example, false confessions are found in 12 percent of cases overall but in more than 20 percent
of homicide cases, and mistaken witness identifications are found in 28
percent of cases overall but are much more common in sexual assault
exonerations, present in two-thirds of such cases.

The exonerations of which we are currently aware are probably un-
representative of the full population of wrongful convictions, making
it difficult to draw any strong conclusions about the root causes of errors. However, what we do know is enough to validate the importance
of innocence advocates' work in trying to free the innocent. Further, the
types of errors identified across many cases highlight areas where general improvements can be made in the criminal legal system, regardless
of the prevalence of wrongful convictions.

Reform

Innocence work has always been closely aligned with policy reform. We find the earliest attempts at policy advocacy related specifically to wrongful convictions in the early twentieth century. Wisconsin passed the nation's first exoneree compensation statute in 1913, followed shortly by North Dakota and California. Edwin Borchard, who began publishing scholarly work on the subject around this time, was involved in the development of a federal compensation law in 1938.[34] Although these early policies were limited and flawed in light of current knowledge, they suggest that innocence was not entirely absent from the criminal justice policy agenda.[35]

For contemporary innocence advocates, policy reform goes hand in hand with exonerating the innocent. Their work on individual cases is often connected to a strong desire to advance reforms designed to improve the fairness and accuracy of the criminal legal system, to ensure that those who are victims of wrongful conviction have ample opportunity to pursue relief, and to provide exonerees with appropriate services in the aftermath of incarceration. Indeed, the New York–based Innocence Project (IP)—by far the largest and most prominent of all innocence organizations—was founded with the goal of not only exonerating innocents through post-conviction DNA testing but also using those cases as catalysts for systemic change.[36] The IP now has a Strategic Litigation Department that pursues legal reform through the courts and a Policy Department that advocates for legislative change, and it is a leader in developing the reform agenda for the innocence movement and other criminal justice issues.

Thus far, the movement has had a number of successes across all levels of policy and practice. This ranges from altering practices in local criminal justice organizations—encouraging police departments to alter their eyewitness and interrogation practices, for example, or working with prosecutors' offices to establish Conviction Integrity Units—to federal policy, such as the passage of the Innocence Protection Act in 2004 and the Wrongful Convictions Tax Relief Act in 2015.[37]

State courts and legislatures also have implemented a variety of reforms to help prevent and discover wrongful convictions and to provide redress in the wake of an exoneration. Several of these policies are discussed in detail and their adoption across the United States analyzed in chapter 2. Here, suffice it to say that in addition to federal policy and local changes, all fifty states and Washington, DC, have on their books at least one of the key reforms tracked by the Innocence Project. These policies vary widely in scope, but it is clear that innocence advocates have made headway in permeating the criminal justice policy agenda.[38]

Research and Education

A third goal of the innocence movement is to provide resources for the education of policy makers, practitioners, and, importantly, the public. In part, this is a direct effect of the casework and policy advocacy done by innocence organizations and the attention it garners. Certainly, innocence reformers directly educate policy makers and practitioners about flaws in the criminal legal system and best practices based on scientific research, but there also is a strategic element tied to public education. From the earliest days of wrongful conviction advocacy, lawyers working on behalf of innocent clients understood the importance of publicity in advancing their cause. Such strategic use of the media—what Innocence Project cofounder Barry Scheck has described as the "power of the press"—has helped not only in fighting for individual clients but also in spreading information about our flawed justice system among the public.[39]

The educational goals of the innocence movement are now baked directly into the fabric of the Innocence Network. For example, the Innocence Project has a Science and Research Department that compiles and analyzes data. This segment of the organization works on many issues related to forensic science at the federal and state levels, but it also produces research reports and scholarly publications. This research goes hand in hand with the organization's policy and legal reform work.

More broadly, the Innocence Network has begun to embrace the academic research community. Each year, its annual conference includes one or more panels on miscarriages of justice research, and it recently developed a Research Review Committee to help local innocence organizations handle research requests that involve the participation of exonerees or staff members.

The collaboration between the innocence advocacy network and the scholarly research community has been vital; as the movement has blossomed, so too has academic interest in wrongful convictions. Each year, dozens of books and hundreds of scholarly articles are published that explore a wide variety of topics related to innocence in the criminal legal system. Many of these articles examine individual incidents of wrongful conviction or sets of cases en masse and have helped us better understand the case patterns described earlier.[40] Other specialized literatures have developed on related topics that explore specific contributing factors, such as eyewitness misidentification, false confessions, and forensic errors, or that focus on understanding the aftermath of wrongful convictions for exonerees and others.[41]

The research and educational goals of the innocence movement extend to broader cultural discourse as well. Many prominent innocence organizations and advocates, as well as exonerees themselves, maintain a social media presence and have virtual mailing lists—one of the coauthors has received more than nine hundred emails as a member of the Innocence Project's mailing list in the past few years—which they often use to promote developments related to wrongful convictions. Further, innocence advocates are often directly involved in writing books or participating in documentary films and series related to wrongful convictions. Recently, for example, the popular streaming platform Netflix released a documentary series called *The Innocence Files*, based on the casework of several Innocence Network organizations.[42] Innocence advocates also participate actively in media coverage of wrongful convictions. Organizations craft their own press releases and are regularly quoted or otherwise highlighted by journalists and in popular media; *Time* even published a special issue to commemorate the twenty-fifth anniversary of the Innocence Project.[43]

The Political Dynamics of the Innocence Movement

Despite the increasing attention and research on wrongful convictions, much remains unknown. Both the scholarly and popular literature remains skewed toward legalistic, journalistic, and case-focused analyses. Certainly, the growth of wrongful convictions as a topic of social science research and scholarship should not be ignored, but there remain many issues related to miscarriages of justice that warrant further examination. More than a decade ago, the law professor Richard Leo argued that the innocence literature lacked strong grounding in social science theory and methods and suggested using theoretical perspectives from disciplines outside of criminology to better understand the many dimensions of wrongful convictions. In the years since, some progress has been made, but many topics remain unexplored or understudied.[44]

One important area that has not yet been the focus of much scholarship is the political dimension of wrongful convictions and the innocence movement. Scholars have highlighted the unique ability of innocence advocacy to merge the ideals of the crime control and due process models of the legal process. As described in the classic work of Herbert Packer, crime control prioritizes repression of crime as the primary function of the criminal justice system, an "administrative" model that resembles an "assembly line" and emphasizes efficiency and finality. This perspective relies on a high level of confidence in the administrative process and the actors who run it. A due process perspective, on the other hand, is less confident in and more skeptical of the process, which it sees as more akin to an "obstacle course"; it emphasizes the protection of individual rights, the presumption of innocence, and error correction.[45]

Packer's two models are often construed as being primarily in competition, with crime control values being more closely associated with political conservatism and due process preferences aligned with political liberalism. However, the law professor Keith Findley has argued that the innocence movement merges the two perspectives. The movement, he writes, "reveals that the dichotomy between crime control and due process concerns was never as stark as sometimes assumed."[46] Findley's assertion is logical and has some empirical support. This is particularly evident in the discussion of actual offenders who escape apprehension when innocents are arrested and convicted. Indeed, the only person who benefits from a wrongful conviction is the real offender; when the wrong person is arrested and convicted, this true perpetrator evades capture and experiences a period of "wrongful liberty." Although research is limited, the available studies suggest that true perpetrators continue to engage in criminal activity and may account for tens of thousands of additional crimes, meaning that there is an element of crime control to addressing wrongful convictions in addition to the more obvious due process concerns.[47]

Certainly, the relationship between wrongful conviction and wrongful liberty suggests that any absolute dichotomy between the crime control and due process models is a flawed one and that the innocence movement can merge both perspectives, thus potentially spanning the ideological spectrum. And, to be clear, innocence advocates have and do sometimes utilize a crime control frame to discuss their work.[48] However, this should not be misconstrued as meaning that the movement is fully bipartisan and nonideological or that it reaches equally across political lines. At a quick glance, it may appear that this is the case— exonerations have occurred in every state, and the leading states (Texas, Illinois, and New York) span the political and geographical gamut; every state has adopted at least one policy, as tracked by the Innocence Project; and the states that have adopted several of them span across regions and the political spectrum, including jurisdictions like California, Colorado, Nebraska, Ohio, North Carolina, and Connecticut.[49] Such surface-level considerations, however, fail to tell the full story and may mask the politics of innocence.

A more nuanced consideration suggests that there is, without a doubt, an ideological element to innocence work. While uncovering exactly when and how wrongful convictions *became* politicized is beyond the scope of this book, the historical record suggests that it is not strictly a contemporary phenomenon. A recent review of writing on the rate of wrongful convictions notes that "ideological divisions reflecting crime control and due process orientations appear in rate scholarship" and that "historical scholarship indicates long-existing divisions between *innocence believers*—those who are concerned with wrongful convictions and tend to believe that they occur with troubling frequency—and *innocence skeptics*—those who believe that wrongful convictions never occur or are vanishingly rare."[50] Further, and more to the point, these divisions have tended to reflect ideological differences, with believers skewing liberal and skeptics skewing conservative, and appeared at least as early as the 1980s, when early innocence scholarship was just beginning to blossom and the "foundations" of the movement "were shifting into place."[51]

Contemporary advocates are aware of the ideological nuances of their work; while some have discussed the "moral accessibility" of the movement and suggest that it is about "just good law enforcement," many recognize that they must be ideologically strategic.[52] In one southern state, for example, an advocate described the crime control angle as the "Republican pitch" for wrongful conviction reform and suggested that innocence advocates had to avoid blending the issue with death penalty abolitionism, which would be a quick route to failure.[53]

Importantly, empirical studies yield differing results regarding the ideological dimensions of the innocence movement. In an analysis of state compensation statutes, the political scientist Michael Leo Owens and the criminologist Elizabeth Griffiths found that government ideology had no statistically significant effect on whether a state adopted a compensation law. On the other hand, a more recent study by the sociologists Stephanie Kent and Jason Carmichael found that partisanship was a significant factor in states' passage of wrongful conviction reforms.[54] It is also worth noting that there is some evidence of ideological variations in innocence beliefs among the public. As Marvin Zalman and colleagues noted in their survey of the public in Michigan, "wrongful convictions ought not to be an ideologically charged issue, as no one supports convicting the innocent," yet some of their results "suggest that in the policy arena, wrongful conviction will have a liberal ideological valence."[55]

Beyond these few examples, there is relatively little attention to the political dynamics underlying the work of the innocence movement. Throughout the remainder of this book, we explore the influence of politics in state policy reforms and public opinion in the realm of wrongful conviction. Our core argument is that politics matter, and in the following chapters, we examine precisely how and why.

2

State Politics, Innocence Advocacy, and Wrongful Conviction Reforms

On April 1, 2009, Cory Session stood before Texas lawmakers to advocate for changes to the state's exoneree compensation law. It was tragedy that brought Session there; he was present on behalf of his brother, Timothy Cole, whose ordeal with the state's criminal legal system began more than two decades earlier.

In early April 1985, Timothy Cole was a twenty-six-year-old Army veteran and student at Texas Tech University in Lubbock, when he was stopped by a detective outside a pizzeria. The interaction led to a decades-long ordeal for Cole and his family.[1]

Two weeks earlier, in March 1985, Michele Mallin, another Texas Tech student, had been parking her car when a man approached and asked if she could help him jump-start his own car. He reached through her window to unlock her door, and she bit his hand. The man then held a knife to Mallin's throat and entered the driver's seat. He drove to a vacant lot, raped Mallin, and then drove back to Lubbock. He stole two dollars in cash and some jewelry before leaving.

Mallin called the police and reported that a young African American man had attacked her. She said he wore a yellow shirt and sandals and smoked cigarettes. At the time, police thought it may have been the "Tech Rapist," a suspected serial rapist responsible for four other attacks in the area. On the basis of the victims' descriptions, police developed a composite sketch, which was placed in the university's newspaper, and they began surveilling campus.

Two weeks after meeting Cole outside the pizzeria, the detective went to his house and took a photo of him. That photo—a Polaroid in which Cole directly faced the camera—was placed in a photo array with five others, mugshots in which the individuals faced sideways to the camera. Mallin identified Cole as her attacker. The next day, she again identified him in a live lineup, though the other four victims were not able to do so. Still, Cole was arrested and charged with the aggravated sexual assault of Michele Mallin.

Cole went to trial in 1986. Mallin testified and identified him in court as her attacker. A forensic examiner testified that semen was present in the rape kit and that serology testing showed evidence of a type A secretor; both Mallin and Cole had type A blood, but only Mallin was known to be a secretor.[2] The examiner also testified that pubic hairs found on the victim's underwear were consistent with Cole's.

Cole's brother and friends testified that he was at home studying while they played cards on the night of the crime. Cole also had asthma and did not smoke cigarettes. The defense sought to present evidence that similar attacks had occurred after Cole's arrest and that fingerprints from a similar attack one month prior to Mallin's did not match Cole, but the judge deemed them to be inadmissible. Cole was convicted by the jury and sentenced to twenty-five years in prison.

Cole's initial appeals were denied. Then, in 1995—after the statute of limitations on the crime expired—a man named Jerry Wayne Johnson, who was serving a life sentence for two similar sexual assaults, wrote to judges, prosecutors, law enforcement, and Cole's defense lawyer, Mike Brown, admitting that he had committed a crime for which one of Brown's clients was incarcerated. Officials never acknowledged the letters.

Cole died in prison in 1999 of an asthma attack without knowing that someone else tried to confess to the crime. The next year, Johnson wrote to another judge, but the case was rejected without comment. However, in 2007, this second letter made its way to the Innocence Project of Texas (IPT) and Cole's family. IPT attorneys requested posthumous DNA testing, and prosecutors agreed. In 2008, results excluded Cole and implicated Johnson as the attacker. The next year, with the Innocence Project and IPT as cocounsel, Cole was officially exonerated.[3]

In the midst of the 2009 hearings that led to Cole's exoneration, advocates in Texas were fighting for changes to the state's compensation policy. State law had long provided some form of compensation for victims of wrongful conviction. Historically, however, the law was rather strict in its approach. In the mid-1980s, eligible exonerees—those who did not plead guilty and who had received a full gubernatorial pardon—could file a claim for compensation. At most, individuals could receive up to $50,000 regardless of how long they had been incarcerated.[4]

This approach persisted throughout the 1990s but was revised several times after the turn of the century. In 2001, the law was amended to allow applicants to seek administrative compensation (if they would forgo their right to file a civil lawsuit) of $25,000 per year of wrongful imprisonment, up to twenty years, as well as counseling services. Eligibility also was expanded; the plea restriction and pardon requirement were removed. Several exonerees, including Anthony Robinson and Maurice Pierce, testified before congressional committees in support of the law, as did Jeanette Popp, whose daughter was the murder victim in the wrongful conviction of Christopher Ochoa and Richard Danziger.[5]

Then, in 2007, the law was altered yet again. Monetary compensation was increased to $50,000 per year of wrongful incarceration, with an additional $50,000 for each year spent on death row. Interestingly, lawmakers also added a provision to cover child-support payments owed and any interest accrued on them. The importance of this latter provision was emphasized by the case of Clarence Brandley, who had been convicted of murder and sentenced to death in 1981. While in prison, he was unable to make his child-support payments and accrued debt as a result. After his 1990 exoneration, he was not compensated for the debt.

Still, Texas's compensation statute was limited, and advocates, including the Innocence Project of Texas, pushed for additional changes. At the heart of the 2009 effort was Timothy Cole's case. Previously, among other shortcomings, state law did not permit an exoneree's family to receive compensation on the exoneree's behalf. Given Cole's experience and the law's limitations, it was especially powerful when his brother, Cory Session, stood in front of the Texas House Committee on Criminal Jurisprudence with their mother by his side and said, "Members, I have an exhibit here. This is exhibit A. The mother of Timothy Cole. In this bill there is a provision for the deceased. We've had disappointments by the score but my mother has a heartache that I cannot even imagine. No amount of money will bring Timothy back. But this bill is a start."[6] Texas lawmakers ultimately passed the Timothy Cole Act, which altered monetary compensation, expanded other services, and included a provision for compensation in cases of posthumous exoneration. Although there have been minor amendments since, this is still the basis for the current

Texas compensation statute, which is among the most comprehensive in the United States.[7]

The state of Texas is not alone in passing an exoneree compensation statute, nor is compensation the only issue on the innocence policy agenda. In this chapter, we explore key policies that have long been on that agenda and use an original data set to explore what factors have influenced states' adoption of wrongful-conviction-related policies.

Wrongful Convictions and Public Policy

The story of compensation reform in Texas begs the question of what influenced the Lone Star State, which historically has been both conservative and highly punitive—it is among the leaders in state imprisonment rate and use of the death penalty—to enact one of the most comprehensive compensation policies in the nation.[8]

In part, the developments in Texas may simply have been influenced by the changing times and the shifting national landscape. Throughout the 1990s, exonerations began to pile up across the United States, and wrongful convictions garnered attention in the national media and among criminal justice officials. By the early 2000s, an organizational network formed, and wrongful conviction advocacy coalesced into the innocence movement.[9] Such broad developments and cultural changes may certainly influence individual states and policy efforts and may have played a role in this case.

Beyond being simply a function of the times, however, other factors probably influenced compensation reform. For instance, Texas has been a significant area of growth for the innocence movement. It currently is a leader in the United States in exonerations since 1989, with four hundred.[10] This, in turn, may be a function of heightened innocence activism in the state; there are currently three innocence projects operating in Texas.[11]

The importance of the presence and activity of innocence advocates should not be understated. They may influence the lawmaking process directly through their policy advocacy efforts and lobbying but also influence it indirectly through their casework. Every exoneration provides a powerful and compelling narrative of injustice, and as seen in Texas, such stories can and are used to advocate for specific policy reforms.

Certainly, the *innocence context* of a state is likely to influence its policy responses. It is unlikely, however, that this alone explains why some states are seemingly more committed to addressing wrongful convictions than others. In this chapter, we analyze the adoption of state policy reforms over the thirty-year period from 1989 through 2018. We provide evidence that while exonerations and innocence advocacy influence policy reform, we must also consider the importance of public opinion and states' political context. In short, we show why and how politics matter.

The Scope of Innocence Reform

Exoneree compensation is far from the only type of reform on the innocence policy agenda, and Texas is not the only state to adopt such reforms. Over the past several decades, state governments across the US have adopted a variety of innocence-related policies. Some of these are designed to reduce the likelihood of wrongful convictions, while others are designed to help identify errors or provide redress in the wake of exoneration.

Any number of reforms to criminal legal practices are related to the innocence movement's agenda; from changes in rules of evidence to law enforcement training to alterations of post-conviction law, there are many ways to potentially address wrongful convictions. However, we focus our analysis on state reforms in five specific areas: (1) eyewitness identification practices, (2) recording of custodial interrogations, (3) preservation of biological evidence, (4) access to post-conviction DNA testing, and (5) exoneree compensation. These are five key areas that were prioritized by innocence advocates for the duration of the innocence movement's life span and are directly related to the production and remediation of errors. Further, they are evidence-based reforms that are directly tied to what we understand about wrongful convictions from known exonerations and existing research. In the following sections, we briefly summarize each of these five issues.

Mitigating Eyewitness Errors

The unreliability of witnesses has long been established, and psychologists and legal scholars have uncovered a number of reasons why.

Generally speaking, the factors that influence eyewitness (mis)identi-
fications are divided into two broad categories: estimator variables and
system variables.[12]

Estimator variables include factors that are outside the control of the
criminal legal system and its actors. Police cannot control, for instance,
the time of day that a crime occurred, the lighting conditions, or how far
away the witness may have been. Nor can they control how stressed or
fearful a witness was at the time, whether the crime involved a weapon,
or the individual characteristics of the witness that may influence their
recall or identification abilities.[13]

This is not to say that system actors have no control over eyewitness
identification outcomes. There are a number of *system variables* over
which police have some control. Consider Timothy Cole's case. In the first
lineup viewed by the victim, Cole's photograph was a Polaroid in which
he faced the camera directly, while the *fillers*—those in the lineup who are
not the suspect—were mugshots in which they faced sideways. While it is
impossible to say whether that difference is the reason Cole was erroneously chosen, there is no doubt that such matters will make one photo in
the lineup stand out above the others. Such are system variables; detectives in Cole's case made the decision to present the lineup in that fashion
but could have (and should have) done things differently. Other system
variables include which officers are present during the lineup, how they
behave, and the like. It is important to recognize that detectives or other
officials involved in the identification process may inadvertently send
suggestive signals to an eyewitness, be it through a hand gesture, nod, or
subtle facial expression. While such factors may be subconscious, they
may be managed through institutionalized policies, such as the use of
double-blind procedures in which the officers administering the lineup
are unaware of the suspect's identity and thus cannot provide feedback.

Eyewitness misidentifications cannot be fully prevented—after all,
human memory is fallible, and people make mistakes, with or without
safeguards in place—but several reforms have been suggested, based on
extensive psychological research, to reduce their likelihood. Some of the
key reforms include the following:

- Instructing witnesses that they do not have to make an identification and/or
  that it is equally important to clear the innocent as it is to identify the guilty

- Using blind procedures such that the officer administering the lineup does not know who the suspect is and therefore cannot give feedback to the witness
- Composing lineups to ensure that the suspect does not unfairly stand out and fillers match the witness's description
- Recording the witness's level of confidence in their selection immediately, prior to receiving any feedback
- Recording identification procedures[14]

Again, these and other reforms cannot prevent witnesses from identifying innocents. However, they have been found to mitigate the consequences associated with the errors in human memory, recognition, and recall and thus may reduce the likelihood of wrongful convictions.

Interrogations and Confessions

A confession is among the most potent forms of evidence that may be presented during a criminal trial and significantly increases the likelihood of a conviction. Thus, as with eyewitness identifications, psychologists and legal scholars have studied interrogations and confessions extensively.[15]

While some false confessions are voluntary and are offered "without prompting or pressure from the police," many are directly related to the nature of interrogations and the direct actions of interrogators.[16] Compliant false confessions, for instance, occur when a suspect, faced with the stress, pressure, and psychological manipulation of a police interrogation, gives in and confesses to escape the situation or to receive some perceived reward, such as a reduction in sentence.[17]

Many factors might influence whether an innocent person confesses to a crime they did not commit. *Situational characteristics* of the interrogation itself may influence a person to confess. Modern interrogations are psychologically intense and intimidating experiences.[18] Suspects are isolated in a stressful environment, sometimes for long periods of time.[19] Other situational characteristics include the strategies used by interrogators to secure a confession, which often are manipulative: lying about inculpatory evidence, for instance, or playing cosuspects against one another.[20]

Beyond the interrogation itself, certain *dispositional characteristics* of the suspect under interrogation might make them more likely to confess. For example, certain groups have been found to be more vulnerable to manipulative interrogation tactics, including juveniles and people suffering from mental illness and developmental disabilities, all of whom are overrepresented among known false confessors.[21]

Due to the complexities associated with interrogations and confessions and the cultural history of the practice, reforming police interrogations so as to reduce false confessions is challenging. Some observers have suggested limiting or banning the use of particularly coercive tactics; others focus on protecting vulnerable populations by limiting the types of strategies used against them, requiring police to participate in specialized training and education on working with vulnerable populations or requiring the presence of an attorney.

The most ubiquitous reform, however, is a relatively straightforward one, at least in theory: requiring police to record custodial interrogations in an effort to "lift the veil of secrecy from the interrogation process."[22] Such a practice might dissuade investigators from using coercive or illegal tactics and provide evidence for the defense should it challenge the confession in court. Importantly, though, recording interrogations may also benefit police by protecting them from inaccurate or frivolous claims of abuse. Furthermore, by having a mostly objective record of an interrogation—rather than relying on the word and potentially flawed memories of participants—judges may be able to better assess the voluntariness of a confession (and thus aid in their admissibility determinations), and juries may be able to better evaluate confession evidence in making their decision to convict or acquit.[23]

Uncovering Wrongful Convictions: DNA Access and Evidence Preservation

Even if reforms designed to mitigate wrongful convictions are adopted and implemented, it is inevitable that such errors—with life-altering consequences—will still occur. Such is the nature of a complex, probabilistic criminal legal system designed and administered by human beings. Thus, another challenge for innocence advocates is identifying those who have already been wrongly convicted and then securing their release and exoneration.

Trying to free someone on the basis of actual innocence brings with it an array of difficulties, many of which are legally complex and beyond the scope of this book. Suffice it to say that, in the United States, once a person has been convicted, the legal system is generally designed not to reconsider the facts of the case but rather to evaluate the procedural mechanisms that led to the conviction. Appellate courts typically consider questions of law as opposed to questions of fact: whether the police violated the defendant's rights during an investigation or whether a prosecutor withheld exculpatory information, for example, rather than whether the convicted defendant was actually guilty.

Beyond the legal challenges associated with exonerations, innocence advocates face a bevy of practical ones, such as finding evidence or tracking down witnesses from cases that may be decades old. Sometimes these come down to nothing more than sheer luck. There are, however, some policy reforms that may be helpful for advocates as they reinvestigate cases and work toward exonerations. We focus here on two of them that are tracked by the Innocence Project and have been historically important to the innocence movement: access to post-conviction DNA testing and preservation of biological evidence.

State laws now grant incarcerated persons the ability to pursue post-conviction DNA testing.[24] Such testing is not automatic, however, as the defendant must petition the court to secure testing. The standards used across states differ, as do the eligibility criteria. For instance, some states specify that only those who are convicted of certain crimes—such as crimes of violence or felonies—are eligible to file such petitions. The legal standard or threshold that the defendant must reach in order for testing to be conducted also varies across jurisdictions. Still, despite these and other differences, the fact that every state has an avenue for at least some defendants to pursue post-conviction DNA testing is a positive step.

However, even if an incarcerated person is eligible for post-conviction DNA testing, the ability to actually conduct those tests hinges on the availability of the evidence. A deep reading into several exoneration cases reveals the role of good fortune; evidence that was thought to be lost was fortuitously found, seemingly, at random. Alan Newton, for example, was convicted in 1985, and his 1994 request for DNA testing was denied because the rape kit from the crime could not be found and was presumed destroyed. It was not until 2005, when the Innocence Project was working the case, that the evidence was located and tested, showing that Newton was not the attacker. Such scenarios highlight the importance of preserving biological evidence and doing so with the proper handling, as many reinvestigations are of cases that are years or decades old.

Many states have enacted laws that put some parameters around the preservation of evidence.[25] As with DNA access laws, the specifics vary as to the types of crimes captured under the law and the types of evidence that must be preserved and for how long. Regardless, if we are to allow reinvestigations to take their course and be done properly, with the goal of ensuring that previous outcomes were factually accurate, it is imperative that there be standards around the handling and preservation of evidence.

Reentry after Exoneration: Compensation Statutes

Once a wrongful conviction is overturned and someone is exonerated and released, they experience myriad challenges in returning to their communities yet are typically provided little in the way of reentry assistance. Generally speaking, exonerees receive less than those who are released on parole or probation. As Saundra Westervelt and Kimberly Cook have written, "justice continues to miscarry for those wrongly convicted of crimes 'when the state fails to assist in their reintegration efforts and recognize its responsibility in their wrongful convictions.'"[26]

Exonerees may be able to pursue civil litigation or private legislative compensation, but such routes are time-consuming and resource-intensive and have low success rates. Most scholars and advocates therefore argue for states to adopt compensation statutes to provide both monetary and nonmonetary assistance for exonerees.[27]

Exploring State Efforts to Reduce Wrongful Convictions

It is undeniable that the policies outlined in the preceding sections—designed to reduce, discover, and remedy wrongful convictions—have

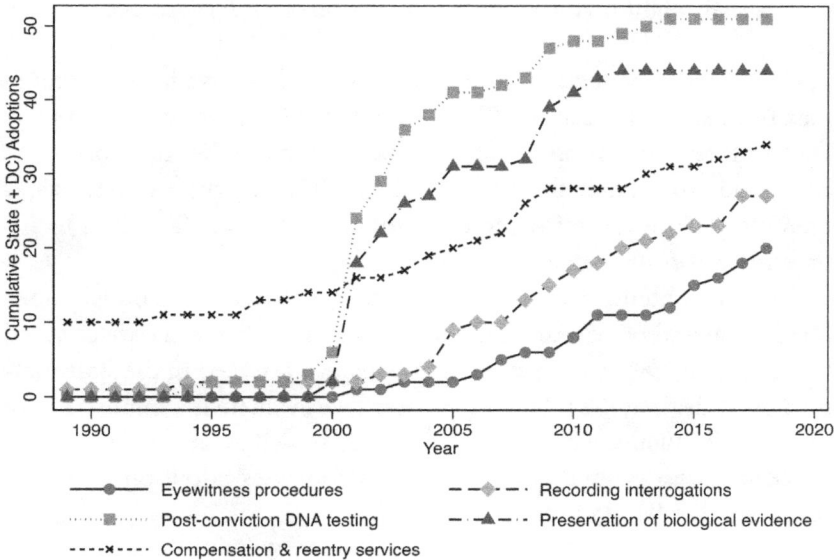

Figure 2.1. Wrongful conviction reforms in the US states

to varying degrees spread across the United States. The question to which we now turn is, why?

We sought to examine the factors that influence states to adopt the five laws outlined in the preceding sections. Using information from the Innocence Project, we compiled a data set of states that have adopted each of the five policies we described in the preceding sections—eyewitness identification reform, recording interrogations, DNA access laws, preservation of biological evidence, and exoneree compensation—each year, over a thirty-year period from 1989 through 2018.[28]

Figure 2.1 shows the cumulative number of states (plus Washington, DC) that have adopted each of these five reforms. We can see that state adoption has trended upward, especially since 2000, but not all reforms have been embraced equally. For instance, by 2015, all state governments had adopted reforms granting convicted persons access to post-conviction DNA testing. At the same time, however, fewer than half of the states had passed laws reforming eyewitness identification procedures and mandating that interrogations be recorded—reforms, that is, that might make wrongful convictions less likely to occur in the first place.

Collectively, evaluating states' adoption of these five laws in totality may offer some indication of how committed those state governments are to addressing wrongful convictions. Yet the number of reforms enacted does not answer the question of why. That is, why are some states seemingly more committed to adopting these reforms (and thus to addressing errors of justice) than others?

Despite contentions that wrongful convictions are a uniquely non-ideological and bipartisan issue (as discussed in chapter 1), we contend that both the *innocence context* and the *political context* in the state matter a great deal. In the following sections, we evaluate the importance of public opinion and electoral competition, as well as the effect of innocence advocacy groups and exonerations, for states' adoption of wrongful conviction legislation.

Public Opinion

There are strong reasons to believe that public opinion is an integral part of the adoption of wrongful-conviction-related legislation. Decades of social science research suggest that policy is responsive to public opinion. Much of this research incorporates the framework of *dynamic representation*, which highlights two ways that public opinion may shape policy.[29] One way that mass opinion can alter public policy is through the replacement of sitting lawmakers. That is, shifts in public opinion can affect policy through the election of new representatives who more accurately reflect the will of the people. The second way is when already-elected lawmakers adapt to changes in public opinion and/or anticipate such changes. Here, lawmakers are concerned about reelection, sense shifts in the political mood of their constituency, and strategically adopt policy in light of changing opinions. In the parlance of dynamic representation scholars, policy makers are "like antelope in an open field, they cock their ears and focus their full attention on the slightest sign of danger."[30] If lawmakers anticipate changes in the preferences of future electoral majorities, they shift the policies they support to parry challenges to their incumbency and enhance their electoral futures.

We think the first route is important; undoubtedly, public opinion might influence policy through the election of different lawmakers. However, like prior researchers, we think the second route is more analytically compelling and, potentially, may matter more for a few reasons. First, prior research consistently finds that replacement is rare. Put simply, incumbents are significantly more likely to run for and win the vast majority of legislative seats compared to challengers, and this is true even when considering the responsiveness of incumbents.[31] This means that the opportunity for policy change to occur via replacement is also rare. Second, we are able to statistically control for replacement by holding constant the partisan conditions of legislative chambers. Third, from a normative perspective, evidence that existing majorities update policy in light of changing public opinion is suggestive of a somewhat functional system of democratic responsiveness in spite of the rarity of incumbent defeat. That is, it is possible that lawmakers respond to constituents' preferences, even with little evidence that voters hold incumbents accountable by electing challengers.

So, what aspects of public opinion do lawmakers look to in their efforts to gauge shifts in the political leanings of their constituency? Given the specificity of reforms to address wrongful convictions and the paucity of survey data on these particular reforms—let alone at the state level—what might policy makers look to? We suggest that when lawmakers support or oppose policies, they consider the broad ideological orientation of their constituents and changes they anticipate in this orientation. After all, lawmakers themselves cannot be policy specialists on every issue but rather are generalists who have to vote on an array of policy considerations each session. In practice, lawmakers have to vote on dozens of issues, often with poor information about how constituents feel about each particular issue on its own. To make electorally sound decisions, then, lawmakers often have little else to guide their votes other than considering broader trends in the public's ideological mood.

While there is some dynamic representation research that examines the link between public attitudes toward a specific practice and corresponding policy shifts—for example, changes in public support for the death penalty and resulting shifts in capital punishment practices—it is more common for scholars to focus on changes in broader, aggregate measures of the public's policy preferences. The classic work by the political scientist James Stimson and colleagues analyzes the public's "policy mood," which is "interpreted as left versus right—more specifically, as global preferences for a larger, more active federal government as opposed to a smaller, more passive one across the sphere of all domestic policy controversies."[32] Other works distinguish between the *economic* and *social* policy aspects of the public's "liberalism" or ideological leaning but still focus on a broad conceptualization of mass opinion and its impact on policy change.[33]

In the context of wrongful conviction reforms, it seems unlikely that state lawmakers measure and assess their constituents' attitudes on policies as specific as alterations to eyewitness identification procedures or exoneree compensation statutes. Rather, we think it is more likely that lawmakers consider the broader ideological mood and liberalism of their constituency when making these types of policy decisions.

How and why, then, is political ideology consequential for people's attitudes toward policies that address wrongful convictions? We believe that the public's liberalism is related to support for wrongful conviction policies such that liberals are more supportive of these types of reforms. We have several reasons for this belief, rooted in what research tells us about the relationship between political ideology and criminal justice policy preferences.

First, several of these reforms—eyewitness identification procedures, recording interrogations, and preservation of evidence—require nontrivial changes to the regulations and policies that guide police practices. Research has shown that conservatives view law enforcement in a more positive light than liberals do and thus may look less favorably on legislation that calls attention to their potential mistakes.[34] Proposing changes to police practices in an effort to reduce the likelihood of wrongful convictions might give the impression that law enforcement, at times, contributes to the underlying errors. Simply questioning police practices may prompt opposition among some members of the public—conservatives, in particular—who disproportionately hold law enforcement in high esteem.

Second, some of these policies require additional funding in order to be successfully implemented. Exoneree compensation statutes are obvious examples, but others may require additional state funds as well. Recording interrogations, for instance, may impose financial costs associated with equipment and data storage, and evidence preservation requires space and storage equipment. This is an important consideration, as studies have long shown that ideology influences public attitudes toward government spending across a host of issues.[35]

Third, while criminal justice preferences may not be strictly divided along ideological lines and are sometimes situational,[36] some classic and contemporary writing suggests that there are notable differences. For instance, conservatives often exhibit a more punitive mind-set, expressing concerns about leniency toward offenders, while liberals are more concerned with issues such as overcriminalization and the protection of suspects' and defendants' rights.[37] These may be indicative of general ideological patterns in people's mind-set toward the *crime control* and *due process* orientations, as discussed in chapter 1, which have often been associated with political conservatism and liberalism, respectively. For our purposes here, this is noteworthy because the innocence movement has often been associated, rightly or wrongly, with a liberal, due process orientation.[38]

Finally, much of the coverage of wrongful convictions highlights the disproportionate risk faced by already-disadvantaged groups, such as racial and ethnic minorities and the poor, in the criminal legal system. Public discourse about wrongful convictions rarely occurs in a vacuum but, like so many criminal justice issues, is inherently intertwined with broader conversations about race, socioeconomic inequality, and more.[39] Such rhetoric, which invokes social group cues, may lead people to structure issues along ideological lines.[40]

For these reasons, we believe there may be an ideological component to public opinion in regard to wrongful convictions and related policies. Unfortunately, to our knowledge, there are no consistent data on public opinion about wrongful convictions and policy reforms in this domain that cover the thirty-year period of interest. However, as discussed earlier, because we suspect that there is an ideological element to wrongful conviction policies similar to other criminal justice issues, we expect that increasingly liberal attitudes among the public more generally are likely to accelerate the adoption of wrongful conviction reforms.

Electoral Context

In line with the framework of dynamic representation we discussed earlier, public opinion may shape policy through lawmakers' adaptation to changes in the public's liberalism. However, it is unlikely that the impact of public opinion on policy adoption is constant across political contexts. There may be electoral environments where lawmakers are particularly inclined to respond to public opinion and other contexts in which lawmakers may feel more insulated from shifts in the public's ideology. In particular, the effect of public opinion on policy may be influenced by the extent to which elections are competitive in a given state. Vulnerable lawmakers or those in relatively more vulnerable chambers probably have a stronger motivation to be responsive to public opinion. After all, scholars have demonstrated that states' electoral competitiveness shapes legislators' behavior and policy outcomes.[41] To the extent that this is true, it also may be the case that lawmakers' behavior is driven just as much by their perception of being vulnerable as it is by real vulnerability, because there is little evidence that citizens actually reward or punish lawmakers for their voting behavior.[42]

We believe that this dynamic may be at work with regard to wrongful conviction reforms. That is, public liberalism will increase the likelihood that states adopt innocence-related policies, particularly in states with more competitive legislative elections. Electoral competition, on the one hand, motivates lawmakers to take risks, by doing things like changing the status quo. Of course, there are dozens of issues that lawmakers could pursue, but they have to also consider the context. Changes in public opinion (or the lack thereof), on the other hand, narrow (or expand) the menu of reasonable choices—and of reasonable issues—from which lawmakers can choose. In a state in which public opinion trends liberal, wrongful conviction reforms probably survive this narrowing of the menu and provide a unique political opportunity for lawmakers who are willing to take a risk and pursue a policy change. Without electoral competition, however, lawmakers have less reason to explore these reforms. It is also possible that wrongful conviction reforms are enough outside the realm of traditional party politics—things like taxes, welfare, education, immigration, and health care, to name just a few—that lawmakers may view them as a useful wedge issue; such reforms may be universally attractive to liberals and potentially split conservatives.

Innocence Advocacy and Exonerations

In addition to public opinion and electoral competition, we expect the presence of innocence organizations to shape states' adoption of wrongful conviction policies. As we discussed in chapter 1, the Innocence Network has now expanded to include more than fifty organizations across the United States. Many of these groups focus primarily on casework—legal efforts to exonerate the innocent—but many also engage in advocacy and public education campaigns. In essence, these innocence projects may be thought of as social movement organizations and/or interest groups, and there are a few ways we think they influence policy adoption at the state level.[43]

Through innocence organizations' casework, they become ingrained in local legal cultures and thus may put issues related to wrongful convictions on the radar of criminal justice and legal practitioners. Perhaps more importantly, though, they regularly contribute to exonerations. Those exonerations often generate media coverage, which, along with organizations' direct public outreach efforts, may raise awareness about wrongful convictions among citizens. The work of innocence organizations may therefore influence public opinion and, as we discussed earlier, prompt responses from lawmakers. Innocence organizations and advocates might also influence policy adoption through direct advocacy efforts in their state legislatures.

Through these various mechanisms—establishing themselves as part of local and state legal cultures, influencing public concern about wrongful convictions, and direct lobbying efforts—innocence organizations are likely to influence the adoption of related criminal justice reforms.

Why Do States Adopt Wrongful Conviction Reforms?

Earlier, in figure 2.1, we showed the number of states that adopted five different policy reforms at different points in time. That figure provides valuable descriptive information, but we wanted to explore the dynamics underlying policy adoption to better understand *why* lawmakers in particular states are more or less inclined to enact policy reforms. Here, we statistically examine why some states are seemingly more committed to addressing wrongful convictions than others are.[44] In the following sections, we describe the data used for our analyses and present the results of a variety of statistical models. These models allow us to explore various features of wrongful conviction reform, such as how time itself matters, while simultaneously controlling for a number of other variables. We describe the key features of our data and analysis here, but interested readers are referred to the appendix for a more thorough discussion of our methodology and results.

Data and Measurement

We relied on a variety of data sources to examine why states adopt wrongful conviction reform. Therefore, state-level policy adoption was our main outcome of interest. Our main independent variables included public opinion, electoral competition, the presence of innocence groups, and the number of exonerations in each state. We also controlled for a number of other state-level variables.

We focus on state governments instead of the federal or local governments/agencies for a few reasons. First, including states instead of local governments and/or agencies is more practically feasible. Police departments and crime labs exist within overlapping, conflicting, and confusing local governmental jurisdictions. Plus, it is often difficult to know which (and whether) local governmental actors have power over criminal justice practices. Building a data set to accurately accommodate the complexity of local government jurisdictions is, at best, practically challenging and, at worst, prone to errors. State governments, additionally, have a clear political advantage to local governments with regard to policy-making power. In legal disputes between local governments/agencies and state governments, state governments almost always win.[45] State governments can preempt local laws and actions, but, importantly, the federal government cannot easily preempt states. Finally, states are a useful venue to test hypotheses about politics and policy. Not only do states have much more autonomy than local governments and agencies do, but states still vary in other empirically relevant and interesting ways. They differ with regard to their demographics, political attitudes, political institutions, histories, and cultures.

State Wrongful Conviction Reforms

Our main dependent variable was state-level wrongful conviction policies. We focused on the five reforms previously outlined in this chapter: (1) changes to eyewitness identification practices, (2) mandatory recording of criminal interrogations, (3) laws governing the preservation of biological evidence, (4) laws that grant convicted persons access to post-conviction DNA testing, and (5) laws providing compensation and other reentry services to exonerees. As we noted earlier, we were interested in the *total number of reforms* enacted by each state as a proxy for how committed it is to addressing wrongful convictions through legislation. We measured whether each reform was adopted and the year in which it was. Our data span the time period from 1989—the year of the first DNA-based exonerations in the United States and the first exoneration year included in the National Registry of Exonerations—through 2018. For each of those thirty years, each state therefore had a value of 0 (if it had not adopted any of these reforms by that year) to 5 (if it had adopted all of them by that point). These data were collected from the Innocence Project's website.[46]

Public Opinion

As we explained earlier, we expected the public's ideological leanings to influence states' adoption of wrongful conviction policies. To capture this dynamic, we used the public opinion liberalism measures developed by the political scientists Devin Caughey and Christopher Warshaw, who estimated liberalism on social and economic policy for each state from 1936 through 2014.[47] Specifically, we employed their social policy liberalism public opinion measure, as this makes more theoretical and intuitive sense as a catalyst for change with respect to criminal justice reform. Indeed, Caughey and Warshaw's research shows that social policy liberalism exerts a stronger influence on policy making than economic liberalism does.[48] On the polls that Caughey and Warshaw used to measure social policy liberalism in 2007 alone, they included survey questions measuring citizens' preferences on the death penalty, immigration, gun control (i.e., assault weapons ban), same-sex marriage, stem-cell research, and abortion. They united similarly worded survey items focused on these policies that were asked in different years and with different samples. These items provide insights into how the public might respond to changes in the criminal justice and/or legal system generally and therefore may influence politicians' decisions on an issue like wrongful conviction.

Electoral Competition

We measured states' electoral competitiveness using the results of state legislative elections.[49] For a given election year, our index included and equally weighted the average margin of victory for contested seats,[50] the percentage of safe elections ("safe" meaning a margin of victory equal to or greater than ten percentage points), and the percentage of uncontested elections across all state legislative seats. We took the average of these three values and subtracted them from 100, so that higher values imply more electoral competition for legislative seats. Given the number, nature, and nonuniform distribution of uncontested elections in state legislatures, such an index was preferable to simple margin-of-victory-style measures.

Presence of Innocence Organizations

To measure the presence of innocence groups, we started by looking at the current listing of all Innocence Network member organizations. Working backward from this list, we identified the founding date for each organization. In most cases, this information was accessible online. In a small number of cases, however, this information was more challenging to uncover. If the information was not available on an organization's website, we searched through media coverage involving the organization and/or called the organization ourselves. We were ultimately successful in finding the founding date of every current member organization.

There are a couple of things we should note about these particular data. First, we missed some organizations. We only included organizations that were members of the Innocence Network as of late 2018, when we began compiling our data, and worked backward from there. There are, however, organizations that may not be members of the network. One such group of which we are aware is Centurion, the longest-standing nonprofit in the United States to focus on wrongful conviction work, but there may be others. In addition, there may be organizations that predate the Innocence Network (which admitted its first members in 2005), were once members of the network but are no longer, or for whatever reason disbanded.[51] Still, we almost certainly captured the majority of organizations, specifically those that are associated with and have the support of the larger Innocence Network.

Another important matter worth noting is that we used the founding date of innocence organizations to create a state-level variable, which was simply the number of innocence organizations in each state and year from 1989 to 2018. If in 1999 a state had no organizations of which we are aware, it was coded as a 0; if there were three organizations, it was coded as a 3. We wanted to give more weight to states and years that had more organizations, and this strategy did so. However, it missed other information about these organizations, such as their size, staff, and funding. Without a doubt, these issues are important to consider in assessing the potential influence such organizations have on state policy development. However, if anything, this particular limitation in our data is only likely to lead to an *under*estimate of their effect.

Exonerations

We included a variable that captures the number of known exonerations in each state, based on those reported in the National Registry of Exonerations. When wrongful convictions are uncovered and overturned, they are often newsworthy events, at least locally (if not nationally). They may generate media coverage and public attention. They indicate errors in the criminal legal system and raise awareness about them. It seems reasonable, then, that lawmakers would be open to reform in light of increasing exonerations. Furthermore, the number of exonerations in a given state, in theory, is likely to be correlated with the number and activity of innocence groups in that state. To tease out the effect of exonerations on policy reforms, we measured exonerations using a moving average that gave more weight to more recent exonerations but still allowed past exonerations to exert some effect.[52]

Control Variables

Finally, we included a variety of control variables. There are other features of states' political, social, criminal justice, and economic contexts that we believe might shape their commitment to wrongful conviction reform. For instance, we took into consideration partisan control of state legislatures and governors' offices, as lawmakers' means and opportunities to reform laws writ large are reduced if the partisan control of state legislatures is narrow or divided.[53] We also accounted for the partisan affiliation of states' citizenry, states' racial and ethnic demographics, and states' violent crime rates. These characteristics may influence wrongful conviction reforms directly, by motivating lawmakers to reform the law, or indirectly, by shaping states' opportunity and means for reform. For example, higher violent crime rates may encourage lawmakers to delegate more power and resources to law enforcement.

Analysis and Findings

We present our findings with respect to public opinion, electoral context, and wrongful conviction reforms in figures 2.2 and 2.3. As laid out earlier, our argument is that the effect of public opinion on states' commitment to wrongful convictions depends on states' electoral context, specifically, that the effect of the public's liberalism depends on state electoral competitiveness. We used an interaction effect in our statistical models to determine whether the evidence supports this idea. And, to cut to the chase, our interaction effect reached conventional levels of statistical significance, thereby supporting our argument. Figures 2.2 and 2.3 demonstrate precisely what these interaction effects reveal, empirically.

Figure 2.2 shows the effect of public liberalism on the number of wrongful conviction policies that a state adopted, depending on that state's level of electoral competition in the most recent election. The right-hand side of this figure captures the effect of public opinion in states with *high* electoral competition (e.g., states whose electoral competition index values are above 55). In these states, we found a strong and positive association between public liberalism and states' commitment to wrongful conviction reforms. Specifically, in states with very

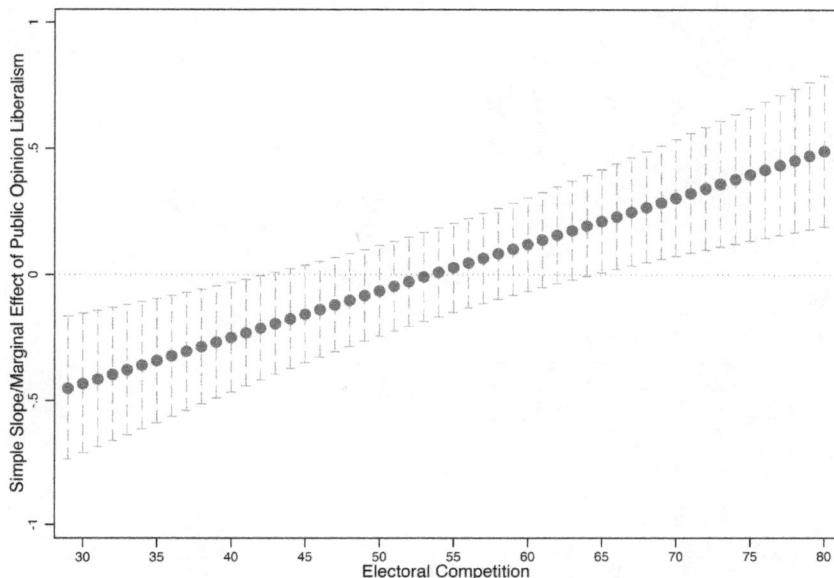

Figure 2.2. The effect of public opinion on wrongful conviction reforms
Note: This figure is based on the first model presented in table A.3 in the appendix.
Other variables are held to their mean values. Vertical lines represent 95 percent
confidence intervals.

high electoral competition (e.g., 81), a shift in public opinion liberalism
from its minimum to maximum value—that is, moving from very conservative on social policy opinions to very liberal—produces 1.9 new
wrongful conviction reforms in a year.

One feature of this figure that is worth noting is the vertical bars.
These vertical bars represent the 95 percent confidence intervals around
the precise effect of public opinion liberalism. These reveal that we can
be confident that public opinion positively affects wrongful conviction
reforms in states with high electoral competition and negatively affects
wrongful conviction reforms in states with low electoral competition.
However, we are less confident in the direction and magnitude of the
effect of public opinion on wrongful conviction reforms in states with
middling levels of electoral competition.

Finally, this figure also reveals that in states with minimal electoral
competition (e.g., an electoral competition index lower than 55), public

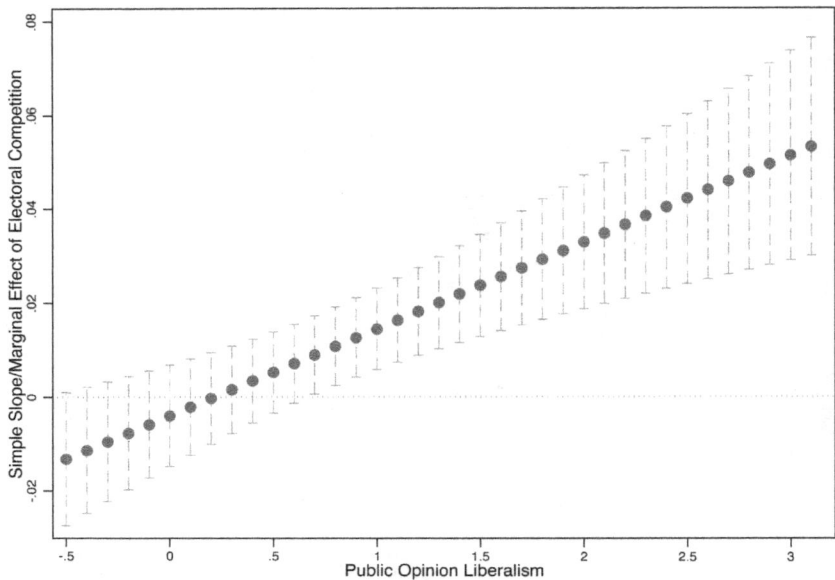

Figure 2.3. The effect of electoral competition on wrongful conviction reforms
Note: This figure is based on the first model presented in table A.3 in the appendix. Other variables are held to their mean values. Vertical lines represent 95 percent confidence intervals.

opinion liberalism actually exerted a *negative* effect on the number of wrongful conviction reforms. This finding raises an important question: Why would increasing public liberalism reduce the number of wrongful conviction reforms? To be clear, it is *not* the case that in states with low electoral competition, lawmakers are *removing* wrongful conviction reforms. Rather, our findings are driven by *inaction*. That is, in spite of large changes in public liberalism, lawmakers who face limited electoral competition are not opposing wrongful convictions reforms but simply avoiding them entirely. Considered this way, this finding is actually fairly consistent with our expectations. We argued earlier that electoral competition fuels legislative action by motivating lawmakers to take more risks, and this graph is consistent with that.

We now turn to figure 2.3, which presents the effect of electoral competition on wrongful conviction reforms depending on states' public opinion liberalism. It reveals how many wrongful conviction reforms a state adopts in light of changing electoral competition, assuming specific levels of public opinion liberalism. Unlike figure 2.2, this one does not provide evidence that the effect changes direction (or at least not sufficiently so) for us to feel more than 95 percent confident. In the most conservative states, increasing the amount of electoral competition has a very weak and *possibly* negative effect on wrongful conviction reforms. That being said, we are very confident that an increase in electoral competition will increase the number of wrongful conviction reforms in states with moderate to liberal public opinion. In fact, in states with very liberal public opinion (e.g., 3.14), an increase in electoral competition from its minimum to its maximum increases the number of wrongful conviction reforms by more than 2.9 in a year.

Clearly, public liberalism and electoral competition might influence the adoption of wrongful conviction reforms, but what about states' wrongful conviction context? Does the presence of innocence organizations or the number of exonerations shape the number of wrongful conviction reforms a state adopts?

Our answer is a clear *yes* to both, although, interestingly, our findings suggest that the presence of innocence groups and the number of exonerations both exert somewhat smaller effects than public opinion does. We present findings regarding these variables in figures 2.4 and 2.5.

First, figure 2.4 shows the expected number of wrongful conviction reforms as the number of innocence groups in a state increases from the minimum to the maximum among states in any year. Here, we found that a state and year with the most innocence groups (versus a state and year with the fewest innocence groups) had roughly 0.66 more wrongful conviction reforms, other things being equal.

Figure 2.5 then shows the expected number of wrongful conviction reforms as the average number of exonerations in the preceding years shifts from its minimum to its maximum value. As with the presence of innocence organizations, states that had experienced many exonerations over the preceding years adopted more wrongful conviction reforms than did states that did not. For example, other things being equal, a state with roughly ten exonerations over the prior four years had about 0.6 more reforms.

To be sure, the effects of both wrongful conviction variables—the presence of innocence groups and the number of exonerations—reached

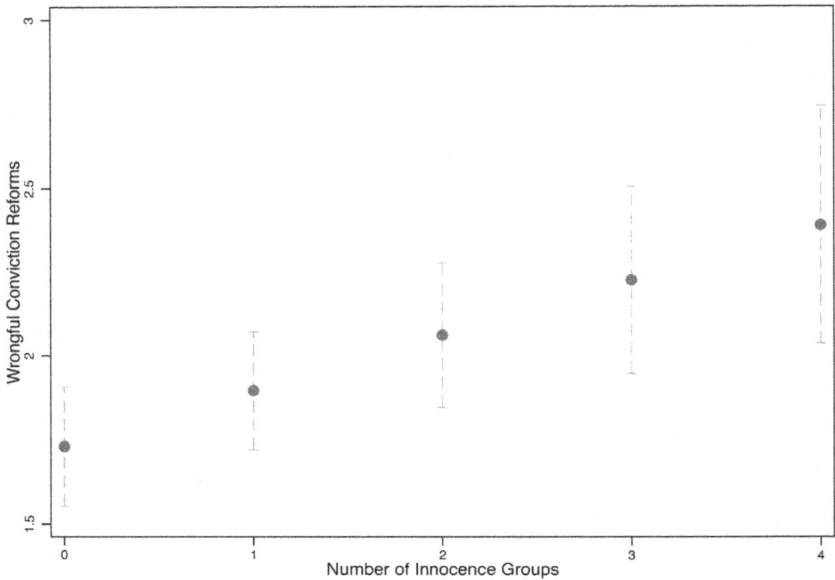

Figure 2.4. The effect of the presence of innocence organizations on wrongful conviction reforms
Note: This figure is based on the first model presented in table A.3 in the appendix. Other variables are held to their mean values. Vertical lines represent 95 percent confidence intervals.

conventional levels of significance in each and every statistical model we fit to these data, but the specific effects for both were smaller than those of public opinion.

Our control variables revealed at least three things about wrongful conviction reforms that we believe are worth discussing. First, time itself has an important effect on states' commitment to wrongful conviction reform. While figure 2.1 demonstrates this, our statistical models indicated that time matters even after adjusting for other variables. Although at different speeds, all states were increasingly likely to adopt these reforms. It appears that there is something of a broader trend across all of the states toward wrongful conviction reform. Figure 2.6 shows the predicted number of reforms in the average state controlling for other variables.

Second, we did not find consistent evidence that states' racial demographics affected the adoption of wrongful conviction reforms, controlling for other variables. Of course, the politics of wrongful conviction reform are intimately related to the discourse on race, equality, policing, and the like. That said, we did not find a statistically significant pattern of evidence that suggests states with relatively more racial and ethnic minorities were any more or less inclined to adopt these reforms than other states—at least not yet. Of course, this very well may change in years to come. Indeed, organizations like the Innocence Project have been involved in broader criminal legal reform that has direct ties to social and racial inequality—discussions about the bail system, the death penalty, and police accountability, for instance—which could lead to innocence-related reform becoming more racialized. We return to these matters later in this book, but suffice it to say, this is something worth keeping an eye on and exploring further in future research.

Third, partisan politics matter somewhat. In a variety of models, we found that states with Democratic governors were more likely to adopt

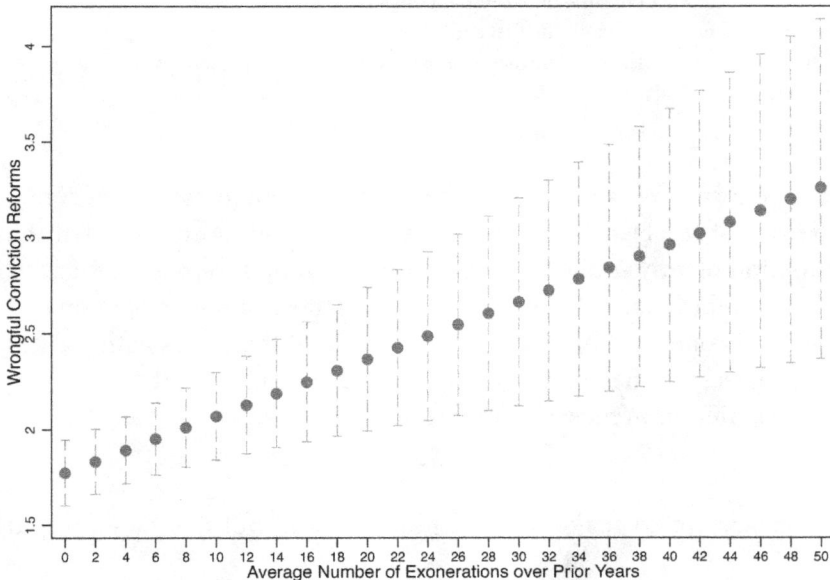

Figure 2.5. The effect of exonerations on wrongful conviction reforms
Note: This figure is based on the first model presented in table A.3 in the appendix. Other variables are held to their mean values. Vertical lines represent 95 percent confidence intervals.

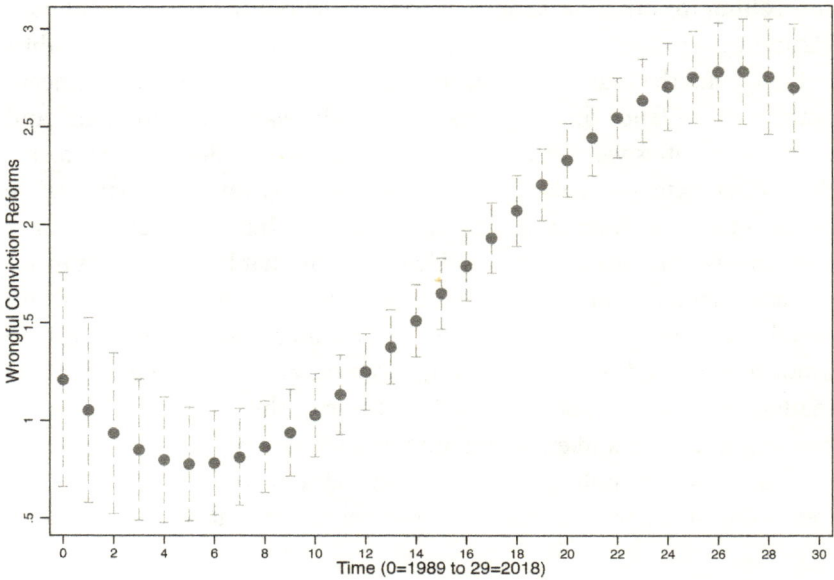

Figure 2.6. The effect of time on wrongful conviction reform
Note: This figure is based on the first model presented in table A.3 in the appendix. Other variables are held to their mean values. Vertical lines represent 95 percent confidence intervals.

these reforms. We also found some evidence, though more mixed, that the size of the Democratic majority in state legislatures affected the adoption of wrongful conviction reforms. To be sure, the substantive effects of these variables were weaker than those of public opinion and electoral competition—for example, we found that states with Democratic governors had on average 0.17 more reforms—but it was statistically significant in most of our models.

* * *

What are we to make, at this point, of the politics of wrongful convictions?

From what we have presented in this chapter, we may draw several tentative conclusions. First, it is clear that state governments are in the midst of experimenting with reforms in an effort to address wrongful convictions. Across the United States, the number of jurisdictions enacting policies that align with the innocence movement's agenda has increased over the past three decades, but policy adoption is uneven across specific issues. DNA-access and evidence-preservation laws are nearly ubiquitous at this point, while alterations to police practices that may help mitigate wrongful convictions—changes in eyewitness identification procedures and interrogation recording, specifically—are less common. Still, it is clear that the innocence movement has had a measurable degree of success in these five priority areas.

Our results also suggest that states' political context—public opinion and electoral competition, in particular—may provide a good explanation for why states differ in their commitments to addressing wrongful convictions. Electorally competitive states whose public opinion trends liberal are more likely to adopt these reforms and to adopt them more quickly.

Given the critical role of public opinion in shaping legislative responses to wrongful convictions, we are left with lingering questions about the public's views regarding wrongful convictions in particular, and we turn next to exactly this subject. Over the next three chapters, we offer critical, in-depth analyses that directly assess the dynamics that underlie citizens' awareness of and beliefs about wrongful convictions, how learning about wrongful convictions influences other attitudes toward the criminal legal system, and the types of political communication and messaging strategies that may best mobilize support for innocence reforms.

As in our analysis of state policy adoption, we pay particular attention to the role of ideology in these matters and emphasize what we have argued throughout: politics matter.

3

Public Awareness of Wrongful Convictions

In 2013, Rabia Chaudry contacted the journalist Sarah Koenig. Years earlier, Koenig had written several articles about Cristina Gutierrez, a defense attorney in Baltimore, Maryland, who was disbarred in 2001 and died in 2004. In 1999, Gutierrez had represented a friend of Chaudry's named Adnan Syed, who was convicted of murder. Chaudry believed he was innocent and asked Koenig, who was the producer of the popular radio program *This American Life*, to look into the case.[1] Koenig was interested and agreed.

Syed's case revolved around the murder of Hae Min Lee, a high school senior who disappeared in January 1999 and whose body was found the next month in a wooded area of a nearby park. She had been strangled. Suspicion fell on Syed, her classmate and ex-boyfriend, and he was arrested in late February.

Syed maintained his innocence, and no physical evidence linked him to the crime. His attorney failed to call a potential alibi witness who claimed to have spoken with Syed at the library around the apparent time of the murder. The conviction rested largely on the word of Syed's acquaintance Jay, whose story changed multiple times but who ultimately testified that Syed killed Lee and that he (Jay) had helped bury the body. Jay also led police to Lee's abandoned car. Finally, there was cellphone-tower evidence that may have put Syed's phone near Lee's burial site, though that evidence has come into question.[2] Despite the uncertainty, a jury convicted the seventeen-year-old Syed in 2000, and he was sentenced to life in prison.

By the time Koenig investigated the case, Syed was thirty-two years old. Her yearlong investigation eventually led her to produce and host a podcast about the case called *Serial*, which was released in October 2014 to critical and popular acclaim. By early December, it had garnered more downloads on iTunes than any other podcast in history, and it remains among the most popular podcasts ever released.[3]

For years, there was considerable public debate about Syed's guilt. Finally, in September 2022, after Syed had spent twenty-three years in prison, a Baltimore judge vacated his conviction, and he was released. A month later, prosecutors dropped the charges against him.[4] Syed's case and the *Serial* podcast about it raised serious questions about the integrity of criminal investigations and the reliability of convictions. Perhaps more importantly for our purposes, *Serial*'s popularity is indicative of the public's thirst for true crime in general and for coverage of wrongful or otherwise questionable convictions more specifically. The series seemingly injected questions about the criminal process and skepticism about its results into the public consciousness on a larger scale than previously seen. As happened in Syed's case, media and other popular attention to these issues does not always come in the form of clear-cut instances in which, for example, DNA evidence exonerates an innocent individual and identifies the real perpetrator. News stories, podcasts, and documentaries may raise awareness of innocence by discussing cases in which there is considerable ambiguity; in fact, these situations may be particularly captivating for readers, listeners, and viewers.

Still, questions remain about the extent to which the American public, broadly, is aware of wrongful convictions, or the potential for errors, in the criminal legal system. In this chapter, we discuss the pervasiveness of wrongful convictions throughout US culture—across various forms of popular media, in the news, in research and scholarship, and in education. We then use data from two original surveys to explore how aware people are about wrongful convictions, their beliefs about how often wrongful convictions occur, and their perceptions about specific issues that may contribute to such errors.

Public (In)Justice

Serial is neither the first nor the only example of a questionable conviction capturing the popular imagination. As we discussed in chapter 1, public attention on errors of justice is not strictly a new phenomenon. Several cases throughout the past century have generated widespread reporting, popular depictions, and celebrity involvement. However, *Serial* seemingly came on the front end of a remarkable wave of popular coverage. Not only was it downloaded hundreds of millions of times and did it become the first podcast ever to win a Peabody Award, a prestigious honor for storytelling in television, radio, or other digital media, but it has also influenced dozens of popular podcasts addressing wrongful convictions and adjacent issues.[5]

The popularity of criminal injustices is not restricted to the realm of podcasts. Virtually all avenues of popular culture have incorporated wrongful or otherwise questionable convictions with success. Feature films like *Conviction* (starring Hilary Swank and Sam Rockwell) and *Trial by Fire* (starring Laura Dern and Jack O'Connell) have made their way to the box office, while various series have become hits. For example, *When They See Us*, a Netflix miniseries directed by Ava DuVernay, tells the story of the Central Park Five (now sometimes referred to as the "Exonerated Five"), a group of Black and Latino teenagers who falsely confessed to the rape and assault of a woman in New York City in 1989. During the time of the investigation and trials, the case generated widespread public outcry—then–real estate mogul Donald Trump infamously spent about $85,000 placing ads in newspapers at the time, calling for New York to "BRING BACK THE DEATH PENALTY"—and resulted in all five defendants being wrongly convicted.[6] The case is among the most widely known errors, and the Netflix series about the case quickly became one of the most watched shows ever on Netflix, apparently viewed by more than twenty-three million accounts within the first couple of weeks after its release.[7] Netflix and other streaming platforms also have consistently added documentaries touching on wrongful convictions to their libraries, kick-started in part by the success of *Making a Murderer*, a 2015 docuseries about the convictions of Steven Avery and Brendan Dassey in Wisconsin. The series was estimated to have been watched nearly twenty million times in its first month of release and rivaled *20/20* with regard to viewership numbers.[8]

Other forms of popular culture also have focused increasingly on wrongful convictions. Dozens of case narratives written by and/or about the wrongly convicted have been published and have achieved commercial success. For example, Anthony Ray Hinton's memoir, *The Sun Does Shine*, was a *New York Times* best-seller and selected for Oprah's Book Club in 2018.[9] Other popular authors have tackled wrongful convictions, such as John Grisham, who has published one nonfiction book about the wrongful conviction of Ron Williamson and at least two novels centered on innocence, one of which features a character based on the Centurion founder, Jim McCloskey.[10] Tayari Jones's novel *An American Marriage* also prominently features a wrongful conviction and was a *New York Times* best-seller and Oprah's Book Club selection.

The increasing attention to wrongful convictions in popular culture has accompanied similar shifts in media coverage of criminal justice issues. The late 1990s and early 2000s marked the beginning of such shifts, which were particularly evident in discourse around capital punishment. As the political scientist Frank Baumgartner and colleagues have shown, more newspaper coverage was devoted to the death penalty throughout the 1990s, "leav[ing] no doubt that the death penalty [became] increasingly prominent on the public agenda."[11] And, notably, the tone of death penalty coverage became more negative toward the practice as the turn of the century approached. By 2000, issues related to innocence, evidence, and flaws in the system were an integral part of media coverage of the death penalty. Importantly, the increasing media attention on wrongful convictions has not revolved solely around capital punishment, nor has it been isolated to individual cases in local newspapers; it has also been featured in major periodicals such as the *Atlantic*, the *New Yorker*, *Slate*, and *Time*.[12]

This explosion in media coverage has coincided with the rise of the innocence movement, which emerged in the early 2000s and brought with it increased attention to wrongful convictions in criminal legal practice and advocacy. The issue has also expanded dramatically within the academy, as wrongful conviction has become a prominent topic for scholars in law, criminology, political science, sociology, psychology, and more. Indeed, while far from a perfect metric, a Google Scholar search for "wrongful conviction" shows the increasing number of publications over time, as presented in table 3.1. In a search for materials published from 1990 through 1999, there was a total of 939 search results. The number then increased dramatically for each five-year period since the turn of the century.[13] And although we have no exact measure for exactly how widespread coverage of wrongful conviction is in the academic world, a number of generalist books and edited volumes have been released, well suited or explicitly designed for classroom use, as more colleges and universities have offered courses on miscarriages of justice in their undergraduate, graduate, and law school programs.[14]

TABLE 3.1. Google Scholar Results for "Wrongful Conviction"

Years included	Number of results
1990–1999	939
2000–2004	1,210
2005–2009	2,390
2010–2014	3,660
2015–2019	4,540

Undoubtedly, over the past twenty or thirty years, there has been a marked uptick in wrongful conviction coverage in the United States across various forms of media and in several different popular arenas. Given the proliferation of scholarship, news stories, and entertainment media focused on miscarriages of justice, it is no surprise that some people have suggested that "the world is now more aware of wrongful convictions than ever."[15] However, we have little systematic, empirical evidence to evaluate the veracity of this claim. Thus, the question remains, just how aware are people of wrongful convictions? This question, interesting in its own right, also raises two related issues: first, that we know relatively little about how frequently people believe wrongful convictions occur and what they perceive as the underlying problems that lead to such errors and, second, that there has been little attention to the characteristics of those who are and are not aware of the issue.

Throughout the remainder of this chapter, we address these questions using data from original surveys. As we demonstrate, a substantial proportion of the mass public is aware of wrongful convictions, they get such information from a variety of sources, and they are able to identify common problems that contribute to such errors. We also find, however, that awareness is not distributed evenly. Rather, consistent with our broader argument throughout this book, politics matter, insofar as people's political interest and ideology color their awareness of and beliefs about wrongful convictions.

What People Know and How They Know It

Given that academic scholarship, traditional news outlets, books, podcasts, movies, and television increasingly discuss wrongful convictions, we wanted to know the extent to which the mass public is aware of the issue.

Public *awareness* is a vague and murky concept. It means different things to different people and can be measured and analyzed in a variety of ways. As such, we designed a survey using a variety of questions that tap into different features of wrongful convictions awareness. This is labeled as "Survey 1" in the appendix.

Our first set of survey items was designed to gauge what people have heard about wrongful convictions and where they got their information. Our second set of questions then examined people's beliefs about the pervasiveness of wrongful convictions. We address each of these matters in turn.[16]

Wrongful conviction stories are often focused on real individuals and narratives, but dramatized fictional accounts are also abundant in books, movies, and television. Because of this, we wanted our questions to distinguish between true and fictional coverage of wrongful convictions.

First, given that some participants might have been uncertain about what we meant by the phrase "wrongful conviction," our survey started with the following introductory statement: "I am going to ask several questions about 'wrongful convictions.' A wrongful conviction occurs when a person is convicted of a criminal offense, but is in fact innocent. In other words, the person did not commit the crime." We then asked respondents, "In the last few years, have you heard any *true* stories about an innocent person who was wrongly convicted of a crime they did not commit?" A solid majority—more than two-thirds—said "Yes."

From the outset, we recognize that these are self-reported measures of awareness and therefore may be subject to social desirability biases. That is, survey respondents may answer questions in ways that they believe will be viewed more favorably by others.[17] As such, it is conceivable that the true number may be slightly lower. However, we have several reasons to think that such biases played little role here and that this percentage is fairly accurate. First, this type of survey question does not have a clear socially desirable response; there is no clear and powerful *good* or *bad* response in a person saying they have or have not heard a wrongful conviction story. Second, we know that wrongful conviction information is abundant in media and popular culture, and prior scholarship has demonstrated that aggregate shifts in news coverage that

TABLE 3.2. How Many People Have Heard of Wrongful Convictions, and From What Sources?

Question	% of total sample	% among those who heard
Heard true story	68.27	
TV news	48.63	71.23
print or online news	18.41	26.96
social media	21.16	30.99
documentary	20.47	29.98
podcast	3.30	4.83
book	6.18	9.05
movie	15.66	22.94
TV show	18.82	27.57
radio	4.26	6.24
Heard fictional story	45.59	
book	13.64	29.91
movie	29.34	64.35
TV show	29.20	64.05
podcast	2.75	6.04

Note: These data come from Survey 1, which we discuss in the appendix. Respondents were allowed to pick multiple options, so these sources are not mutually exclusive. Many respondents heard both true and fictional stories from multiple sources.

increasingly feature "innocence issues" are tied to shifts in public support for capital punishment over time.[18] Thus, it is not unbelievable that a majority of people report having heard these true stories. Finally, as we discuss later, there was predictable variation between individuals in their level of awareness, and it seems unlikely that social desirability biases only apply to particular subsets of the population.

In addition to understanding how many people were aware of wrongful convictions, we wanted to know the sources of their information. For those who said that they had heard true wrongful conviction stories, we asked a follow-up question to learn where they heard them. Television news was the most common response; nearly three-fourths of respondents who had heard a true story about a wrongful conviction also said that they heard it from television news. The next two most common sources of true stories were social media and documentaries, although they were much less common—less than one-third of respondents who heard a true story indicated each of these as their source. Respondents were least likely to indicate that they had heard true wrongful conviction stories from books, radio, and podcasts. Thus, even though podcasts like *Serial*, mentioned at the outset of this chapter, might garner widespread popular attention, they represent only a small portion of where people receive this type of information.

Although we do not explore it in detail here, we note that the precise percentage of respondents selecting each option differed predictably by demographic characteristics. For example, we performed chi-squared tests that revealed significant differences in whether respondents reported having heard a true story about a wrongful conviction, on the basis of their race and age. Black respondents were the most likely to have heard a true story about a wrongful conviction, with 83 percent saying that they had. Indeed, Black respondents were two and a half times more likely than white respondents to report that they had heard a true story about a wrongful conviction.[19] On the other hand, respondents who identified as Hispanic or Latino were only slightly more likely than non-Hispanic white respondents to have head a true story about a wrongful conviction: 70 percent of Hispanic/Latino respondents said that they had heard a true story, while only 66 percent of non-Hispanic white respondents said the same. With regard to age, younger respondents were more likely than older respondents to have heard a true wrongful conviction story, with 81 percent of eighteen- to twenty-four-year-olds saying that they had. This age group was two and a half times more likely than thirty-five- to fifty-year-olds and two times more likely than fifty-one- to sixty-five-year-olds to say that they had heard a true story about a wrongful conviction. Interestingly, the oldest age group, respondents over sixty-five years of age, were only slightly less likely compared to the youngest cohort to have heard a true story about a wrongful conviction, with nearly 79 percent saying that they had. Finally, respondents with college degrees were more likely to have heard a true story (71 percent) than were noncollege graduates (66 percent), but this difference was not statistically significant.

It is also useful to consider the broader sample with regard to the sources of wrongful conviction information. For example, while a large majority of people who had heard a true story said that they did so from television news, just under half of our *full sample* (49 percent) had heard a true wrongful conviction story from TV news, and only about one-fifth of our full sample had heard a true story from social media or documentaries, respectively. We also gave respondents an "Other" option, where they could type in an information source in case our list was not exhaustive. A few respondents chose this option and reported things such as "From [a] close, personal friend who was wrongfully convicted" or "personal experience." We even had an individual comment that a respondent had heard about wrongful convictions from a relative who was the head of an innocence project. However, because these data were collected through an anonymous online survey, we were unable to follow up with these individual respondents to verify reports and collect more information.

Whereas a solid majority—more than two-thirds of our sample—said that they had heard *true* stories, fewer than half of our respondents said that they had "heard any *fictional* stories (not true) about an innocent person who was wrongly convicted of a crime they did not commit." That we observed variation between the true and fictional accounts of wrongful convictions bolsters our earlier point that social desirability biases were probably not driving the "Yes" responses, because if that had been the case, we would expect similar percentages for both questions. Thus, a majority of the people sampled had heard true stories, and almost half of them heard fictional depictions of wrongful convictions. Unsurprisingly, by far the most common sources of the fictional accounts were movies (64 percent) and television (64 percent), with books (30 percent) as the distant third.

In addition to asking people whether they had heard stories about wrongful convictions, we wanted to know whether people were aware of innocence advocacy efforts, so we asked respondents, "Have you ever heard of the Innocence Project?" As we have discussed, there are numerous innocence organizations throughout the United States, but the New York–based Innocence Project is by far the largest and most prominent; and the organization (or others like it that use the "Innocence Project" name) is often mentioned in media coverage of exonerations. In response to this question, 43 percent of the sample said that they had heard of the Innocence Project.[20] This is an interesting finding and speaks to the success of innocence advocates in spreading their brand into mainstream coverage. As is the case with any social advocacy movement, making the public aware of key individuals and/or organizations may be vital to the health of the Innocence Project, the Innocence Network, and the broader coalition of innocence advocates.

Who Is Aware of Wrongful Convictions?

We have shown that a substantial proportion of people have heard stories of wrongful conviction and have heard of the Innocence Project, but we also explored the characteristics of those in our sample who were (and were not) aware of wrongful convictions. To learn more about these groups of people, we applied statistical models to each of the three types of awareness described earlier: people who had heard of the Innocence Project, people who had heard true stories of wrongful convictions, and people who had heard fictional stories of wrongful convictions. These models allowed us to evaluate the extent to which respondents' political predispositions shaped their level of awareness, controlling for other demographic characteristics such age, race, sex/gender, and educational attainment.[21]

The full results of our statistical models are included in the appendix and show that two political variables predicted respondents' awareness of wrongful convictions. First, there were significant differences between respondents on the basis of their political ideology, particularly when it came to hearing true stories of wrongful convictions and hearing about the Innocence Project. Figure 3.1 elaborates on our statistical models by showing the likelihood that a self-reported liberal, moderate, and conservative report having heard of the Innocence Project or true or fictional stories of wrongful convictions, controlling for other characteristics.

Figure 3.1 shows that liberals were much more likely to report having heard of the Innocence Project and having heard a true story about a wrongful conviction, relative to conservatives. For example, controlling for other variables, the probability that a liberal had heard a true story about a wrongful conviction was 64 percent, while the probability that a conservative had heard the same was only 50 percent. The gap between liberals and conservatives was even greater when it comes to those who had heard of the Innocence Project. The probability that a liberal had heard of the Innocence Project was 42 percent, while the probability

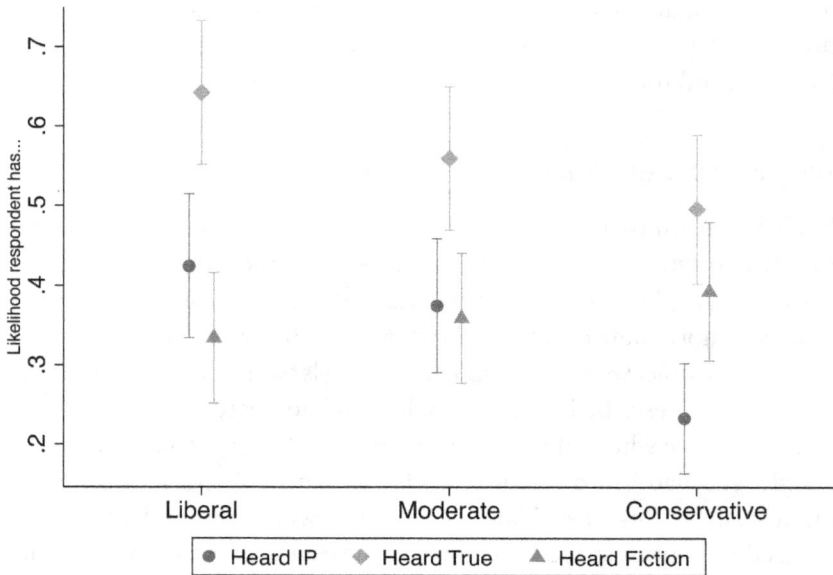

Figure 3.1. Ideology and wrongful conviction awareness
Note: These quantities are based on the models presented in table A.4 in the appendix. Other variables are held to their median values. Vertical lines represent 95 percent confidence intervals.

for a conservative was just 23 percent. These two differences—in hearing true stories of wrongful conviction and in hearing of the Innocence Project—were statistically significant. Interestingly, however, the differences between liberals and conservatives in their exposure to *fictional* stories about wrongful convictions were statistically *in*significant.

These findings—that liberals and conservatives differ in how likely they are to hear about the Innocence Project and to hear true stories of wrongful conviction but not fictional stories—is interesting and begs the question, why?

One plausible explanation is that there are more pronounced ideological differences in the selection of news media—the primary source of information about true wrongful conviction stories—than in entertainment media. Political communication scholars have debated the role and consumption of ideologically driven media. Some have suggested, and some evidence supports the notion, that as the public has become increasingly polarized politically, "media choices increasingly reflect partisan considerations."[22] To the extent that this is true, and given the ideological differences often found in criminal justice preferences, it seems plausible that political conservatives who rely on conservative media may be less likely to hear true stories of wrongful conviction that may call into question, for example, the actions and integrity of the police. This issue of potential ideological differences in news coverage of wrongful convictions is one we discuss more in the conclusion. On the other hand, it is less likely that liberals and conservatives differ as dramatically in the types of movies and television shows they consume. We might, then, consider the implications of this. If conservatives are primarily only exposed to this type of information through fictional entertainment, it may have consequences for their beliefs about the extent to which wrongful convictions and related problems occur in the criminal legal system, a matter to which we return later in this chapter.

In addition to ideological differences in awareness of wrongful convictions, we suspected that there might be differences based on people's political interest. For decades, scholars have noted that some individuals are more interested in politics than others, and research has demonstrated that political interest is consequential for a wide range of political attitudes and behaviors. As the political scientist Markus Prior has stated, the "interested seek out more news, learn more about politics, and participate at higher rates."[23] Given that the politically interested are inclined to stay informed about current events and political happenings, it seemed plausible that they would be more aware of wrongful convictions than those who are less interested, and that is precisely what we found. Respondents' self-reported interest in politics was the most consistently significant variable explaining their level of awareness. Controlling for other variables, respondents who described themselves as interested in politics were more likely to have heard stories about wrongful convictions and to have heard about the Innocence Project. It is worth noting that these models include ideology, so this is not driven by interested liberals or interested conservatives only. Rather, political interest, in and of itself, appears to independently drive awareness of wrongful convictions.

Figure 3.2 shows the likelihood that respondents had heard true or fictional wrongful conviction stories or had heard about the Innocence

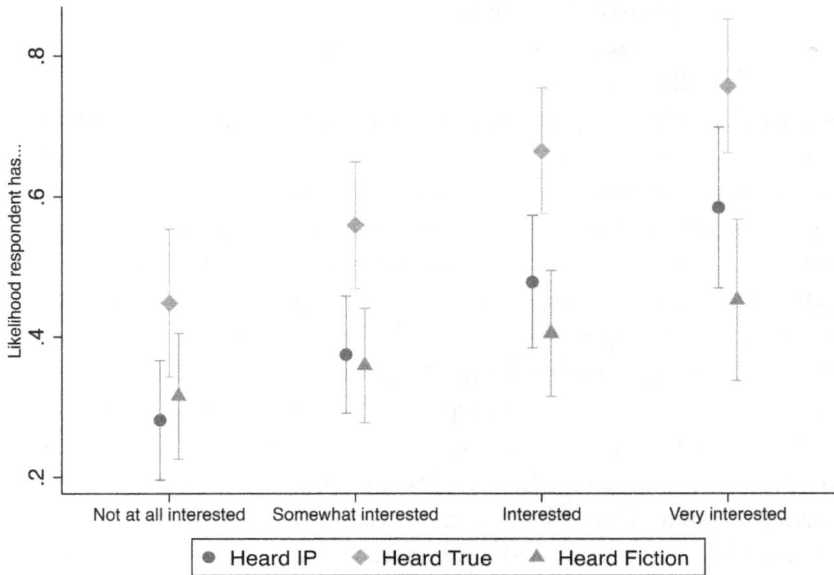

Figure 3.2. Political interest and wrongful conviction awareness
Note: These quantities are based on the models presented in table A.4 in the appendix. Other variables are held to their median values. Vertical lines represent 95 percent confidence intervals.

Project, on the basis of their level of political interest. The relationship between political interest and awareness of this issue was particularly evident for the outcome measuring whether respondents had heard true accounts of wrongful convictions. Other things being equal, respondents who reported being very interested in politics were nearly thirty-one percentage points more likely to have heard a true story about a wrongful conviction than respondents who reported that they were not at all interested (76 percent versus 45 percent, respectively).

This finding that higher political interest is associated with an increased likelihood of hearing a true wrongful conviction story is intuitive given that the people most interested in politics are more likely to seek out news information. Still, it is an important consideration, as it may have consequences for innocence advocates as they work to garner support for reforms and encourage people to engage in activism. Indeed, Markus Prior notes that the most interested are "more likely to be mobilized and attempts to encourage political participation often have significantly greater effects on individuals who are politically interested to begin with."[24] Thus, not only are the politically interested more aware of wrongful convictions; they might also be the ripest for political mobilization.

Although we do not show the results in a graphic here, we implemented another survey ("Survey 2" in the appendix) to see if this same pattern of results emerged in a different sample implemented at a different point in time. The results are shown in table A.6 in the appendix and confirm the findings shown here. Ideology was a significant predictor of hearing true accounts of wrongful convictions and awareness of the Innocence Project but was not associated with hearing fictional accounts. We found, other things being equal, that liberals were nearly twenty percentage points more likely to have heard about the Innocence Project and sixteen percentage points more likely to have heard a true story about a wrongful conviction, relative to conservatives.[25]

Across two studies, then, the pattern was consistent. It does not appear to be a fluke that ideology is related to awareness of wrongful convictions, as measured by hearing factual accounts of wrongful convictions and being aware of the Innocence Project. Additionally, as with the first survey, the second one showed that people with higher levels of political interest were significantly more likely to be exposed to information about wrongful convictions (across all three measures) than were the less politically interested.

The Perceived Scope of Wrongful Convictions

Hearing about wrongful convictions and the organizations that fight to overturn them is one aspect of awareness. A related but slightly different feature of awareness is rooted in people's beliefs about the frequency and scope of wrongful convictions. To understand this, we asked people how often they think innocent individuals are convicted of crimes they did not commit, whether they think an innocent person has recently been executed, and how often they think various types of errors occur in the criminal legal system (e.g., witness misidentification, mishandling of evidence, false confessions). As in the previous section, we first discuss the views of the broader population and then analyze the subsets of people that hold particular beliefs.

Perceived Frequency of Wrongful Convictions

We first wanted to know beliefs among the general public about the rate at which wrongful convictions occur. Informally, this is something we have regularly asked our students to kick-start class discussions about the criminal legal system and it generally yields a wide variety of responses, but there has been relatively little empirical attention paid to the topic. One 2005 survey of Michigan residents found that a majority of respondents believed that wrongful convictions occur "occasionally"; when asked to choose among specific categories of error rates, the most common choice was "4–5%," and more than four out of five respondents chose estimates between 1 and 10 percent. The survey also found that a majority of respondents believed that "wrongful convictions occur frequently enough to justify major changes in the criminal justice system."[26]

When designing our survey to gauge the public's perception of the frequency of errors, we thought it possible that people might think that wrongful convictions occur at different rates for different types of crimes. For instance, people might believe that more serious crimes are associated with more careful investigations and thorough trials involving a closer scrutiny of evidence, thus leading to lower error rates than for less serious crimes. To account for this possibility, we asked two separate questions. First, we asked, "Overall in the United States, of all people who are convicted of *felonies* (serious crimes that lead to a prison sentence), what percent do you think are wrongly convicted?" We then asked the same question about "people who are convicted of *misdemeanors* (less serious crimes that lead to short jail sentences or fines)." For both questions, there were several categories of responses that ranged from "less than 1%" to "more than 25%."

Figure 3.3 summarizes the results of these first two questions. The median response category for beliefs about the percentage of people who are wrongfully convicted for both felonies and misdemeanors was 5–6 percent. It is noteworthy that this percentage is fairly consistent with many scholarly estimates of the rate of wrongful convictions, the most empirically grounded of which tend to fall in the 3 to 6 percent range.[27]

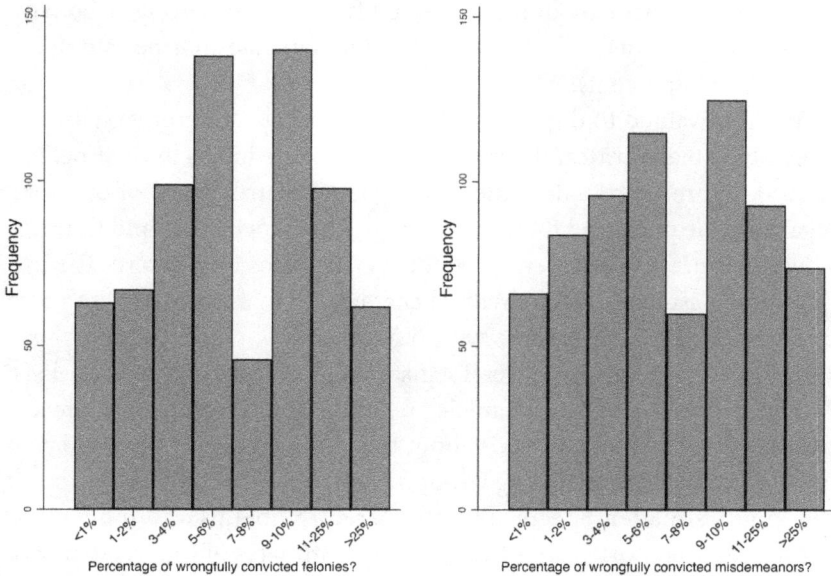

Figure 3.3. How frequently do people believe wrongful convictions occur?
Note: These data are derived from Survey 1. See the appendix for more information.
5–6 percent represents the median category for both.

This suggests that not only does the mass public hear these stories but that they also are quite reasonable in their evaluations of the pervasiveness of the problem.

Although not our main focus here, we briefly juxtapose these results regarding people's beliefs about the actual rate of wrongful convictions with a comment on the rate they deem acceptable. In addition to the questions about their perceived rate of errors, we also asked, "While it would be ideal to have a perfect justice system, some people recognize this is not possible. There are different errors that may lead innocent people to be wrongly convicted of crimes they did not commit. In your opinion, what is a tolerable rate of wrongful convictions?" In response to this question, the modal response category, chosen by nearly half of our respondents, was "less than 1%," and the median category of tolerable rates was "1–2%." There is thus a gap between people's beliefs about the state of the criminal legal system (what they believe *actually* happens) and what they believe is tolerable (what they think *should* happen). That is, the median estimate of the perceived frequency of wrongful convictions (5–6 percent) is higher than the median rate that people deem tolerable (1–2 percent).

We also wanted to dig deeper than these simple descriptive statistics, which may mask critical differences between individuals in their beliefs. Indeed, figure 3.3 reveals somewhat bimodal distributions of opinions regarding the perceived frequency of wrongful convictions, and the considerable variation between respondents' estimates underscores the importance of isolating the individual characteristics associated with these disparate views. Therefore, as with our analysis of basic awareness presented earlier, we relied on several statistical models to explore these beliefs.

The full results of these models are presented in table A.5 in the appendix, alongside other details about the models themselves. Similar to our earlier findings regarding wrongful conviction awareness, we found that politics matter. Specifically, compared to liberals and moderates, conservatives reported significantly lower estimates of the frequency of wrongful convictions for both felonies and misdemeanors, and respondents with higher levels of political interest reported higher estimates than those with lower levels of political interest.

Race and age, controlling for other things, also shape respondents' perception about the frequency of wrongful convictions. Black respondents and Hispanic/Latino respondents, for example, tended to think that wrongful convictions are more common than non-Hispanic white respondents did, with respect to both felonies and misdemeanors. Our models suggest that, after holding other variables to their median values, Black respondents are more likely to be in the 7–8 percent category for the frequency of felony wrongful convictions, while white respondents are likely to be in the 5–6 percent category. Age was also important, with young respondents more likely to think that wrongful convictions occur more frequently than older respondents were. The youngest cohort, eighteen- to twenty-four-year-olds, was a full unit higher on the outcome than was the oldest cohort, which includes people over the age of sixty-five.

Perceptions of Wrongful Executions

In addition to asking people about how often they perceive wrongful convictions to occur in felony and misdemeanor cases, we wanted to

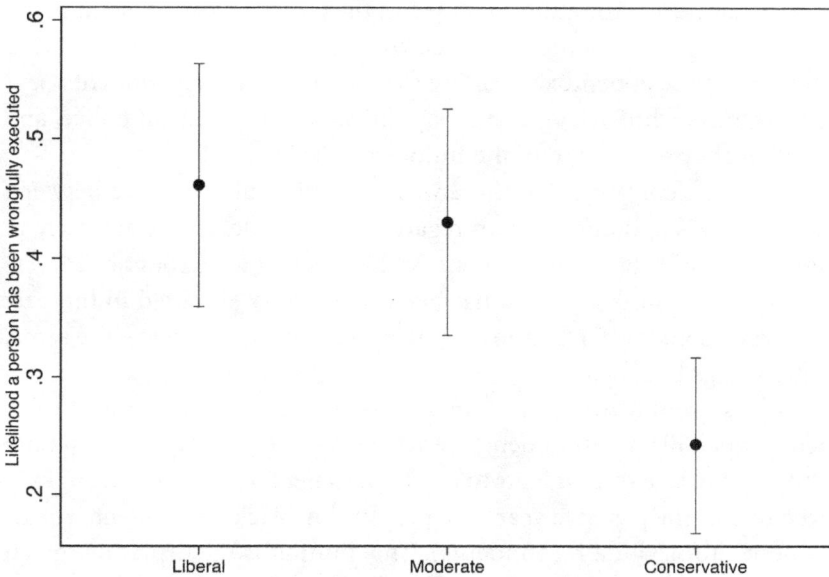

Figure 3.4. Ideology and beliefs about wrongful executions
Note: These quantities are based on the final model presented in table A.5 in the appendix. Other variables are held to their median values. Vertical bars represent 95 percent confidence intervals.

know about people's perceptions regarding wrongful executions. To assess this, we asked the following yes-or-no question, similar to one that has been asked in Gallup polls: "Do you think that a person has been executed under the death penalty in the past five years who was, in fact, innocent of the crime he or she was charged with?" More than half of our respondents (52 percent) said yes in response to this question. Our results are in line with previous Gallup poll results for this question; when the question was last asked in October 2009, 59 percent of people thought that an innocent person had been executed in the past five years. This finding is also consistent with a significant body of scholarship that suggests that the rise of the "innocence frame" in media discourse has played a crucial role in the declining support for the death penalty over the past two decades.[28]

Again, we wanted to know whether this belief was related to respondents' ideology. Figure 3.4 plots the probability that someone believes a person has been wrongfully executed in the past five years depending on their ideology. The figure is derived from the third model presented in table A.5 in the appendix, meaning that it controls for respondents' sex/gender, race, ethnicity, age, level of political interest, trust in police, and whether they have heard of the Innocence Project.

Figure 3.4 confirms that there was a meaningful difference between conservatives and liberals with regard to their belief in the accuracy of our system of capital punishment. While liberals were roughly 46 percent likely to think a person has been wrongfully executed in the past five years, conservatives were only 24 percent likely to believe the same, other things being equal.

We also found important differences by race as well. Other things being equal, Black respondents were twenty-six percentage points more likely than white respondents to think that a person has been wrongfully executed in the past five years (69 percent for Black respondents versus 43 percent for white respondents). This finding is unsurprising, given that previous research has demonstrated a significant racial gap in various attitudes related to the criminal legal system, particularly in regard to the death penalty. Indeed, earlier scholarship has demonstrated that Black and white individuals not only differ in their support for capital punishment generally but also respond differently to various arguments about the death penalty, including those related to innocence.[29]

Finally, although not the focus of our study, we found that age also shapes people's attitudes. Specifically, respondents in the youngest age group (eighteen- to twenty-four-year-olds) were forty-four percentage points more likely to think an innocent person has been wrongfully executed in the past five years than were respondents in the oldest age group (people over sixty-five).

Beliefs about Specific Errors

As a final assessment of people's beliefs about the pervasiveness of errors associated with wrongful convictions, Survey 1 presented respondents with a list of various issues that may occur in the justice system and have been known to contribute to wrongful convictions. For each one, we asked them to "indicate how often [they] think it occurs." The response options were on a five-point scale that included options for "Almost never," "Rarely," "Occasionally," "Regularly," and "Almost always." We were particularly interested in learning whether respondents' ideology affected their perceptions of these specific issues.

We begin by discussing a set of items that asked about problems associated with police investigations and/or police conduct. Respondents were asked how often they think each of the following occurs:

- A witness intentionally identifies the wrong person in a lineup.
- A witness unintentionally identifies the wrong person in a lineup.
- An innocent person voluntarily falsely confesses to a crime they did not commit.
- An innocent person is coerced into falsely confessing to a crime they did not commit.
- An innocent person is convinced that they committed a crime they did not commit and falsely confesses to the crime.
- Police investigators or officials engage in illegal practices.
- Police investigators or officials engage in unethical practices.

Figure 3.5 presents our findings with respect to these seven items. Specifically, this figure shows the mean category selected for each item by liberals (represented by squares on the figure) and conservatives (represented by diamonds). The horizontal bars extending beyond the nodes represent the 95 percent confidence intervals for each mean value. When these confidence intervals do not overlap on a given item, we can be fairly confident that there are real differences between conservatives and liberals.

A quick glance at the figure reveals a consistent pattern: the boxes (liberals) are always to the right of the diamonds (conservatives). Although not every ideological difference was significant, these means suggest that liberals generally thought these particular errors occur more frequently than conservatives did. As figure 3.5 shows, the gap between conservatives and liberals was small and insignificant in regard to witnesses intentionally misidentifying the accused or innocent people falsely believing they committed a crime (i.e., a persuaded or internalized false confessions). On the other hand, the most notable gaps between liberals and conservatives were on the items that suggest negative actions by police. For instance, we found prominent gaps on the items

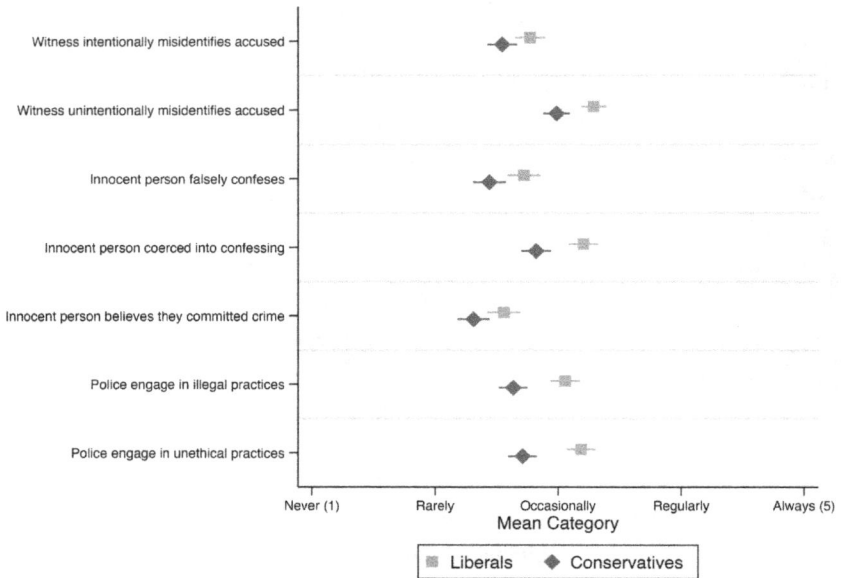

Figure 3.5. Ideology and opinions about problems with police investigations and conduct
Note: These data are derived from Survey 1. See the appendix for more information.
Horizontal bars extended from the nodes represent 95 percent confidence intervals.

pertaining to coerced false confessions, illegal police practices, and unethical police practices. This is intuitive; as we have previously discussed, conservatives tend to have more sanguine perceptions of law enforcement than liberals do and thus perceive errors that speak to policing problems as less frequent.

In addition to issues related to police investigations and practices, we also asked respondents about problems with the handling and presentation of scientific evidence, as well as the flawed use of criminal informants. Specifically, we asked respondents how often they believe the following issues occur:

- Forensic or scientific evidence is collected or handled incorrectly.
- A forensic or scientific expert makes a mistake in analyzing evidence or interpreting the results of scientific tests.
- A forensic or scientific expert makes an unintentional mistake when testifying about evidence to the jury.

- A forensic or scientific expert intentionally misleads the jury when testifying.
- An informant provides false information in exchange for something, such as money or a break on their own case.

We present our findings with respect to these items in figure 3.6. There are two notable features to this figure. First, there was virtually no difference between liberals and conservatives in their perception of how often informants provide false information in exchange for some benefit or reward. Second, while the differences between liberals and conservatives in their perceptions of the handling and presentation of scientific evidence were clearly smaller than those related to police investigations and conduct, liberals still were generally more likely to believe that these types of errors are more common. For example, on average, liberals thought it is more common for forensics experts to make mistakes, unintentionally and intentionally, than conservatives did.

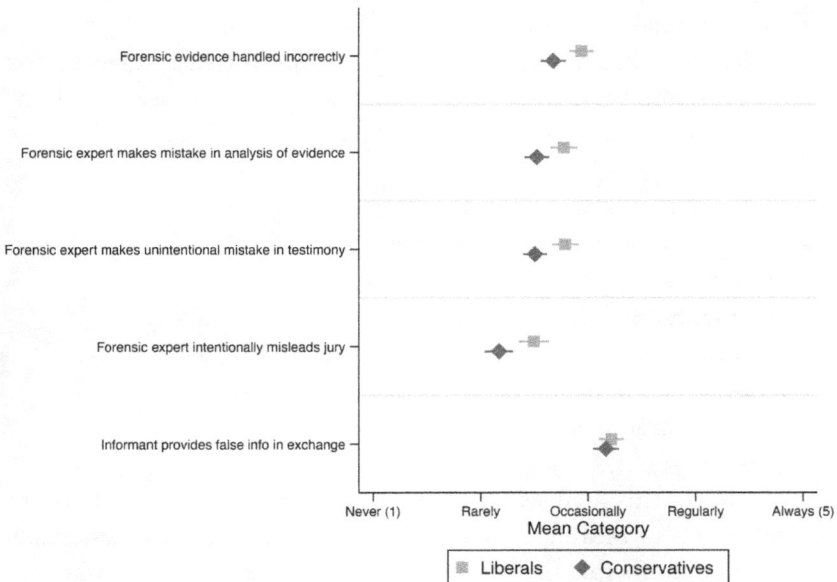

Figure 3.6. Ideology and opinions about scientific evidence and informants
Note: These data are derived from Survey 1. See the appendix for more information. Horizontal bars extended from the nodes represent 95 percent confidence intervals.

Unlike the ideological difference in perceptions of police errors just described, the findings regarding perceptions of forensic experts are less intuitive. In general, conservatives tend to be more skeptical or hold more negative views toward science and scientific experts, while liberals tend to have more positive views.[30] It follows, then, that liberals would be *more* confident in forensic experts and thus perceive scientific errors to be less frequent, but we found the opposite: liberals believed that forensic errors were more likely to occur. Unpacking the specific reasons for this pattern of results is beyond the scope of our current endeavor, but we speculate that this finding may be due, in part, to a couple of things. First, it may be that liberals' heightened skepticism of forensic experts is a reflection of their general distrust in the criminal legal system—of which those experts are a part—rather than a broader distrust in the scientific process and forensic experts. Second, liberals' support and belief in the scientific process may also lead them to be aware of the potential for human error. Our study design does not allow us to determine the precise causal mechanisms underlying these ideological differences, but doing so seems like a fruitful opportunity for future inquiry.

Finally, we asked about people's perception of issues surrounding court proceedings and key legal actors. Specifically, we asked respondents how often they think the following occur:

- An innocent person pleads guilty to a crime they did not commit.
- Prosecutors engage in illegal practices.
- Prosecutors engage in unethical practices.
- Defense attorneys do a poor job of defending their clients.
- Judges are biased (not impartial) when upholding the law.
- Juries are biased (not impartial) when making decisions.
- Juries do not accurately interpret the evidence.

The results for this final set of items are shown in figure 3.7. Relative to our other sets of findings, these results are somewhat more nuanced. It appears that liberals thought prosecutors engage in illegal practices significantly more often than conservatives did, which falls in line with perceptions of illegal and unethical police practices. As discussed earlier, this is perhaps unsurprising: police and prosecutors represent the state,

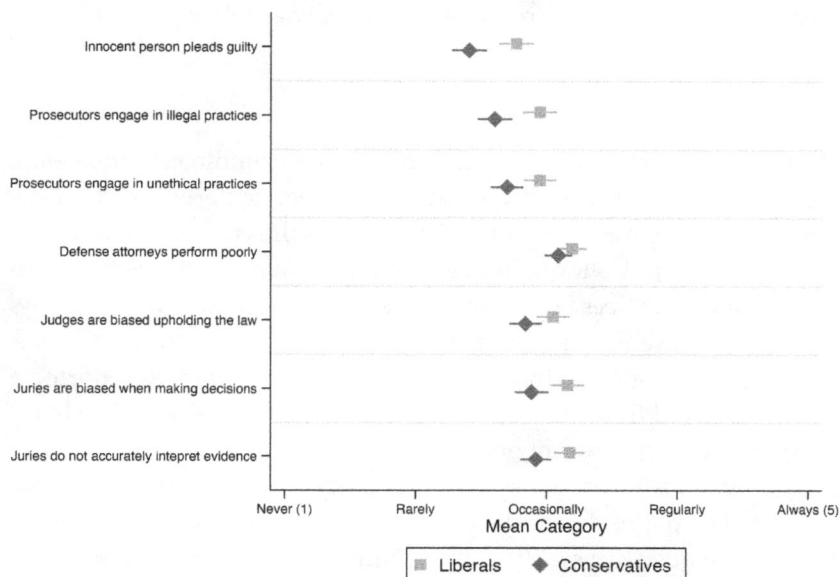

Figure 3.7. Ideology and opinions about issues with court proceedings
Note: These data are derived from Survey 1. See the appendix for more information.
Horizontal bars extended from the nodes represent 95 percent confidence intervals.

or those who are tasked with enforcing the law and ensuring that guilty parties are captured. Interestingly, there also was a significant difference in the perceived frequency with which innocent defendants plead guilty, such that liberals perceived these scenarios to be more frequent than conservatives did. Given that pleas account for more than 90 percent of criminal convictions in the United States, this suggests that conservatives generally have more faith in the accuracy of case outcomes. On the other hand, both ideological groups generally agreed about how often defense attorneys perform poorly and how often judges are biased when upholding the law.

Collectively, the findings presented throughout this chapter suggest that liberals and conservatives differ in their opinions about the frequency and nature of errors in the criminal legal system. While the exact differences vary across different questions and measures, they generally suggest that ideology shapes the public's view of wrongful convictions and related problems, specifically as related to police and prosecutors.

* * *

We think it pertinent to pause and reflect on our findings to this point. Political ideology is thought to capture people's preferences about the size and role of government in society, and it is thus reasonable to expect ideology to shape policy opinions on topics ranging from health care to taxes to social services (and many issues in between). Across our surveys thus far, we have found that ideology goes beyond this to color beliefs about the state of the criminal legal system. Conservatives reported a lower perceived frequency of wrongful convictions and were less likely to believe that an innocent person has been executed.

Of course, we cannot say with certainty how often innocents are convicted or put to death. We can, however, say that wrongful convictions are an objective reality in the criminal legal system, and we found that ideology shapes people's perceptions of that reality. It may be comforting to assume that political leanings do not distort perceptions of reality, but it is a false assumption. Our evidence is consistent with a body of research that suggests that, at times, political views alter beliefs about objective matters, such as economic indicators like changes in unemployment rates and inflation.[31] In the context of wrongful convictions—the frequency with which they occur, their sources, and their consequences—politics transform beliefs.

It is not just people's ideological preferences—conservatism or liberalism—that shape their views. We also found strong evidence that political interest is a predictor of people's awareness of wrongful convictions, and these things shape other perceptions, such as whether they believe that an innocent person has been executed in recent years. In short, those who are most interested in political happenings are the most aware of wrongful convictions and are more likely to see the problem as pervasive.

The findings from this chapter might offer insights for readers and activists concerned with garnering support for wrongful conviction advocacy and reforms. At a basic level, the difference in what people believe occurs (the perceived rate of wrongful convictions was generally in the 5–10 percent range) and what they find tolerable (generally, less than 2 percent) suggests that people believe or can be persuaded that there is room for improvement. Liberals and those who are interested in politics are most aware of the issue, and previous research makes clear that the interested are often more easily mobilized for political action. Thus, since the politically interested know more about the problem and are already more inclined to participate in political activities, they may only need to be targeted with mobilization messages rather than general education about the issue. By contrast, the less politically interested are less likely to hear about wrongful convictions or believe they are widespread. These individuals may be better targeted with general information about the problem itself, as they may be less supportive of policy reforms simply because they are less likely to be aware of the problems associated with wrongful convictions. Activists might also benefit from targeting the forms of media through which the majority of people get their information, namely, news, film and television, and social media.

We think that awareness of wrongful convictions as we have conceptualized it here is important in its own right, as much research in the area of public policy formulation and adoption has emphasized the critical role played by public attention to an issue, problem definition, and agenda setting.[32] Indeed, awareness of wrongful convictions among the mass public may be crucial to policy change, and the findings presented in this chapter illuminate some dimensions of what the public already knows and thinks about wrongful convictions.

What we have not uncovered yet, however, is how people respond to information about wrongful convictions. That is, does learning about these errors of justice alter public policy preferences or trust in the system? And how do different messaging strategies influence public perceptions? We turn to these matters in the following chapters.

4

How Wrongful Convictions Shape Public Opinion

On July 25, 1983, nine-year-old Dawn Hamilton disappeared in a wooded area in eastern Maryland.[1] Two young boys—ten-year-old Christian and seven-year-old Jackie—said they saw Dawn at a nearby pond. They said she had gone into the woods with a man they did not recognize. Their description was of someone approximately thirty years old with blond hair and a mustache.

Hours later, as police officers scoured the woods, Dawn's shorts and underwear were found hanging from a tree. Officers then found her body. She had been raped and murdered.

The boys from the pond, Christian and Jackie, initially disagreed about the strange man's look but worked with police to form a composite sketch. Days later, an anonymous caller informed police that the sketch resembled Kirk Bloodsworth, a local man who had left work and whose wife had filed a missing-persons report. Police tracked him down and inserted him into a lineup. Christian identified Bloodsworth, despite his red hair that the boy did not remember; Jackie did not make an identification.

Bloodsworth was arrested two weeks after the murder. Five witnesses later claimed to have seen him either with the victim or near the crime scene. In addition, an expert testified that marks on the victim's body could have come from a pair of his shoes, and Bloodsworth allegedly said that he had "done something terrible." In his defense, Bloodsworth had several alibi witnesses who testified that he was at home or with other people on the day of the murder.

In March 1985, Bloodsworth was convicted and sentenced to death. His conviction was overturned on appeal, but he was retried and again convicted, this time sentenced to life in prison.

In 1992, the evidence from the investigation was reexamined, and forensic analysts found a small spot of semen from the victim's underwear that had gone undetected. The DNA test results excluded Bloodsworth, and he was released in June 1993. That December, he was given a full gubernatorial pardon. In 1994, Bloodsworth was awarded around $300,000 in compensation for his ordeal, and in 2021—nearly three decades later—he was awarded another $400,000 from the Maryland Board of Public Works.[2]

Kirk Bloodsworth stands as the first person in the United States to be sentenced to death and later proven innocent and exonerated through post-conviction DNA testing. His case was instrumental in the passage of federal legislation pertaining to wrongful convictions—a portion of the 2004 Innocence Protection Act was named after him—and in Maryland's abolition of the death penalty in 2013.[3] His case is among the most important in modern criminal legal history and was popularized in a book and a feature-length documentary.[4]

Bloodsworth's case, like so many others in recent years, reached the eyes and ears of many members of the American public. But what does that mean for how the public views the criminal legal system? Would hearing Bloodsworth's story influence people to view the death penalty differently? Further, would it make them less trusting in the criminal justice system in general or in police specifically? In this chapter, we explore exactly these questions. We use data from three original surveys to better understand how information about wrongful convictions—whether presented as a single story or in the form of general information—influences public opinion.[5] In doing so, we also analyze the messages that do and do not resonate with liberals and conservatives alike. Our argument is rooted in framing theory and suggests that such information does influence public opinion but that its effects depend on the method of communication and the specific types of attitudes we examine.

Wrongful Convictions and Public Opinion

Kirk Bloodsworth's case received a significant amount of coverage in the popular media and within legal circles, but it came during the early years, when advocacy and activism around wrongful convictions was only beginning to blossom and had not yet coalesced into an organized movement. However, as we have discussed throughout this book, such information about wrongful convictions has become more ubiquitous in recent years. In chapter 3, we noted the immense popularity of podcasts like *Serial*, documentaries like *Making a Murderer*, and series such as *When They See Us*. In addition, John Grisham's first and only nonfiction book, *The Innocent Man*, which covered the wrongful conviction of Ron Williamson, was a national best-seller and served as the basis for a docuseries on Netflix.[6] Bryan Stevenson's best-selling memoir, *Just Mercy*, told the story of Walter McMillian's wrongful conviction and was made into a major motion picture in 2019.[7] These and many other books, shows, and films have captured the attention of millions of people.

Traditional news sources have followed suit, frequently reporting on wrongful convictions and related issues. The stories are not only featured in major news outlets like the *New York Times*, the *Washington Post*, and *USA Today* but in local news as well.[8] In fact, as we were initially drafting this chapter, a headline story in the *Lawrence Journal-World*—the local Kansas newspaper of one of the authors—caught our eye. It covered the post-exoneration experiences of Floyd Scott Bledsoe, who was wrongly convicted of murder in 2000 and spent fifteen years in prison.[9] Then, while we were editing this book, Kirk Bloodsworth was awarded a second round of compensation (after nearly thirty years), which received headlines in the *Washington Post* and other outlets.[10]

Clearly, the *innocence frame* is pervasive in media discourse surrounding the criminal legal system. In chapter 3, we showed that although there is variation among people, large swaths of the population are aware of wrongful convictions and that people learn about them through a variety of sources. Further, in line with national Gallup polls, we found that a majority of people believe that an innocent person has been executed for a crime they did not commit. Beyond this, people are adept at identifying specific issues in the legal system that contribute to wrongful convictions, such as eyewitness errors, false confessions, and forensic mishaps.

Given that wrongful convictions are increasingly covered in popular discourse and much of the public is aware of them, we now consider a related but distinct question: What effects does this information have on public opinion?

Unpacking the Innocence Effect

Does information about wrongful convictions alter people's opinions about the criminal legal system? The intuitive response is probably *yes*, but previous research, most of which has focused on support for the death penalty, fails to provide a clear answer.

Some research suggests that media attention to wrongful convictions has significantly influenced the decline in public support for the death penalty, in the aggregate, over the past two decades.[11] Indeed, Gallup polls show that support for capital punishment has decreased from around 70 percent in the early 2000s to around 55 percent in 2020. Perhaps more importantly, recent polls show that life imprisonment without parole is now favored by a majority of Americans. These shifts in aggregate public opinion have occurred alongside the development and growth of the innocence movement, and when survey respondents are asked a follow-up question about why they oppose the death penalty, concerns about wrongful convictions are among the most commonly reported reasons.[12]

On the other hand, studies that have directly analyzed the effects of wrongful convictions on attitudes about capital punishment at the individual level have reached mixed conclusions. Some studies found that news articles or statements that call attention to innocence shifted attitudes in an expected (negative) direction, but the effects were small and statistically *insignificant*; others detected small but *significant* attitudinal shifts.[13] It also may be that not all individuals respond similarly to such information. For example, the political scientists Mark Peffley and Jon Hurwitz presented survey respondents with the argument that "some people say that the death penalty is unfair because too many innocent people are being executed." They found that this statement significantly reduced death penalty support among Black respondents, by sixteen percentage points, but it had almost no effect on white respondents.[14]

Taken together, previous research offers mixed evidence regarding the effects of wrongful convictions on public opinion. Further, there are two notable limitations to much of the existing scholarship that make it difficult to draw any firm conclusions.

First, most researchers have focused on death penalty attitudes. This is understandable and intuitive, as wrongful convictions provide a fundamental challenge to the practice of capital punishment—the execution of an innocent person may be seen as a worst-case scenario for our criminal legal system—and the innocence movement has, rightly or wrongly, often been tied to the anti-death-penalty movement.[15] However, people's beliefs about capital punishment, while important, represent only one category of public opinion that may be influenced by wrongful convictions, and others may be equally or more important than death penalty views. We remain curious about the broader effects of such errors of justice, for instance, whether they shift opinion beyond the death penalty and influence attitudes toward the broader criminal legal system or toward other specific organizations or actors within it. For example, Kirk Bloodsworth's case might certainly influence someone to change their views on capital punishment, but his case also involved questionable investigation and courtroom proceedings. It is plausible that his case might also influence broader views about the criminal legal system.

A second limitation of the existing research is that, by and large, it does not account for the fact that information about wrongful convictions is communicated in different ways and that these different methods of communication may influence the effects of this information. The political scientist Frank Baumgartner and others have documented the rise of wrongful convictions in media discourse about criminal justice and highlighted their contribution to reducing support for the death penalty, but this "innocence frame" is broad and encapsulates a wide variety of information related to wrongful convictions.[16] However, the differences in type and presentation of information may influence what effects it has.

We hope to address these limitations here. In order to understand the effects that wrongful convictions have on public perceptions of the criminal legal system, it is imperative that we examine a variety of opinions that include the death penalty but also extend beyond the ultimate punishment. We also demonstrate that the way in which wrongful conviction information is communicated changes the effects it has. Our argument builds on theoretical insights from the rich literature on framing and offers insights about how researchers should draw conclusions about framing effects.

Innocence Frames and Attitudes toward the Legal System

In the most general sense, "framing" refers to the way in which information is communicated and presented. Researchers have long found that the way information is framed can shape how people conceptualize an issue and what considerations come to mind. A framing effect occurs when different presentations of information alter attitudes, beliefs, and/or behaviors. Framing theory has been used to understand the effects of public rhetoric on a variety of social and political attitudes, including those related to law and criminal justice.[17]

One common distinction in framing techniques is that between *episodic* and *thematic* frames. As explained by the political scientist and political communication scholar Shanto Iyengar, *episodic frames* concentrate on specific events or cases, while *thematic frames* discuss political or social issues in a broader, more general context.[18] For example, "a news story about cuts in government welfare expenditures substantiated by statistical figures is an empirical example of thematic framing," while "a news story about an elderly disabled woman unable to get public home care is an empirical example of episodic framing."[19] Both frames call attention to reductions of welfare provisions, but they do so in different ways that may be important when considering how they might influence public opinion.

We can clarify the distinction between thematic and episodic frames in the context of communicating information about wrongful convictions by thinking of them as numbers and narratives. That is, a thematic frame might present the *number* of known exonerations or an estimate of how many people are wrongly convicted in a particular state or country. By highlighting such figures, this presentation places the information in a broad societal or systemic context. On the other hand, an episodic frame might present a *narrative* about a single case in which someone was wrongly convicted and later exonerated. In contrast to communicating wrongful conviction information in a broad societal context, a narrative provides an individual's story. So, while other scholars have documented the rise of innocence-related information in media discourse about criminal justice, this information can be communicated in different ways, as numbers or narratives, and we argue that these different approaches to framing may have different effects on people's attitudes.

Given these different ways of communicating information, which type of frame is likely to be more powerful? Is a narrative about a single exoneree more persuasive than a statistic about the thousands of individuals who have been wrongfully convicted? We argue that the answer to these questions depends on the type of attitudinal outcome we examine. Therefore, when designing our surveys, we had different expectations for specific *policy preferences* and for *broader attitudes* toward legal systems, organizations, and/or actors.

In regard to altering *policy preferences*, there was reason to believe that both wrongful conviction numbers and narratives may be effective but that narratives would probably be the more powerful and persuasive framing technique. Prior research has shown that thematic frames can change policy attitudes and may be particularly compelling if they provide novel information.[20] However, scholars have argued that episodic frames may be more effective because narratives sometimes prompt counterfactual thinking—a process by which people consider potential alternatives to what happened or what they think they know—and catalyze persuasion to a greater degree than numerical information does.[21] A narrative can transport the person consuming it into the story and consider how an issue might impact them.[22] Although this was not our main focus, one of the surveys we discuss in this chapter provided some evidence that such transportation occurs. In the second study we discuss, we found that the presentation of a wrongful conviction narrative significantly increased people's personal concern that they or someone they knew might be wrongfully convicted. Specifically, compared to respondents in our control group—those who were not exposed to any wrongful conviction information—respondents exposed to a narrative frame were 2.9 times more likely to be "extremely concerned" (versus "not concerned at all") that they or someone they know might be wrongfully convicted. By contrast, respondents exposed to a numbers frame were only 1.6 times more likely to feel "extremely concerned." These contrasting numbers illustrate the point that these two types of frames operate in different ways.

In addition to shifting attitudes through transportation, episodic frames are particularly powerful when emotional reactions are amplified, and it is difficult to imagine a narrative about the travails of a wrongfully convicted individual not eliciting some type of emotional response from most people.[23] Finally, in further support of our notion that an episodic frame would be more persuasive than a thematic one in shifting policy attitudes, we might consider the growing literature on the *narrative policy framework*, which highlights the ability of narratives to shape a wide range of policy preferences.[24] In line with this research, we expected a narrative about a person who was wrongfully convicted and sentenced to death to be particularly powerful.

For the reasons we just described, we expected both the wrongful conviction numbers and narrative to affect support for capital punishment but suspected that the narrative would be more powerful.[25] On the other hand, we expected the numbers to have a greater effect on *broader attitudes* toward the criminal legal system. The reason for this is rooted in the key distinction between thematic and episodic frames described earlier. Specifically, thematic frames and general statistical information place issues in a broader context. They "emphasize[] general patterns in society" and encourage people to think broadly about social and governing systems; research has found that thematic frames thus prompt governmental attributions of blame and responsibility.[26] Numerical information about exonerations may thus encourage respondents to think about systemic patterns in the criminal legal system over a given time frame. We therefore thought that a thematic frame comprising wrongful conviction statistics would reduce trust in the criminal justice system and the officials within it. On the latter point, there are multiple organizations and individuals associated with the criminal legal system—courts, lawyers, police, judges, and so on—but we focus here on one of the most central categories of actors associated with the legal system and wrongful convictions: law enforcement. We thought that numerical information not only should reduce trust in the justice system generally but also might erode trust in police.

To summarize, we agree with other scholars that wrongful convictions can influence public opinion but argue that their persuasive power depends on the method of communication and the type of attitude we seek to change. In approaching our survey, we expected that both exoneration numbers and a wrongful conviction narrative would reduce support for the death penalty but that the narrative would prompt more substantial effects. Conversely, we expected exoneration numbers to re-duce trust in the justice system and trust in police, while the narrative would not.

Support for Capital Punishment

The death penalty is among the most studied topics in the realm of public opinion and criminal justice. One theme flowing through the existing literature is that, for many people, these opinions are fairly well entrenched and resistant to change. Rather than people being persuaded, such attitudes may, in fact, be subject to reinforcement. A fundamental example of this type of reinforcement comes from a 1979 study by the psychologist Charles G. Lord and colleagues. Their research demon-strated that exposing people to evidence that challenged or affirmed the death penalty as a deterrent to crime not only failed to change opinions but rather led existing beliefs to become further entrenched. That is, death penalty supporters became more supportive and opponents more opposed.[27]

The study by Lord and colleagues helped establish the foundation of the contemporary literature on *motivated reasoning*, which unpacks various psychological processes and biases—namely, confirmation and disconfirmation biases and belief perseverance—that create obstacles to persuasion and attitude change.[28] Motivated reasoning suggests that people have unconscious drives (or *motivations*) to seek out information that bolsters their existing attitudes (confirmation bias), counterargue information and messages that challenge their views (disconfirmation bias), and, ultimately, process and respond to information such that it reinforces their opinions and beliefs. If, for instance, someone supports the death penalty, they might be hesitant to read an article with a title in-dicating that it will discuss racial disparities associated with the practice. On the other hand, if someone opposes the death penalty, they might avoid an op-ed in support of capital punishment written by a prosecu-tor. And, in either case, even if a person chooses to read an article with information that challenges their views, in their head, they are likely to counterargue each point made. Importantly, most people are not ac-tively trying to engage in biased information searching and processing but rather are doing so outside their conscious awareness.

In addition to these core psychological barriers to persuasion, altering death penalty attitudes faces another challenge, in that it is a morality policy—an issue in which divisions are rooted in conflicts over basic moral values that do not lend themselves to compromise. As Baumgartner and colleagues note, "The death penalty, like abortion, is a moral issue on which most Americans' views are solidly fixed."[29] It should come as no surprise, then, that efforts to change death penalty attitudes frequently fail and may even have the opposite of any intended effect. For example, in the study by Peffley and Hurwitz mentioned earlier, the authors found evidence of a troubling "backlash effect," whereby white respondents became more supportive of capital punishment when presented with a racialized argument. Specifically, in response to the statement that "the death penalty is unfair because most of the people who are executed are African Americans," white respondents reported a twelve-percentage-point *increase* in support for the death penalty.[30]

Despite these challenges, there is reason to believe that wrongful convictions might have the persuasive power to shift support for capital punishment, in line with aggregate-level findings. Although often discussed in the abstract, the death penalty is, as Baumgartner and colleagues note, "multifaceted."[31] The risk of executing the innocent raises tangible concerns that may fundamentally challenge the institution in ways that other issues—constitutionality, for example, or its potential deterrent effect on crime—may not. Again, however, the ways in which the issue of wrongful convictions is framed is key to understanding its effect on support for capital punishment. A thematic frame—information about how many people have been exonerated—might communicate a clear message about innocence and the death penalty with which some people are unfamiliar or, if they are familiar, make those considerations more salient. An episodic frame—a narrative about a wrongful conviction case—might transport the message recipient into the story and raise tangible concerns about the death penalty, prompt counterfactual thinking and/or transportation, and generate emotional responses, all of which are mechanisms through which attitude change may occur.

To test our expectations regarding the effects of different wrongful conviction frames on support for the death penalty, we carried out two online survey experiments.[32] We designed the first study as an initial examination of only the thematic frame (exoneration numbers). We then used it to inform the design of our second study, in which we examined both numbers and narratives.

Our first study (Survey 3) involved a simple two-condition survey experiment in which respondents were randomly assigned to one of two conditions. First, participants in a control group were simply asked about their support for the death penalty without receiving any additional information. The second group was first presented with the following thematic frame about wrongful convictions: "According to the National Registry of Exonerations—which is managed by the University of Michigan and Northwestern University Schools of Law—more than 1,800 people were found to be innocent after being convicted for a crime they did not commit since 1989. More than 155 of these people were sentenced to death for crimes they did not commit, but were later found to be innocent."[33] After reading this information, respondents in this treatment group were asked about their support for capital punishment.

We measured support for the death penalty in the same way for both the control and treatment groups. We used a similar approach to that of previous researchers and Gallup polls.[34] Respondents were asked, "Do you support or oppose the death penalty for persons convicted of murder?" There were four response options that ranged from "strongly oppose" to "strongly support."

With this simple initial test, we found that our statement of exoneration numbers reduced support for the death penalty. Figure 4.1 shows the probability that a respondent "strongly supported" the death penalty depending on whether they were exposed to our message. Respondents in the control group (those who did not receive the information) were nine percentage points more likely to strongly support the death penalty, other things being equal. Clearly, the thematic frame provoked a substantively and statistically significant effect on respondents' support for the death penalty.

Given that Survey 3 showed that a thematic innocence frame could influence death penalty support, we designed a follow-up study (Survey 4) to examine the effects of both numbers and narratives. In this survey, respondents were randomly assigned to one of four conditions: no frame (control group), a numbers treatment (thematic frame), a narrative treatment (episodic frame), or a combined treatment (both numbers and narrative).

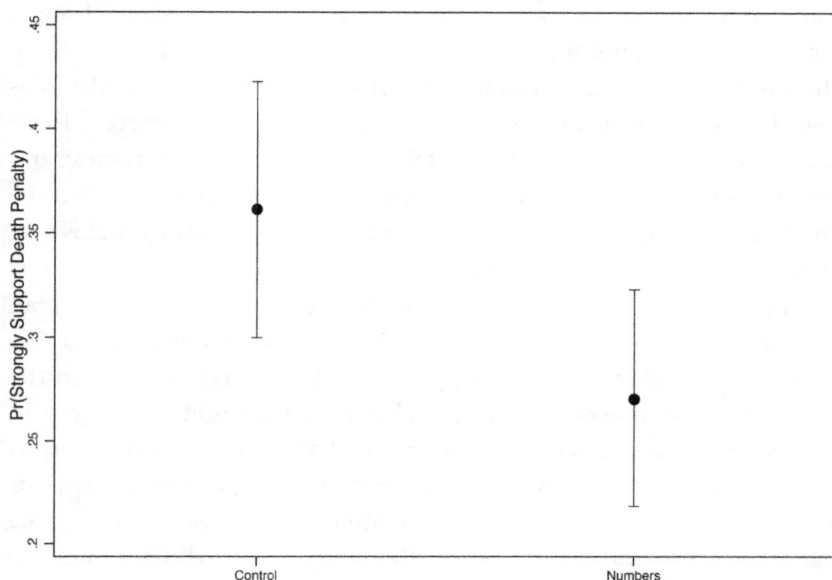

Figure 4.1. Numeric exoneration information and death penalty support
Note: Quantities are derived from table A.7 in the appendix. Vertical bars represent 95 percent confidence intervals. Other variables in the model—ideology, sex/gender, race/ethnicity, education, and political interest—are held their median values.

We made four changes to the thematic frame from Survey 3. First, we updated the number of exonerations, which had increased to more than two thousand by the time we conducted Survey 4. Second, we dropped reference to "the University of Michigan and Northwestern University Schools of Law." Although this reference was originally included to raise the perceived credibility of the information, we removed it in case it actually reduced polarized perceptions of credibility, as polls suggest that some people have negative perceptions of universities.[35] Third, we incorporated a sentence that stated, "Additionally, there may be as many as 100,000 innocent people currently in prisons across the United States for crimes they did not commit."[36] Finally, we wanted to connect our numbers treatment to a related public-safety concern about wrongful convictions: when an innocent person is wrongly convicted, it means that the guilty offender may remain free.[37] To do so, we added the following statement: "An official from the National Institute of Justice said, 'These numbers show that not only have thousands of people been wrongfully jailed, but that just as many criminals remain free, roaming the streets. Every year a person spent wrongfully incarcerated also represents a year in which the actual perpetrator remained at-large.'" These last two changes are both consistent with thematic numeric framing and are evident in political discourse.[38] Further, they helped ensure that the treatment messages for our thematic and episodic frames were closer in length.

In addition to a thematic frame, we wanted to test the effects of an episodic frame, or a narrative about a single wrongful conviction. We had several goals when designing our message. First, we wanted the narrative to be short and realistic, akin to what might be covered in a brief newspaper article. Second, given what we know from prior research about the qualities of persuasive narratives, we also wanted our story to evoke sympathy in the reader and help transport them into the narrative. Third, for the purposes of this study, we also did not want our narrative to trigger racial cues, so we used a racially ambiguous name for the individual who was wrongly convicted. Finally, we wanted the reader to feel confident that the person was innocent, rather than uncertain about whether they had committed the crime. We therefore kept the inculpatory evidence to a minimum and made the case involve a DNA-based exoneration.[39] To accomplish our four goals, we initially based our narrative loosely on the true story of Kirk Bloodsworth, told at the beginning of this chapter, but added several changes to fit our purposes. Our final narrative treatment read,

> In 2002, Michael Williams, a U.S. military veteran, was arrested for murder. The only evidence against Williams included two child witnesses who claimed to have seen him near the crime scene, a pair of shoes that could have fit him, and marks on the victim's body that might have come from those shoes. Yet, Williams had several alibi witnesses who said that he was with other people on the day of the crime. Williams was convicted and sentenced to death. He spent almost nine years in prison, during which he was assaulted numerous times. While incarcerated he became estranged from his wife and two children.
>
> Michael Williams came within 12 hours of his execution. He ordered his last meal, was measured for his burial suit, and his parents made

arrangements for his funeral. Shortly before the scheduled execution, DNA testing proved that Williams was not the offender and he was released from prison. After his release, Williams encountered harassment from his community, had difficulty finding employment, struggled financially, and was homeless for a period of time. He continues to struggle to adjust to life after his wrongful conviction.

The final treatment group received both the narrative and the numbers in a single message.

Unlike Survey 3, we measured death penalty support in two ways in the second one. We used the same question from Survey 3—"Do you support or oppose the death penalty for persons convicted of murder?"—but this time provided seven response options that ranged from "strongly oppose" to "strongly support." However, inferences about support for the death penalty may be shaped by question wording. For example, Gallup polls have recently found that when asked a yes-or-no question about support, approximately 55 percent of respondents said yes, while 43 percent said no; when provided an alternative punitive option and asked for their preferences, however, 60 percent of respondents said they preferred life imprisonment without parole, while only 36 percent preferred the death penalty.[40] We did not want our findings to hinge on the wording of a single question, so in addition to the general support question, we also asked respondents, "Do you favor capital punishment, life imprisonment with no possibility of parole, or imprisonment with the possibility of parole for murderers?" The answer options included, "capital punishment (the death penalty)," "life imprisonment without the possibility of parole," or "imprisonment with the possibility of parole at some point in time." We randomized the order of the two death penalty questions to avoid any potential question-order-effects.[41]

Figure 4.2 displays our findings by showing the *effect* of each of our innocence frames on death penalty support. To determine these effects, we fit a simple regression model to our seven-point outcome; this model and one based on the alternative outcome are presented in table A.8 in the appendix. In these models, we also controlled for other relevant characteristics about the respondents, such as their race/ethnicity, age, political ideology, political interest, sex/gender, and education.

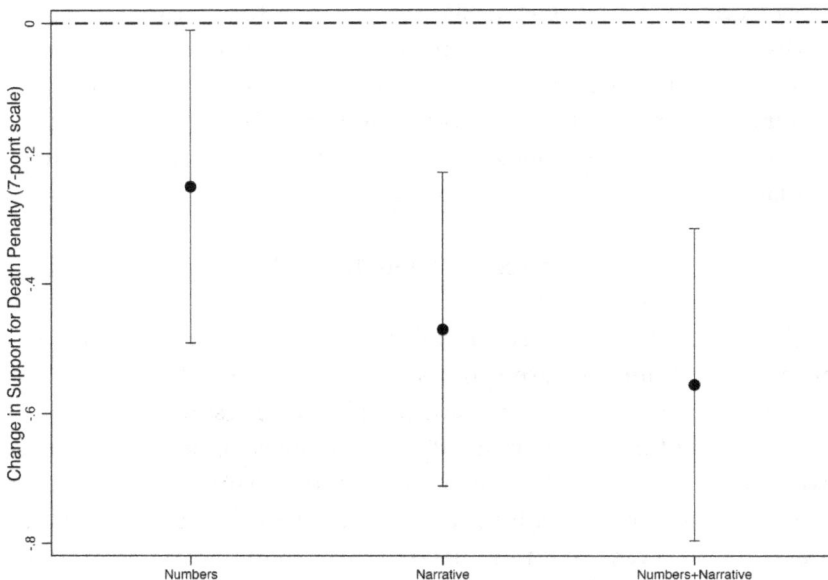

Figure 4.2. Effects of different frames on support for the death penalty
Note: Quantities are derived from the first model in table A.8 in the appendix. Vertical bars represent 95 percent confidence intervals.

The dashed line near the top of the figure (at 0 on the y-axis) represents the control group, which received no wrongful conviction information. Clearly, all three innocence frames reduced death penalty support compared to the control group, but it is also clear that the frames that included a narrative, whether alone or combined with numbers, more strongly persuaded respondents than the numbers-only frame did. In fact, the effect size of the combined frame is more than twice as large as the effect of the numbers alone. Other things being equal, the narrative frame and the combined frame reduced death penalty support by half a response category or more.

We also analyzed the alternative outcome that asked respondents which form of punishment they prefer. This test revealed that our findings are robust to different measures of death penalty support. For example, respondents in the control group were more than twice as likely to prefer capital punishment (compared to life with the possibility of parole) than those who viewed the combined frame.[42] Furthermore, compared to respondents who were exposed to the narrative-only frame, respondents in the control group were almost twice as likely to prefer capital punishment relative to life imprisonment with the possibility of parole.

All told, we found that wrongful conviction information significantly eroded support for capital punishment, but as we expected, the magnitude of the effect depended on how that information was communicated. Both studies made clear that exoneration numbers have the power to persuade, which is interesting on its own given that capital punishment preferences have often been thought to be quite stable and resilient. Despite this impressive finding, our results also showed that narratives are more influential than numbers for altering death penalty attitudes. Specifically, a narrative (episodic) frame seems to exert a stronger effect than a numbers (thematic) frame, and the combination of both may be the most influential.

These findings are not particularly surprising when considered within the context of framing research more generally. However, it would be rash to draw firm conclusions about the persuasiveness of episodic and thematic frames on the basis of only an assessment of death penalty preferences. As we discussed earlier, different framing techniques raise different considerations and may therefore influence other attitudes in different ways. We have only explored one main outcome—support for capital punishment—so any conclusions would be inaccurate or, at least, incomplete. In order to better understand how wrongful convictions might affect public opinion, we must also consider broader attitudes toward the criminal legal system.

Trust in the Justice System and Police

People's views of capital punishment are important to consider but represent only one element of the criminal legal system. A wide variety of scholarship has explored public opinion related to other aspects of the justice system, perhaps most notably, views of law enforcement.[43] One key issue that has received some attention recently is the possible erosion of trust and perceived legitimacy of police and of the legal system more generally.[44] In part, these discussions are tied to much-broader social, cultural, and political movements that are well beyond the scope of this book—the Black Lives Matter movement and protests in response to police violence, critiques of mass incarceration, and the prison abolition movement, to name a few—but on a basic level might also be related to the issue of wrongful convictions.

There is an intuitive connection between factual errors and perceptions of the criminal legal system. After all, wrongful convictions involve cases in which our justice system failed to secure justice, in which officials and organizations and systemic protections failed to accomplish what are arguably their most fundamental goals: to apprehend the guilty and protect the innocent. It follows, then, that as the public learns more about such miscarriages of justice, they may begin to lose trust in criminal justice officials and perceive the system to be less legitimate.

On the other hand, existing research has raised doubts regarding the extent to which beliefs about the justice system are malleable, or at least suggests that such malleability is dependent on a number of factors. To highlight the potential nuance here, we might consider two earlier published studies that we conducted on attitudes toward police.

In the first, we examined whether information about racial disparities in traffic stops reduced people's trust in police. We found that only a small subset of people responded negatively to such information, and it depended on what "cause" they attributed to those disparities. Specifically, people who believed that the disparities were due to racial profiling by police became slightly less trusting, while those who attributed the disparities to Black drivers committing more violations became slightly more trusting; but neither group consistently or substantially shifted their views of law enforcement. The only group that showed considerable movement included those who attributed the disparities to a more institutional or organizational reason—that police are more likely to be in areas with more Black drivers. That is, only those whose attributions were seemingly less polarized—they did not blame officers or citizens but had something of a "middle-ground" institutional explanation for disparities—were responsive to new information in a consistent and meaningful way.[45]

In a second study, we wanted to explore whether the recent barrage of stories about police violence was influencing people's views of law enforcement. We found that both text-based and video-based depictions of police use-of-force against Black citizens—both lethal and nonlethal—not only generated a variety of emotional responses but also influenced a number of specific attitudes toward police: support for body-worn cameras, approval and trust in police, beliefs about excessive force and training, and the like. Unlike the previous study of traffic stops, the use-of-force stories generally altered attitudes across groups of respondents.[46]

Of course, it may simply be that statistics about racial disparities in police practices are unclear, perceived as inaccurate, or for some other reason unlikely to change attitudes, while instances of police violence are emotionally evocative and compelling. Regardless, these two studies suggest that, when it comes to views of police and criminal justice, persuasion may be a nuanced process.

So, how might this relate to wrongful convictions and their effects on systemic trust and perceived legitimacy? There are a number of ways we might think about this question. Compared to a text-based or visual depiction of a person being harmed or even killed by police, the story of a person who is the victim of an unjust conviction and later exonerated, while encompassing a wide range of emotions, may be less evocative. But it seems reasonable that basic figures about exonerations may be more influential than those about racial disparities in traffic stops or other police practices; they may be perceived as simpler and more straightforward and as less controversial.

We noted earlier that thematic frames prompt people to think about issues broadly in societal or governmental contexts. Such framing of wrongful conviction information—numbers of exonerations—might then trigger considerations about police practices broadly and about the criminal justice system and thus reduce overall trust in these institutions. On the other hand, narratives and episodic frames typically focus on singular cases and events and, as such, are narrowly constructed around the individuals involved. It is possible that such a narrative might affect evaluations of the officer(s) or other individuals involved in the case described, but it is unlikely to alter opinions regarding law enforcement as a whole or of the entire criminal legal system.

We wanted to examine these ideas and embedded an initial test of them in Survey 4 described earlier that included four experimental conditions. After support for capital punishment was measured, we asked all respondents about their trust in the justice system and, separately, about their trust in law enforcement. We used measures similar to those used by the political scientist Charles R. Epp and colleagues in their 2014 book *Pulled Over*. Specifically, respondents were asked, "How much trust do you have in the criminal justice system to treat people fairly?" This was followed by asking, "How much trust do you have in police officers to treat people fairly?" Both questions had five-point response options that ranged from "none at all" to "a great deal."

For the sake of simplicity, we discuss these results in order, beginning with those regarding people's trust in the criminal justice system. As with our analysis of death penalty support discussed earlier, we isolated the effect of each of our frames—exoneration numbers, a wrongful conviction narrative, and the combined frame—on respondents' level of trust using ordinary least squares regression models. Doing so allowed us an opportunity to learn the extent to which respondents who were randomly exposed to different information reported different levels of trust, while also controlling for other characteristics. Because the frames were randomly assigned, the control variables had little influence on the quantitative effect of the frames. Still, including our control variables nonetheless increased our confidence in the findings and provided additional insights into other things that may shape respondents' level of trust in the criminal justice system.

The full results are presented in table A.9 in the appendix. Here, we focus on the effect of the different frames on respondents' average level of trust in the criminal justice system. This is shown visually in figure 4.3. The horizontal dashed line represents the control group—those who did not receive any wrongful conviction information—and each vertical node then represents the effect of one of our frame conditions. The first node on the left indicates that the numbers frame reduced trust in the criminal justice system by nearly 0.15 units. The vertical bars represent the confidence interval and show that this effect reached conventional levels of statistical significance. We can confidently reject the hypothesis that respondents in the control group have equivalent levels of trust relative to respondents who were exposed to the numbers frame. However, as shown by the middle node, we cannot say the same for respondents who received only the narrative frame, as there is no evidence that the story alone influenced people's trust in the system. Finally, the combined treatment significantly reduced trust, but interestingly, the effect

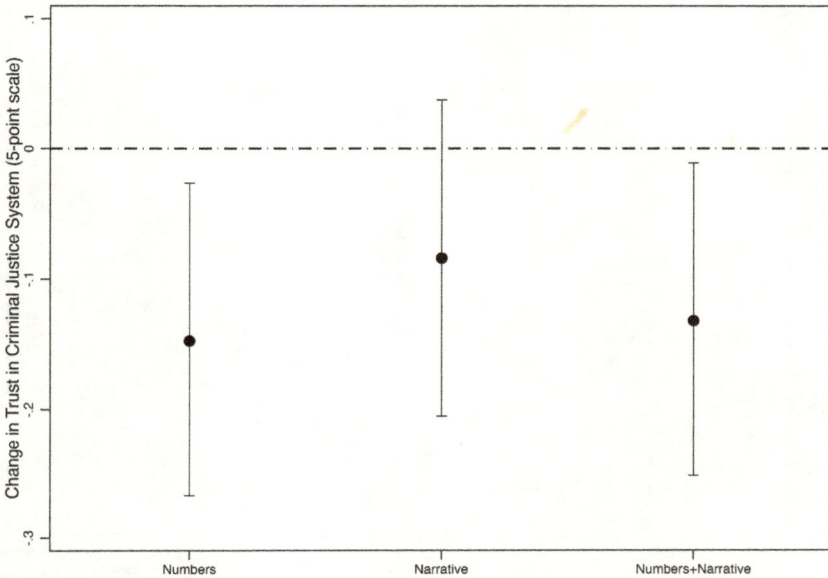

Figure 4.3. Experimental frames and respondents' trust in the criminal justice system
Note: Quantities are derived from the first model in table A.9 in the appendix. Vertical bars represent 95 percent confidence intervals.

was statistically indistinguishable from that of the numbers alone. That is, whether someone received just the numerical information or received the numerical information along with a story did not matter; it appears that the numbers did the heavy lifting with regard to altering people's trust in the criminal justice system, probably by encouraging them to think broadly about the system. Uncovering this sort of nuance in what types of information persuade people is critical for our understanding of how people perceive the criminal legal system.

We now turn to the question of trust in police, and on this outcome, our findings were decidedly more mixed. Here, we again used an ordinary least squares regression model, controlling for other respondent characteristics, to determine whether randomly assigning respondents to different messages altered their level of trust in police. On the one hand, we found something similar to trust in the criminal justice system: the numbers frame reduced respondents' trust by just over 0.1 units relative to no message at all (the control group), while respondents in

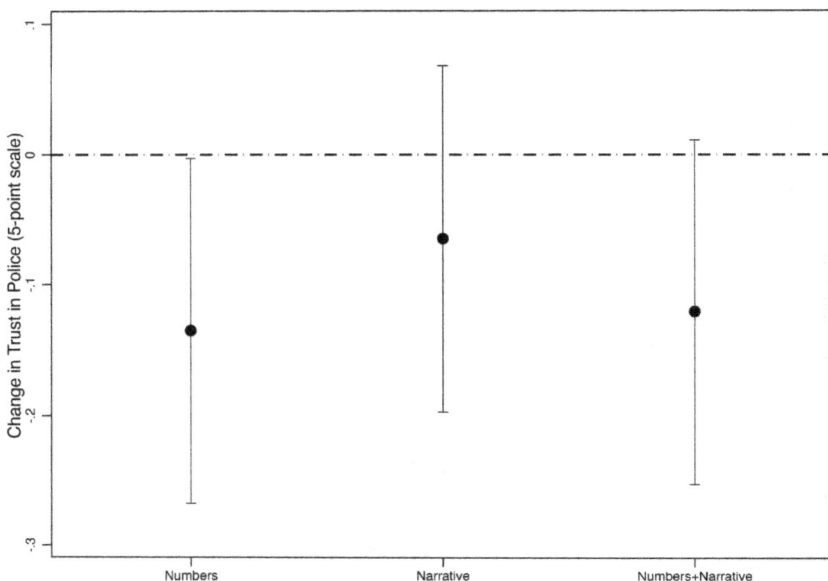

Figure 4.4. Experimental frames and respondents' trust in police
Note: Quantities are derived from the second model in table A.9 in the appendix.
Vertical bars represent 95 percent confidence intervals.

the narrative-only group were not any different from the control group. On the other hand, as shown in figure 4.4, our 95 percent confidence intervals were much wider and, in two of three conditions, included zero (indicated by their intersecting with the dashed line, which represents the control group). Even in the one condition where trust was significantly reduced—the numbers-only treatment—the substantive effect was quite small on the five-point scale. In short, the evidence that wrongful conviction information reduced trust in police is less compelling than with trust in the criminal justice system.

We were initially puzzled by the findings that the numbers frame reduced trust in the criminal justice system but had much more muted and uncertain effects on trust in police. There were two initial reasons we considered for the lack of meaningful movement in people's trust in police. On the one hand, our expectations about attitudes toward police may have been incorrect; that is, we thought numbers could persuade people on this topic, but maybe they cannot. On the other hand, perhaps there were particular features of our survey design that produced the muted results. Indeed, our numbers frame did not provide any information about law enforcement and made no explicit connection between police actions and wrongful convictions. After all, for information to catalyze persuasion, it must raise considerations that are applicable and salient, and we failed to make a direct connection between our treatment message and our outcome.[47] It is also possible that the result was tied to our outcome question; we only had one measure of attitudes toward law enforcement—trust in police to treat people fairly—but there is a wide range of alternative questions. Would a different measure yield a different conclusion?

Given these potential issues, we designed another follow-up survey (Survey 5), in which we linked wrongful conviction numbers directly to law enforcement and added additional measures of attitudes toward police. We again used a survey experiment with four conditions. However, our focus here was not on comparing numbers and narratives but on whether numbers have the persuasive power to alter attitudes toward police. As such, we no longer included a narrative treatment or questions about trust in the justice system generally.

For this study, respondents were randomly assigned to one of four conditions. First, those in the control group were told, "A wrongful conviction is a case in which an innocent person is convicted of a crime they did not commit." They were then asked about their attitudes toward law enforcement.

A second group was given a shortened version of the numeric frame from the previous experiment (with updated numbers as of implementation). They were told, "A wrongful conviction is a case in which an innocent person is convicted of a crime they did not commit. According to the National Registry of Exonerations, there have been more than 2,150 wrongful convictions since 1989. More than 155 of these people were sentenced to death. Experts believe that many more errors are never discovered, and there may be as many as 100,000 innocent people in prisons across the United States." As in the previous study, there was nothing in that treatment that directly mentioned or implicated law enforcement as contributing to wrongful convictions. As such, we designed a new treatment message that explicitly tied wrongful convictions, in part, to misconduct by law enforcement. This third group was told, "A wrongful conviction is a case in which an innocent person is convicted of a crime they did not commit. More than 70% of wrongful convictions directly involve misconduct by law enforcement. Much of this misconduct is connected to police practices such as coercive interrogations and the handling of eyewitnesses." Finally, a fourth group was given *both* the basic numeric information and the text that attributed wrongful convictions to misconduct by law enforcement. This was our main manipulation.

After all respondents had received the information for their respective group, they were asked three questions that gauged their evaluations of law enforcement. First, they were asked the same question as in the previous experiment: "How much trust do you have in police officers to treat people fairly?" They were given the same five response options as before.

We wanted to include additional measures of trust in police, so we asked all respondents two more questions, both of which used seven-point scales ranging from "strongly disagree" to "strongly agree." Everyone was asked the extent to which they agreed or disagreed with the statements "that the police can be trusted to make decisions that are right for the people in their communities" and "that people's basic rights are well protected by the police." These items were drawn from the vast literature on police legitimacy, which includes trust but is a broader concept that involves procedural fairness, equity, and protection of rights, among other things.[48]

Again, our full results are presented in table A.10 in the appendix. The effect of all three of our frames was similar across all three outcome measures, and *none* of them prompted a significant change in attitudes. For the sake of comparison to the previous survey, figure 4.5 shows the effect of the experimental frames on the first measure of trust—whether respondents said they trust police officers to treat people fairly. As with the previous figures, the horizontal dashed line represents the control group, and the vertical bars for each node represent 95 percent confidence intervals. Clearly, none of our frames led to significantly reduced trust in police relative to the control group, regardless of what numerical information was presented.

This was the case across all three treatments and all three outcome measures; there was little movement in attitudes toward law

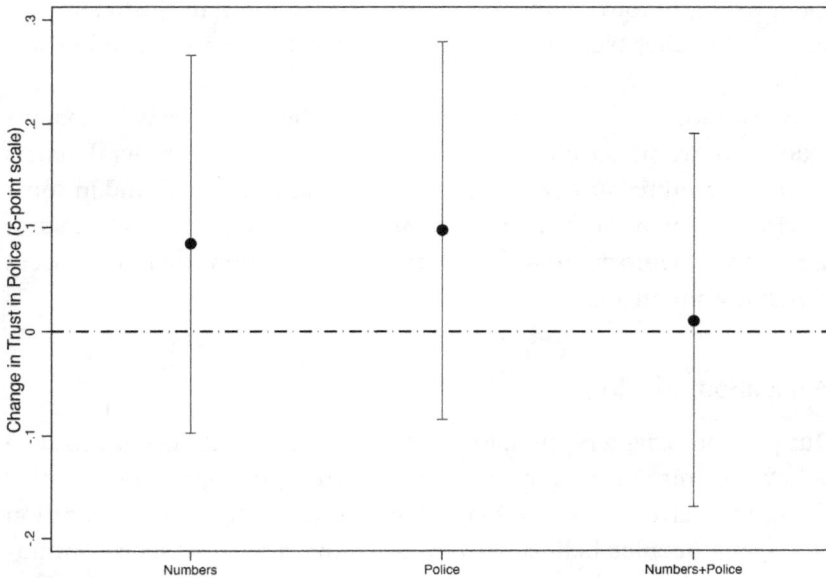

Figure 4.5. Experimental frames, police-specific cues, and trust in law enforcement
Note: Quantities are derived from the first model in table A.10 in the appendix.
Vertical bars represent 95 percent confidence intervals.

enforcement, regardless of the information we gave people and which question we asked them about the police. While we anticipated that wrongful conviction statistics would reduce trust in police and prompt more negative evaluations of law enforcement, we found little evidence that this actually occurs across two different surveys. In short, there is little or no evidence that numerical information about wrongful convictions, whether explicitly tying them to police practices or not, reduces trust in police.

What do we make of these findings?

Taken together, the results of our two studies suggest that the power of wrongful convictions to alter attitudes toward police is limited and may be more similar to information about racial disparities in police stops than to information about police use of force. If we connect our findings regarding trust in police to those regarding trust in the criminal justice system generally, we can say only that our argument about the effects of thematic frames only has mixed support. Numerical information about wrongful convictions did, indeed, erode trust in the justice system but failed to alter trust in police in a significant, consistent, and meaningful way.

We cannot say with certainty why this is the case. It may be that attitudes toward police are simply more entrenched than general beliefs about the criminal justice system as a whole, as has been found in some previous research. At the very least, they appear more resistant to change in response to information about wrongful convictions than other areas of public opinion are.

What about Ideology?

Our previous chapters emphasized the role of political ideology in state policy reforms and public awareness of wrongful convictions. In this chapter, we have focused thus far on the role of political communication in altering people's beliefs. However, it is possible that such communication influenced people's opinion unevenly, depending on their ideological leanings. That is, maybe the messages we provided resonated more strongly with liberals, while conservatives were more resistant to them. Alternatively, these messages may have had a greater impact on conservatives. After all, we established in chapter 3 that, in general, conservatives are less likely to be exposed to true stories of wrongful convictions and tend to think that such errors occur less frequently than do liberals. Perhaps, then, our messages were more likely to provide novel information for conservatives and were therefore more informative for a larger number of conservatives than liberals in our sample of respondents.

To explore whether our wrongful conviction messages had different effects on conservatives and liberals, we used a series of statistical models that included interaction effects, which made it possible to test whether the treatment effects in our experiments were contingent on respondents' political ideology.

We present these models in table A.11 in the appendix. Suffice it to say that we found minimal evidence that the effect of political communication was dependent on respondents' ideology, as most of the interaction effects failed to meet conventional levels of significance. However, we did find that conservatives (relative to liberals) were more likely to change their opinion on capital punishment when exposed to the thematic frame—exoneration numbers—but not the narrative frame. Take, for example, the survey question, "Do you favor capital punishment, life imprisonment with no possibility of parole, or imprisonment with the possibility of parole for murderers?" Our models indicated that the probability that a conservative in the control group—that is, a conservative who was not given any wrongful conviction information—preferred capital punishment was just under 70 percent. However, when exposed to the numerical information, that probability was significantly reduced to 52.5 percent.[49] This represents a large—more than seventeen percentage points—reduction in support for capital punishment among conservatives who were exposed to our thematic frame. On the other hand, liberals exposed to that information only dropped seven percentage points in their preference for capital punishment.

This decline in support for the death penalty appears to be driven by movement toward a preference for life without parole. Conservatives who were exposed to the numbers frame were nearly sixteen percentage points more likely to support life without parole (compared to conservatives in the control group), while liberals were *equally* likely to support life without parole whether they received no information or numerical information. Put simply, the numbers frame pushed more conservatives from preferring capital punishment to preferring life in prison without parole than it did liberals.

It is important to note that we remain somewhat uncertain about the extent to which this finding—that numerical information influences conservative opinions more than liberal ones—is robust to alternative question wording. When conservatives are given alternatives to the death penalty, such as life imprisonment without the possibility of parole, we find that numerical information reduces their support for capital punishment. However, we also tested a different question to measure attitudes about capital punishment, one that offers no alternatives. That question asked, "Do you support or oppose the death penalty for persons convicted of murder?" Respondents were allowed to choose their level of support among answers varying from "Strongly Oppose" to "Strongly Support." Our point estimates in table A.11 reveal that conservatives who were exposed to the numbers frame were less supportive of the death penalty than were conservatives in the control group.

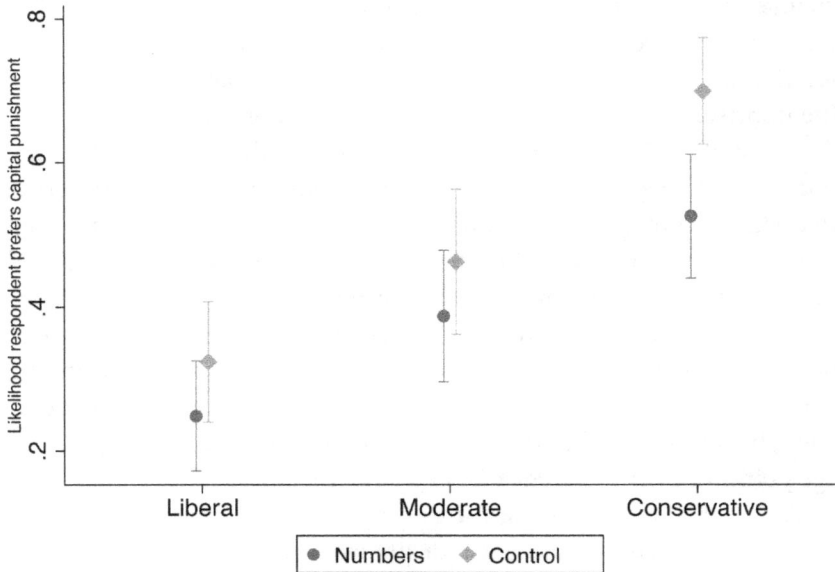

Figure 4.6. The effect of the numbers frame depending on ideology
Note: We derived these estimates from the second model presented in table A.11 in the appendix. We hold the values for the control variables to their medians. The vertical bars represent 95 percent confidence intervals.

However, the p-value associated with the interaction effect, which we use to determine whether the interaction effect is statistically significant, was slightly higher for this support question ($p \approx 0.051$, compared to $p \approx 0.049$ with the preference question) and just north of the conventional level used to determine statistical significance ($p < 0.05$). Still, taken together, the findings presented in table A.11 persuade us to believe that the numbers frame is more successful at changing conservatives' opinions than liberals'.

Figure 4.6 shows the conditional effect of the numbers frame depending on a respondent's ideology. This figure presents the probability that a respondent preferred capital punishment to life imprisonment with or without the possibility of parole. The point estimates in the figure are based on the second model in table A.11 in the appendix. This figure shows two important things. First, liberals, regardless of treatment, are less likely to prefer capital punishment compared to conservatives.

Second, conservatives significantly differ among themselves between those who were exposed to the numbers frame and those who were not. Simply put, the numbers frame exerted a stronger effect on conservatives than on liberals or moderates.

None of this is to say that our episodic frame—the narrative about the wrongful conviction of Michael Williams—had no effect. We have already established that, overall, the narrative had a more pronounced effect on death penalty beliefs than the numbers did. Rather, we found that conservatives and liberals were *equally* moved by the narrative but *differentially* moved by the numbers.

These findings beg the question about why ideology might alter responses to the numeric frame. One potential answer may lie in the treatment message. Recall that the second thematic frame discussed earlier emphasized a public-safety consideration. That is, it included a line that stated, "These numbers show that not only have thousands of people been wrongfully jailed, but that just as many criminals remain free, roaming the streets. Every year a person spent wrongfully incarcerated also represents a year in which the actual perpetrator remained at-large." We suspect that this type of public-safety argument, which emphasizes that a wrongful conviction means that the true perpetrator was not convicted and may still be free, is a point that may resonate more strongly with conservatives. The "perpetrator-at-large" rhetoric may simply be more persuasive for conservatives than for liberals. Our narrative, on the other hand, did not include such a public-safety dimension, and, in turn, its effects are not contingent on ideology. It is certainly possible that the effects of a wrongful conviction narrative that includes a true perpetrator would also be moderated by ideology.

An alternative explanation is rooted in the findings from chapter 3. That is, in Survey 1, conservatives reported hearing true stories of wrongful convictions less often and expressed a belief that such errors occur less frequently than liberals did. Therefore, it may be that the numbers frame presented in this survey was more likely to provide novel information for conservatives than it did for liberals and thus challenged their underlying beliefs and assumptions about wrongful convictions. That said, we suspect that the best explanation for this pattern is more likely to reside in the framing of the issue, particularly with respect to the public-safety dimension of wrongful convictions. We believe this to be the case because while we found a significant interaction effect between ideology and the experimental treatment when it included public-safety language, we were unable to find a similar significant interaction effect in Survey 3, which did not include language associated with the public-safety dimension.

Regardless of the specific mechanism, these findings suggest some ideological differences in receptivity to wrongful conviction information vis-à-vis capital punishment preferences, but what about our other outcomes—trust in the criminal justice system and trust in police to treat people fairly? Interestingly, we found no evidence that political ideology shaped the effect of our messages on either of these outcomes. We examined interaction effects in models using our trust outcomes, from both surveys, and they never met conventional levels of statistical significance. Thus, with respect to trust in police and in the criminal justice system, it appears that political messages exert similar effects on respondents regardless of their ideology.

There is one other caveat about our findings that we want to make abundantly clear. Independent of the messages we provided, we found that conservatives have very different opinions on capital punishment, trust in criminal justice system, and trust in police than liberals do. Tables A.8, A.9, and A.10 show that conservatives consistently report higher levels of support for capital punishment and significantly higher levels of trust in the criminal justice system and in police than do liberals. Thus, despite the fact that our findings regarding differential effects of wrongful conviction information on the basis of ideology are mixed, we have little doubt that, overall, political leanings matter when it comes to public opinion about wrongful convictions and the criminal legal system.

* * *

We began this chapter with a relatively simple goal: to understand whether and how information about wrongful convictions alters people's attitudes. Given the incredible growth of coverage dedicated to this issue across various forms of media and entertainment, it seems pertinent to consider its implications for public opinion.

We found, quite clearly, that information about wrongful convictions shapes public opinion but that it does so in somewhat nuanced ways, depending on both how information is framed and what attitudinal outcomes we examine. Episodic frames—narratives of individuals who are victims of wrongful conviction—have the power to diminish people's support for the death penalty and make people more concerned that they or someone they know could be wrongly convicted. On the other hand, thematic frames—factual information about numbers of wrongful convictions—affect death penalty attitudes to a lesser degree but reduce people's overall trust in the criminal justice system (where the narrative had no effect). Our findings collectively contribute to the literature by establishing that there may not be one framing strategy that is universally more persuasive than another on a given topic but that it depends on the persuasive goal.

More broadly, we might consider our results in light of the contemporary discourse surrounding the criminal legal system. For instance, the death penalty has undoubtedly been in decline throughout the twenty-first century by virtually every measure, including public support. Our survey results are in line with aggregate findings regarding public support for the death penalty, specifically, that the rise of the innocence movement is at least partially responsible for the decreased support for capital punishment in recent decades. On the other hand, questions remain about the extent to which wrongful convictions have influenced any wider movement toward more negative views of the criminal legal system. Our data suggest that information about such cases may reduce trust in the system generally but provide little evidence that it significantly influences attitudes toward police. Perhaps, then, any negative swing in general views toward law enforcement that has occurred in recent years is not tied to the work of the innocence movement, specifically, but to a more collective critical discourse around policing that may include wrongful convictions but also bigger issues such as racial disparities in police contact and police use of force.

Finally, while we found differences between conservatives and liberals with regard to their overall views and beliefs about the death penalty, the criminal justice system, and police, we found little evidence that ideology moderates people's responses to information about wrongful convictions. That is, by and large, conservatives and liberals *responded* similarly to our messages. This is a positive finding, as it suggests that the innocence movement may have the ability, at least in some respects, to cut across the political spectrum. Further, where we did observe a notable difference—conservatives responded more strongly to one of our thematic messages—it is possible that we uncovered evidence of a message that is particularly powerful for this group. In particular, it may be that conservatives are more responsive when wrongful convictions are framed as a public-safety issue. Indeed, research suggests that there is a significant crime control element to innocence work, in that wrongful convictions may ultimately generate thousands of additional crimes. But it is also an intuitive point that is not lost on innocence advocates; one prominent member of an innocence organization described the "true-perpetrator angle" as the "Republican pitch" for wrongful conviction reform.[50] Our findings suggest that this person may be correct and that such a pitch may be particularly effective.

Innocence advocates might (and should) take these findings as positive. While to this point we have shown that ideology is powerful and may create obstacles to policy reform in several ways, the messages at the heart of the innocence movement appear to cut through some of that political noise. People across the spectrum are open and responsive to information about wrongful convictions. Further, we did not test the source of the messages, and it is possible that were they to come from criminal justice officials, innocence advocates, or, perhaps most powerfully, exonerees themselves, such information would be even more persuasive.

We focused in this chapter on views of capital punishment and general trust in the system and police. However, innocence advocates often fight for specific reforms designed to reduce wrongful convictions and to provide redress after exoneration. How do members of the public view those reforms? And are there ways to generate support for such policies? It is to these questions we turn in chapter 5.

5

Public Support for Innocence Reforms

In 2020, the major New York publisher Doubleday released *When Truth Is All You Have*, a memoir by Jim McCloskey, who founded Centurion Ministries in 1983, the first nonprofit in the United States to focus on wrongful conviction work. The foreword to the book was written by the famed lawyer-turned-novelist John Grisham, who lamented the lack of care among the public about wrongful convictions and its absent desire to make things better:

> There are thousands of innocent people convicted and locked away in prison. Most Americans, or most white ones anyway, do not believe this. Those with darker skin know better because they have seen and lived this reality. But since the vast majority of Americans will never be affected by wrongful convictions they are not concerned with them. . . . Wrongful convictions are on no one's list of our most important problems. Occasionally, when an exoneree retaliates with a big lawsuit and the taxpayers are forced to pay millions in damages, this gets attention and causes resentment but nothing changes. We hear the common refrain that "the system is broken" but there is little effort to fix it. . . . Life goes on for the rest of us.[1]

The first part of Grisham's statement—that "most Americans" do not believe that wrongful convictions occur—is not fully accurate. As we have shown in previous chapters, many people are aware of wrongful convictions and learn about them through various sources, though, as Grisham suggested, perceptions of the problem do appear, unsurprisingly, to differ based on race (and political ideology).

But what about the second piece of Grisham's argument—that people seemingly care little about fixing the problems associated with wrongful convictions? He is probably correct insofar as wrongful convictions are unlikely to be at the top of the policy-priority list for most people.

Indeed, as one of the authors of this book has previously written, the "innocence movement . . . has generally been able to achieve some success without major public support or outcry. . . . [Wrongful convictions are] far from the forefront of the public political consciousness."[2]

Innocence advocates are aware of the potential for public apathy. "I'm still not sure that anybody cares," one advocate previously said.[3] The public "is still naïve," said another.[4] And yet another questioned whether the public views wrongful convictions as a real problem: "People feel the injustice of it when they see it, but I don't think it's something in front of their face like their health insurance. They just don't see it affecting them."[5]

Our previous surveys revealed that not only is the public aware of wrongful convictions, but people do respond to information about them in meaningful ways. Certain communication strategies even generated personal concern about them. But do awareness and concern translate to support for specific policy reforms associated with the innocence movement?

In this chapter, we examine the extent to which people support police investigatory reforms designed to mitigate wrongful convictions. Perhaps more importantly, we explore the strategies that most effectively garner support for such policies. After all, the innocence movement extends beyond legal casework; it also emphasizes the development and implementation of policy reforms designed to reduce the likelihood of wrongful convictions, to assist in the identification of those that have already occurred, and to provide postrelease support for the exonerated. And if, as we argued earlier, public opinion is consequential for policy adoption, it is important to understand what factors shape public support for specific policies that are part of the innocence movement's agenda.

We present data from four surveys to isolate the characteristics of individuals and the specific types of messages that do and do not increase support for reforms, and we incorporate insights from political communication that highlight the power of framing and priming particular considerations to generate policy support. As in chapter 4, we shine a light on the unique power of narratives to generate attitude change, but we also find utility in priming—encouraging people to think about certain issues in order to foster change.

The story told by these findings is clear and consistent with what we have argued throughout this book—that politics matter—and the considerations we raise have implications for innocence advocacy and criminal legal reform.

Who Supports Policy Reform?

Wrongful convictions are not a new problem, and the research that underlies reforms is rooted in decades of psychological and legal scholarship. However, innocence as an advocacy movement is still a relatively recent phenomenon, and a majority of the policy changes that have been enacted have occurred in the past couple of decades.[6] As such, there is little empirical research directly focused on public attitudes toward policy reforms that are on the innocence movement's agenda. A previous study by Marvin Zalman and colleagues found that a majority of survey respondents believed that "wrongful convictions occur frequently enough to justify major changes in the criminal justice system," but we want to explore attitudes toward specific reforms on the innocence movement's agenda and unpack the communication strategies that influence support for them.[7] Our analyses account for a wide range of individual characteristics such as race, sex/gender, age, trust in police, and more, but we emphasize the role played by two specific variables: political ideology and awareness of wrongful convictions.

As we discussed earlier, it might seem like wrongful conviction reforms—recording interrogations, preserving biological evidence, and compensating exonerees, for example—should cross ideological lines. These policies are, after all, designed to protect innocent defendants (and thus to help prevent actual offenders from experiencing "wrongful liberty," committing more crimes, and claiming additional victims) and to provide redress after an error is discovered and overturned.[8] Therefore, as we and others have noted, trying to prevent wrongful convictions should appeal to proponents of both crime control and due process and thus seems like a noncontroversial goal that could mobilize support across the political spectrum. Still, there is reason to believe that public opinion on wrongful conviction policies is divided along ideological lines. More precisely, it is likely that liberals are more supportive of policy reforms designed to address wrongful convictions. The reasons for this expectation were outlined in chapter 2, but we briefly revisit them here.

First, wrongful conviction reforms require meaningful changes to the policies that guide police practices. Studies have shown that conservatives have a more sanguine perception of police and prosecutors than liberals do, and it follows that people who have positive feelings toward law enforcement may be less favorable toward reforms that call attention to errors in the criminal legal system, which are tied directly to police practices.[9]

Second, some wrongful conviction policies may require additional state and local funds for implementation and may cost, or be perceived as costing, a significant amount of money.[10] Since political ideology influences public attitudes on government spending, it seems plausible that conservatives would be less inclined to support increases in expenditures, especially those tied to policies that could be perceived as questioning the integrity of criminal legal system.[11]

Third, although wrongful convictions (and the associated freedom of true perpetrators and their continued crimes) may hold appeal across the ideological spectrum, people on the political right and left are likely to have different preferences and priorities. A considerable literature has demonstrated that conservatives tend to be more punitive, with preferences that fall more in line with law-and-order politics, compared to liberals, who often exhibit a stronger due process orientation.[12]

The fourth and perhaps less obvious reason is that media coverage and elite discourse about wrongful convictions often emphasize the disproportionate risk that disadvantaged groups, such as racial and ethnic minorities and people from low-income backgrounds, face in the criminal legal system.[13] That is, discussions of wrongful convictions are not independent from broader issues of racial and economic disparities in the system. Racial disparities exist throughout the criminal process, for example, in the rates at which people are stopped by police, sentencing outcomes, and imprisonment.[14] This information is increasingly discussed in the media, and rhetoric that invokes social-group cues often leads people to organize political issues along ideological lines. If wrongful convictions are discussed alongside issues of race and income inequality, it seems plausible, if not likely, that liberals and conservatives may view policies designed to address the problem through an ideological lens tied to social groups they find more or less sympathetic.

For these reasons, it seems reasonable to expect ideology to influence people's level of support for wrongful-conviction-related policies. In chapter 2, we found that, depending on a state's electoral context, the ideological leaning of the state's public affects the adoption of innocence policy reforms. While that revealed the nuanced influence of public opinion on state policy adoption, it did not directly test whether liberals and conservatives in the general public differ in their support for these policies. In this chapter, we remedy that.

Ideology and Policy Support

To test our expectations regarding ideology and support for innocence policies, we measured both political ideology and support for policy reform across four different surveys (Surveys 1, 4, 5, and 6). We measured ideology by asking survey respondents to place themselves on a seven-point scale ranging from "extremely liberal" to "extremely conservative." We gauged support for policy reform by first providing respondents a brief but balanced description of innocence-related police reforms and then asking about their level of support for those reforms on a scale from "strongly oppose" to "strongly support." The measure of policy support used for analyses throughout this chapter is the following survey item: "Research suggests that reforms to police investigation practices, such as eyewitness procedures and interrogations, may reduce the likelihood of wrongful convictions. However, they may also increase the difficulty of obtaining accurate convictions. Do you support or oppose these types of policy reforms?"[15] To ensure that any relationship we observed between ideology and support for reforms was not spurious, we analyzed the survey data using regression models with controls for a wide range of predictors of support. In this chapter, we present figures with visual indicators of our key results; the full regression tables with results and controls are presented in the appendix.

The results painted a clear and consistent picture: ideology was a statistically and substantively significant predictor of support for policy reform. Liberals were more inclined to support innocence reforms than conservatives were, and the results were quite robust. Figure 5.1 shows the relationship between ideology and innocence policy support across our four surveys. Figure 5.1 reveals a consistent finding that

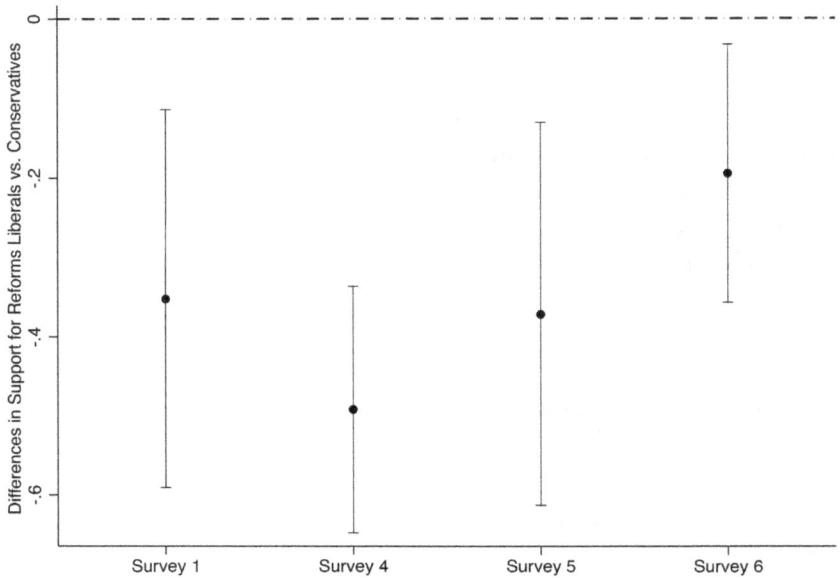

Figure 5.1. Support for wrongful conviction reforms and ideology
Note: Estimates are based on the models presented in table A.12 in the appendix. Vertical lines represent 95 percent confidence intervals. Negative values indicate that conservatives have lower levels of support than liberals do.

respondents' ideology significantly shaped their support for reform. The circular nodes in this figure show the *difference* in support for reforms between conservatives and liberals on average, while controlling for other characteristics about them. For example, our analysis of Survey 4 showed that, on average, liberals' support for reform was about 4.1 on a scale of 0 to 6; in contrast, conservatives' average level of support was 3.6. The circular node on the far left shows this 0.5-point difference. In more substantive terms, this means that conservatives' support for police reforms was 12 percent lower than that of liberals. The vertical bars show the 95 percent confidence intervals and make us reasonably confident that the difference between conservatives and liberals in Survey 4 was not an artifact of sampling error but rather represents a systematic difference between these two groups.

Perhaps the most notable takeaway from figure 5.1 is the consistency of this finding—we found significant, systematic differences between conservatives and liberals across four separate surveys, with distinct samples, administered across four years, and all based on statistical models that control for other respondent characteristics. All of this raises our confidence in the key finding that ideology plays an important role in whether a person supports police reforms related to wrongful convictions.

We found not only a consistent relationship between ideology and innocence policy support but a strong one as well. The magnitude of the effect of ideology rivaled or, in many cases, exceeded that of other potential predictors. Consider the effect of race, for instance, where some people might expect to find differences. We found a statistically significant difference in support for reforms between white and Black respondents in only one of our four surveys; in the other three, Black and white respondents reported similar levels of support. And, even in the one instance in which we found a difference, the gap between Black and white respondents was smaller than the gap between conservative and liberal respondents. We found essentially the same pattern in regard to sex/gender: there was a significant difference between men and women in only one of our four surveys, and again, the difference was smaller than that between conservatives and liberals.

Clearly, as we have stressed throughout this book, political ideology matters in a consistent and significant way.

Wrongful Conviction Awareness and Policy Support

Beyond ideology, we wanted to test whether people's awareness of wrongful convictions is itself a predictor of support for policy reforms. Specifically, we thought that those who reported higher levels of awareness would be more supportive of reforms than those who were less aware.

Our suggestion that those who are more aware of the problem are more likely to support related policies may seem obvious. It is certainly an intuitive point. However, as we showed in chapter 3, although many people have heard about wrongful convictions, there is considerable variation in the extent to which they have done so and in what they think or know about the problem. For example, 68.3 percent of people surveyed said they had heard true stories about an innocent person who was wrongfully convicted, but only 42.8 percent said they had heard of the Innocence Project, the largest and most prominent innocence advocacy organization. And while fictional accounts of wrongful convictions are increasingly featured in entertainment media, a slight majority of people reported that they had *not* been exposed to such fictional stories. In short, some people hear about wrongful convictions and others do not, and we think it is important to examine if and to what extent this awareness influences policy support.

People who are more aware of wrongful convictions have probably heard about the hardships endured by those who experience them. They probably have heard the emotionally evocative stories of those whose lives were upended by a seemingly flawed and unjust criminal legal system. They might also have been exposed to facts and figures about wrongful convictions and thus have learned about the potential pervasiveness of the problem. In chapter 4, we demonstrated that these types of information—both narratives and numbers—have the power to alter people's attitudes and increase their personal concern about wrongful convictions. This all leads us to expect that awareness of wrongful convictions should prompt a desire for changes to policy and practice.

Although the survey data analyzed in chapter 3 provided numerous measures of *awareness* of wrongful convictions, we focus our attention here on one in particular: whether people had heard of the Innocence Project. We chose this measure of awareness because of its precision and because familiarity with the Innocence Project reveals a relatively high level of awareness.[16]

Our analyses of the relationship between awareness of the Innocence Project and support for wrongful conviction reform (with controls for ideology and other variables) indicated that awareness was a strong and significant predictor of support. Using data from Survey 1, figure 5.2 shows that people who said that they had heard of the Innocence Project were more supportive of reform than were people who had not, controlling for other factors. Specifically, the average level of support for respondents who indicated that they had heard of the Innocence Project was about 3.8, other things being equal, while it was about 3.4 for people who had not. This 10.5 percent difference was nearly as large as the difference between conservatives and liberals, and it was statistically significant.

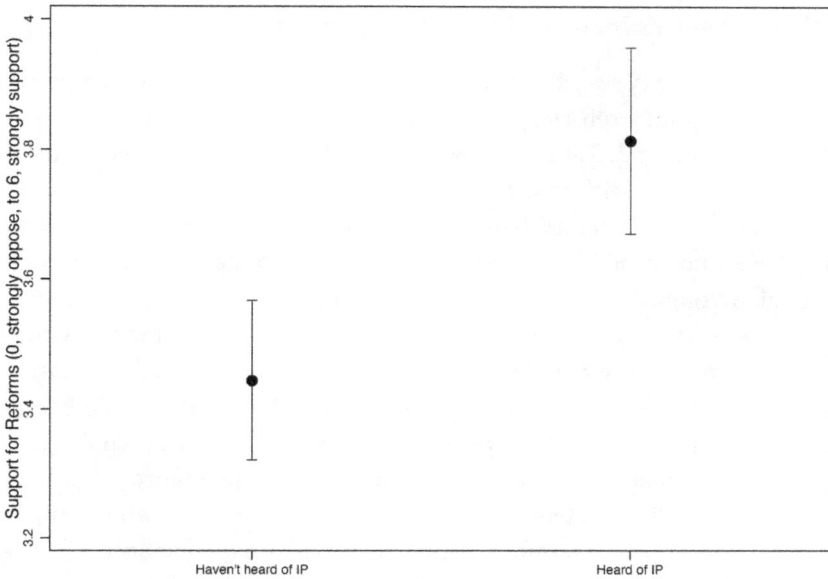

Figure 5.2. Support for wrongful conviction reforms and Innocence Project awareness
Note: These quantities are derived from the model presented in table A.13 in the appendix. Vertical lines represent 95 percent confidence intervals. Other variables are held to their mean values.

One limitation of our tests of the effects of awareness was that our measure was contingent on self-reported awareness, and while we do our best to account for rival explanations through statistical controls, inferences about the effects of awareness are correlational and do not yield strong causal evidence. In addition, these tests did not account for the specific types of wrongful conviction information that people received (because they were simply reporting whether they had heard about the Innocence Project), and as we showed in chapter 4, the manner in which information about wrongful convictions is presented is important. Specifically, we showed that different types of information triggered different attitudinal responses.

In the next section, we not only address these limitations but also isolate specific messages and types of political communication to better understand what does and does not affect support for innocence-related policy reforms.

What Strategies Increase Support for Policy Reform?

To identify the types of messaging that generate support for wrongful conviction policy reforms, we again utilize insights from framing theory, as in chapter 4. There, we demonstrated that different presentations of information—different *frames*—have different effects on attitudes toward the death penalty, trust in the criminal justice system, and trust in police. Specifically, we found that an episodic frame (a narrative about a single wrongful conviction) had a more substantial impact on people's death penalty preferences than a thematic frame (factual information about the number of people exonerated). In short, we argued that narratives elicit emotional responses, prompt "transportation" of the message recipient into the story and counterfactual thinking (e.g., it could happen to me or people close to me), and, in turn, facilitate more prominent changes in policy preferences than do thematic frames, which might convey novel statistical information to a message recipient and shift relevant policy preferences but to a lesser degree. However, in chapter 4, the only policy preference we examined was in regard to capital punishment. Here, we test the effects of framing techniques—narratives versus numeric information—on support for police reforms designed to mitigate wrongful convictions. Consistent with the framing literature and the findings in chapter 4, we expected a narrative about a person who was wrongfully convicted and sentenced to death to increase support for policy reform to a greater degree than information about the number of exonerations.

To test our expectations, we turn back to Survey 4, described in chapter 4. There, we discussed the effects of alternative frames for trust in the justice system, trust in police, and support for capital punishment. Now, we focus on the effects on support for innocence policy reform.

Survey respondents were randomly assigned to one of four experimental conditions, and all respondents were asked the question described earlier about their support for reforms to eyewitness identification practices and police interrogation. To prevent redundancy, we simply summarize our four conditions here (see chapter 4 for the full content of each treatment message).

First, participants in a control group were asked about their support for policy reform without receiving any additional information.

A second group was first presented with a thematic frame that provided information about the number of people exonerated and a statistical estimate of the number of people currently incarcerated for crimes they did not commit. The thematic presentation of wrongful convictions links the information to a concern about the number of guilty offenders who remain free. After reading this information, these respondents were asked about their support for policy reforms.

A third group first received an episodic framing of wrongful conviction information in the form of a narrative, designed to be similar to what one might find in a newspaper. The narrative described the wrongful conviction and eventual exoneration of "Michael Williams" and was based loosely on the true story of Kirk Bloodsworth. The narrative described the role played by child eyewitnesses in Williams's conviction and death sentence. It stated that Williams spent nine years in prison, noted the hardships he endured before DNA testing proved that he was not the offender, and commented on his struggle to adjust to life after the wrongful conviction. After reading the story, people in this group were asked about their support for policy reforms.

The fourth group received both the numeric information and the narrative before being asked about their support for policy reforms.

As with previous analyses, the full results are presented in the appendix. Figure 5.3 shows the effects of each frame on support for police investigatory reforms. To summarize our findings, quite simply, the narrative mobilized support for policy change, while the numbers did not.

As anticipated, survey respondents who were provided the story of Michael Williams (narrative) were significantly more supportive of policy reform than were respondents in the control group, who received no wrongful conviction message (as represented by the dashed line at 0). More specifically, the average level of support for reform among respondents in the control group was 3.72, other things being equal, while the average level of support for respondents who received the narrative frame was 3.94. This represents a roughly 6 percent increase in support, which was statistically significant.

Interestingly, the average level of support for reform among respondents in the dual-frame condition—that is, those who were exposed to both the numbers and the narrative—was nearly equivalent to the level of support for those who were exposed to only the narrative. In other words, similar

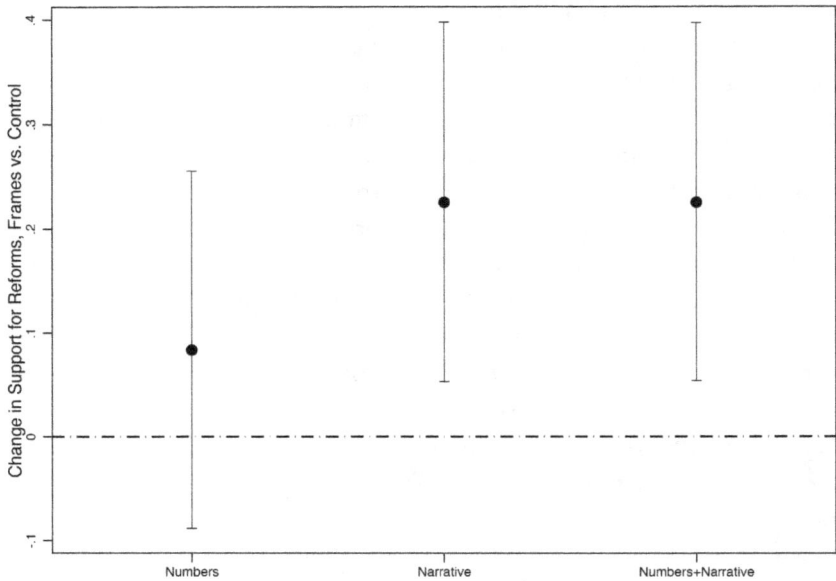

Figure 5.3. Support for wrongful conviction reforms and experimental frames
Note: These quantities are derived from the first model in table A.14 (Survey 4) in the appendix. Vertical lines represent 95 percent confidence intervals.

to what we found in chapter 4, the narrative appears to be what primarily drove persuasion on a policy preference; coupling the two frames together did not have an effect beyond what the narrative achieved on its own.

However, the numeric information on its own had no significant impact on support for policy reform. While we had anticipated the narrative to have a greater effect than the numbers, we thought that providing people with statistics about the prevalence of wrongful convictions would also be persuasive, as it was with support for the death penalty, as presented in chapter 4. That the numeric information did little to generate support for policy reform was therefore puzzling.

What might account for this unexpected finding regarding the failure of numeric information to heighten support for reforms? One potential explanation rests in the content of our numeric frame. A "strong" frame raises considerations that are cognitively available, accessible, and applicable.[17] In our earlier analysis of support for the death penalty (chapter 4), both the numbers and narrative treatment texts provided information about death sentences that were later overturned, and we observed corresponding changes in attitudes toward capital punishment. Here, regarding support for policy reform, our narrative specifically mentioned an eyewitness misidentification that led to a wrongful conviction, and again, we saw the hypothesized effect when using a police reform measure that mentions changes to eyewitness identification procedures. That is, the treatment frame contained information that was directly *applicable* to the outcome measure. However, the numbers treatment mentioned neither eyewitness testimony nor police interrogations; thus, it produced no change in support for reforms focused on those topics. Because our numbers treatment did not explicitly provide any text that was directly applicable to the police reform outcome, we were left to ponder what would happen if our thematic frame included such information about the proportion of wrongful convictions caused by eyewitness errors or coerced confessions.

Unsatisfied with this lingering puzzle, we designed a follow-up survey experiment to determine if there was a way to present a thematic frame that contained numerical information that mobilized support for policy reform. The study again had four conditions and was described in detail in chapter 4 (Survey 5). In that chapter, we discussed how we used this follow-up study to better understand how various types of wrongful conviction information altered—or, in that case, did not alter—trust in police. We now explore whether it influenced support for policy reforms. Again, the full text of our treatment messages was provided in chapter 4, so we only summarize them briefly here.

The control group was simply told, "A wrongful conviction is a case in which an innocent person is convicted of a crime they did not commit." Respondents were then asked about their support for reform, using the question described earlier in this chapter.

A second group was provided a shortened version of the numeric information from the previous experiment (with updated numbers). On the basis of the results of that previous survey, we suspected that this information would fail to garner support for police investigatory reforms because there is nothing in the text that discusses how errors made by law enforcement can lead to wrongful convictions.

The third condition therefore had a treatment message that explicitly attributed wrongful convictions, in part, to misconduct by law

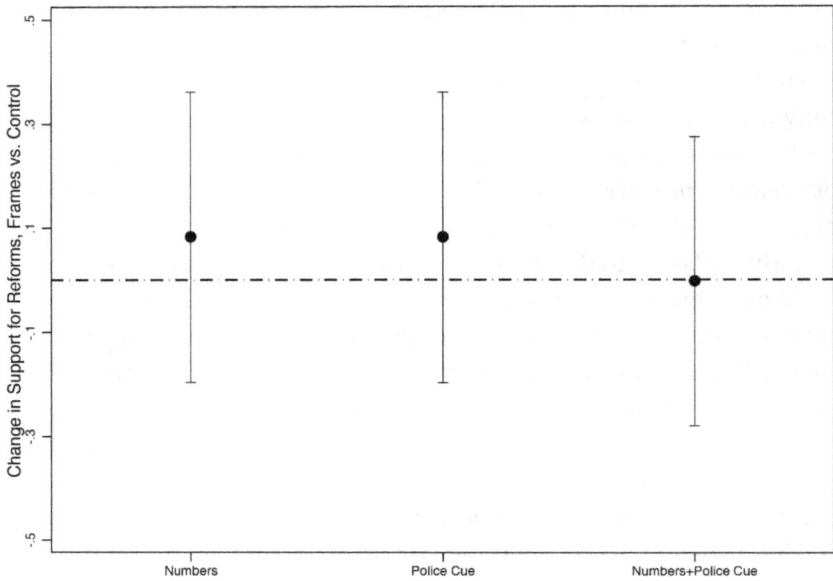

Figure 5.4. Follow-up survey: support for wrongful conviction reforms and experimental frames

Note: Vertical lines represent 95 percent confidence intervals. We derive estimates from an ordinary least squares model that also controls for respondents' ideology, education, sex/gender, race and ethnicity, age, political knowledge, and trust in police.

enforcement. Further, the message specifically linked the police misconduct to interrogations and eyewitnesses—the things mentioned in our measure of support for policy reform.

The fourth group constituted our main manipulation; participants were given both the numeric information and the text that attributed wrongful convictions to misconduct by law enforcement.

As in the previous experiment, we found that the basic numeric information had no effect on innocence policy support. Interestingly, though, this lack of an effect held even when that information was coupled with text that attributed the blame for wrongful convictions to law enforcement. Relative to the control group, none of the treatments prompted a statistically significant increase in support for police investigatory reforms, as shown in figure 5.4.

Taken together, the results of our experiments tell a consistent story. An episodic frame—an individual story about someone who was wrongly convicted—effectively mobilized support for policy reform. However, despite our efforts to convey numeric information in a relevant and persuasive manner, facts and figures about wrongful convictions failed to shift attitudes on innocence reforms, specifically, changes to police investigatory practices. While statistics about a given society over a particular time period changed broader attitudes toward the justice system (as we showed in chapter 4), they did little to increase support for policy reforms specific to wrongful convictions.

Beyond the Frame: Priming and Public Opinion

Framing is but one theoretical lens that tells us how to communicate information in a persuasive manner. As a final test of how to increase support for wrongful conviction policies, we designed a study around theoretical insights from the literature on *priming*.

Priming is related to, but distinct from, framing. By calling attention to particular considerations and making them salient, priming changes the "standards that people use to make political evaluations" and may change the criteria that people use when forming policy preferences.[18] Priming is a useful framework for understanding how media coverage can shape perceptions of an issue. As the communication scholars Dietram Scheufele and David Tewksbury have written, "By making some issues more salient in people's mind (agenda setting), mass media can also shape the considerations that people take into account when making judgments about political candidates or issues (priming)."[19] For example, if the media repeatedly discusses unemployment during a political campaign, voters may evaluate candidates on the basis of how they think each candidate would handle unemployment; this would be a priming effect. This is distinct from framing, in that the media could discuss unemployment statistics (a thematic frame) and/or present a story about an unemployed individual (an episodic frame).

In the context of wrongful convictions, it is possible that those who are advocating for innocence-related policy reforms may find utility in priming specific considerations. Here, we focus on two in particular: *trust in police* and *compensation for the wrongly convicted*.

First, we explore whether priming people to think about how much they trust police will increase support for wrongful conviction reforms. While trust in police is high for some individuals, the vast majority of people do not have *complete* trust in police. Indeed, in the two trust-in-police measures we discuss here, only 7.7 percent of respondents selected the highest level of trust on both measures. Thus, for most people, encouraging them to reflect on how much they actually trust police might make it cognitively salient that they do not have complete trust in law enforcement. This, in turn, should lead them to consider that imperfect trust when forming an evaluation of policy reforms designed to improve police practices and increase their support for such changes.

Second, we think that the effects of priming trust in police can be accentuated by also priming financial considerations associated with wrongful convictions. As we discussed in chapter 2, many states have adopted compensation statutes that provide varying levels of financial restitution and, in some states, other reentry services to exonerees after their release.[20] Although the true "cost" of a wrongful conviction cannot be captured in dollars and many of these laws do not function especially well in practice, in theory, some states provide compensation to exonerees, and thus there is a direct monetary toll associated with wrongful convictions and exonerations.[21] Priming people to think about the financial damage associated with wrongful convictions should increase their support for reforms designed to prevent such miscarriages of justice.

To test the effects of priming trust in police and compensation on support for wrongful conviction reforms, we designed a question-order survey experiment (Survey 6) in which respondents were randomly assigned to one of three conditions.

Respondents in the control group were simply asked about their support for reforms addressing police investigation practices (see the question wording described earlier in this chapter).

To prime people to consider their trust in police, respondents in a second group were first asked two questions gauging their attitudes toward police before they were asked about their support for reforms. Specifically, they were asked, "How much trust do you have in police officers to treat people fairly?" and "To what extent do you agree or disagree that the police can be trusted to make decisions that are right for the people in their communities?"

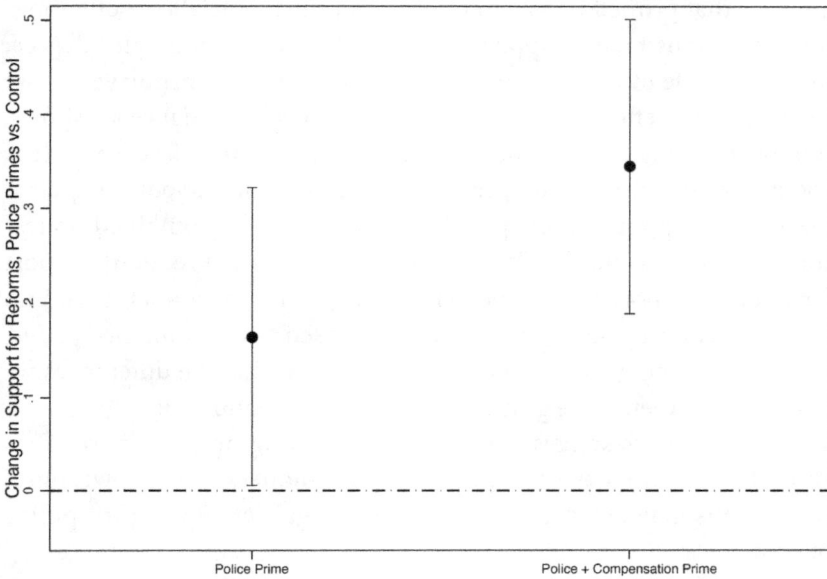

Figure 5.5. Support for wrongful conviction reforms and experimental primes
Note: These quantities are derived from the model presented in table A.15 in the appendix. Vertical lines represent 95 percent confidence intervals.

A third condition was designed to prime respondents to consider the financial cost of wrongful convictions in addition to their trust in police. This group was provided the following: "People who are wrongfully convicted for crimes they did not commit face many challenges when released from prison. Research shows that compensation laws that provide money and services for people when they are released can help them reintegrate into society. However, they may cost the states a significant amount of money. To what extent do you support or oppose these types of policies?" They were then asked the same trust-in-police questions described earlier and finally were asked about their support for policy reform.[22] To be clear, this third condition simultaneously primed both financial costs and trust in police; in doing so, we were unable to isolate the effect of only priming the financial cost.

The results of this survey are presented in figure 5.5. As we expected, priming people to consider their trust in police increased support for innocence-related reforms.[23] Furthermore, uniting the police cue with a message that primed people to think about the financial cost of wrongful convictions raised support for reforms to an even greater degree; the magnitude of the combined police/compensation prime was more than twice the effect of the police prime by itself. As figure 5.5 shows, support for reform among people who were not primed in any way (the control group represented by the dashed line at 0) was about 0.34 points lower than support among people who received the combined police/compensation prime. In effect, the absence of a prime reduced support for reform by more than 10 percent, from 3.36 for respondents with no prime to 3.7 for respondents who were exposed to the combined prime, other things being equal. Figure 5.5 also reveals that the differences we observed between these groups was statistically significant.

These findings suggest that simply encouraging people to pause and reflect on their trust in police and the monetary toll of wrongful convictions may be an effective strategy to garner support for policy reform.

Do Experimental Primes and Frames Affect Liberals and Conservatives Differently?

As in chapter 4, we also evaluated the extent to which liberals and conservatives reacted differently to the experimental frames and primes that we have presented in this chapter. While we found some evidence in chapter 4 that conservatives were more persuaded by the numbers frames than liberals were with respect to capital punishment preferences, we did not find any evidence of the same with respect to support for police investigatory reforms. That is, liberals and conservatives responded similarly to our framing and priming strategies with regard to the changes they produced in policy support.

None of this is to say that ideology does not influence people's support for policy reforms related to wrongful convictions. Rather, as we showed earlier, ideology matters a great deal in shaping people's attitudes toward these reforms. It means only that we were unable to reject the hypothesis that our messages, whether designed to frame or prime, affect liberals and conservatives differently.

* * *

Overall, our survey results tell a strong and coherent story: if innocence advocates wish to mobilize support for wrongful-conviction-related reforms, they should pay careful consideration to what strategies they use to communicate their messages.

Across four surveys, we found that political conservatives are, on average, less supportive of police investigative reforms that may reduce the likelihood of wrongful convictions. However, we also found that irrespective of ideological preferences, those who are simply more aware of wrongful convictions are more supportive of innocence policies. A first step for innocence advocates, then, is simply to continue to spread awareness about wrongful convictions, through both the media and the proliferation of popular culture that brings attention to wrongful convictions. Importantly, our specific measures suggest that those who are more aware of the Innocence Project are more supportive of reforms. As with our analyses in chapter 2, which showed that the presence of innocence organizations influences state policy adoption, our survey results suggest that making the public aware of innocence groups may increase support for the wrongful conviction reform agenda, which thus speaks to the immense value of such nonprofit organizations. They can be, and are, instrumental in promoting positive changes in our criminal legal system.

We also found that priming certain considerations may increase support for innocence policies. Specifically, encouraging people to think about their less-than-complete trust in law enforcement may serve to increase their support for innocence reforms related to police practices, and combining these considerations with financial ones seems to be even more effective. Perhaps most importantly, both liberals and conservatives responded to the messages provided in our surveys. So our surveys suggest that, despite differing baseline levels of support, people across the ideological spectrum are responsive to information about wrongful convictions.

Innocence advocates should take some measure of solace in these findings. As we noted at the outset of this chapter, there has been some consternation—both within the innocence movement and among outsiders like John Grisham—that the public remains apathetic about fixing problems in our criminal legal system that contribute to wrongful convictions. While it remains true that wrongful convictions are unlikely to be among the public's top policy priorities, there are strategies that generate public support for reforms, and those strategies may well cut across the often firm lines of political ideology. Understanding those strategies is vital, as public support may be a key component of ensuring that the noble ideals of the innocence movement—and other movements aiming to generate social change and legal reform—become a reality.

Conclusion

The Politics of Innocence 2.0

When we designed our first survey related to wrongful convictions and public opinion in mid-2016, there were just over eighteen hundred cases listed on the National Registry of Exonerations. As of this writing, there are more than three thousand, an increase of more than 60 percent.[1] The increasing number of exoneration cases has brought with them a heightened level of attention to flaws in the criminal legal system in the news media and popular culture, as we have discussed throughout this book.

In the realm of criminal justice policy and practice, too, the salience of wrongful convictions has increased dramatically. For instance, a 2011 study by one of the authors found that ten states had eyewitness identification reform policies and nineteen had policies regarding the recording of interrogations; by 2018, the numbers of states with such policies had increased to twenty and twenty-seven, respectively.[2] It is a similar story with exoneree compensation statutes: a decade ago, twenty-seven states and Washington, DC, had such policies; at the time of this writing, thirty-seven states and DC have one.[3]

Still, there is much we do not—and, possibly, cannot—know from a research perspective. We cannot say with any measure of certainty whether the number of wrongful convictions or the frequency with which they occur has increased or decreased. We do not yet know the long-term practical consequences of eyewitness or interrogation reforms with regard to case outcomes. We know that many existing compensation laws are flawed both in writing and in practice, but we do not yet have a firm grasp of their many complexities in action. Yet there is one thing we can say with some confidence: the innocence movement does not appear to be going away anytime soon, though it is evolving in interesting and important ways.

The question, then, is what does the research we have presented throughout this book tell us about the current state of the innocence movement and the future of advocacy and activism around wrongful convictions?

Innocence Is Political

We said at the outset that much of the discourse and conventional wisdom surrounding wrongful convictions suggest, implicitly or explicitly, that the issue is largely apolitical. And, in some respects, it may be: errors occur everywhere, regardless of political culture, and few people (aside from actual offenders) would advocate for the conviction of the innocent. Still, to suggest that this issue is fully nonideological and bipartisan is inaccurate. Political ideology plays a key role in the adoption of state policy reforms and is a powerful force in shaping public awareness of and opinions about issues related to wrongful convictions. As such, to ignore political ideology is to miss an important component of the innocence movement's successes, failures, and future prospects.

As we showed in chapter 2, state policy reform in the wrongful conviction realm is tied to state-level politics and public opinion. For decades, political scientists have analyzed the linkage between public opinion and public policy. Does public policy change when public opinion shifts on an issue? Are public policies consistent with the preferences of the majority? Scholars have examined the extent to which government policy—formed at different levels of government and in different branches of government—is congruent with and responsive to the preferences of the citizenry.[4] It is understandable that so much scholarly attention is dedicated to this topic; it strikes at the heart of whether a government represents the will of the people. Our analyses in chapter 2 contribute to this rich literature and add important nuance. We found that public opinion—public liberalism, in particular—influences the adoption of state-level innocence reforms. Importantly, however, we found that its effect depends on states' electoral context. Specifically, our analyses suggest that a more liberal constituency increases the likelihood that states adopt these reforms, but only in states where lawmakers experience, relatively speaking, more competitive elections. Thus, the political leaning of a state's mass public is consequential for policy adoption, but mostly in states in which lawmakers are electorally vulnerable. Further, the political party of the governor influenced policy adoption, such that states with Democratic governors were more likely to adopt innocence reform legislation.

We also found that the presence of innocence groups shapes policy adoption. That we observe an effect for the presence of innocence groups while also accounting for exonerations and public opinion suggests that the political advocacy efforts of these organizations are an integral part of policy change. These organizations are doing more than fighting to exonerate the innocent; they help alter public policy and thus have the potential to alter the criminal legal landscape. They are, in short, effective as interest groups and/or social movement organizations.

Taken together, chapter 2 provides considerable evidence that politics matter for the passage of policies related to wrongful conviction. In other words, innocence reform is not apolitical.

Public awareness of and beliefs about wrongful convictions also are inextricably connected to political ideology. Chapter 3 provides information about the extent to which the mass public is aware of wrongful convictions and the various sources of this information. Notably, we found predictable and nontrivial differences between liberals and conservatives in whether they had heard true stories of wrongful convictions and whether they had heard of the Innocence Project. However, that we did not observe ideological differences in whether people had heard *fictional* accounts of wrongful convictions is telling. It suggests that ideological differences in awareness may be tied to ideological differences in news selection and the extent to which different news outlets cover these issues.

Political differences extend beyond simply hearing true accounts of wrongful convictions; our findings suggest that ideology is linked to beliefs about the frequency with which they occur and the sources of such errors. Perhaps most tellingly, we found that liberals were significantly more likely than conservatives to think that an innocent person has been executed in the past five years. This ideological gap was also evident in people's beliefs about the percentage of both misdemeanor and felony convictions that involved innocent defendants. And interestingly (but perhaps not surprisingly), liberals believed that errors associated with police actions—coerced false confessions and illegal and unethical police practices, for example—occur more frequently than conservatives did. On the subject of wrongful convictions, then, it seems that liberals and conservatives have two fundamentally different perceptions of reality.

Importantly, though, awareness is not only about ideology; it is also shaped by political interest. The people who are most interested in news and politics are, understandably, more keenly aware of factual errors in the legal system. Given that the politically interested are more likely to be mobilized for political action, these individuals provide a potential base that innocence advocates could target for support.

Understanding the sources of people's awareness is important, in part, because awareness is positively associated with support for wrongful conviction reform policies, as we showed in chapter 5. People who had heard of the Innocence Project were significantly more supportive of reforms to police investigation practices than were people who had not heard of the organization. Thus, advocates for reform should care about who is and who is not aware of the issue and seek to increase awareness to the extent possible, because this awareness is directly tied to support for policy change. In part, innocence advocates should continue to use the press, social media, and other outlets to amplify their message. If media and popular attention to wrongful conviction stories continues to increase as it has in recent decades, it will probably increase awareness and, perhaps, calls for policy reform.

Political ideology and interest also exert independent effects on support for policy reform. In fact, perhaps the clearest evidence that debunks the notion that the innocence issue is apolitical is what we showed in chapter 5. Across four separate surveys, political ideology was a significant predictor of people's support for reforms designed to reduce the likelihood of wrongful convictions, and the effect persisted while controlling for rival explanations for these attitudes. In addition, political interest was a positive predictor of support for policy reform in every survey we administered.

Taken together, our survey results demonstrate that there is a chasm between liberals and conservatives in their beliefs about the frequency with which innocents are convicted of crimes they did not commit and in their support for related policy reforms. Liberals believe that such errors are more common and are thus more supportive of police reforms that may mitigate them. To reiterate a point we mentioned earlier, there were significant differences in the likelihood that conservatives and liberals have heard true stories of wrongful conviction, but no such differences were evident for whether people heard fictional accounts. If ideologically driven selective exposure to news media occurs and news outlets differ in their coverage of wrongful convictions, it helps explain the patterns we observe.

As an anecdotal example of this ideological difference in media coverage, around the time we were drafting the conclusion of this book, we noticed a couple of news stories that addressed wrongful or questionable convictions, and they provide a telling example of how different outlets cover them (and thus how the public is likely to learn about them). On November 17–18, 2021, the *New York Times*' online home page featured a story about Julius Jones.[5] Jones had been convicted and sentenced to death in 2002 for the murder of a man named Paul Howell. From the outset, the conviction was questionable, as the result of a trial that was awash in racial bias. The case eventually became a cause célèbre, receiving coverage in a variety of outlets including nontraditional news sources such as ESPN.[6] Jones, on Oklahoma's death row for nineteen years, always maintained his innocence. Finally, on November 18, 2021, Governor Kevin Stitt commuted Jones's sentence just hours before his scheduled execution.

The *New York Times* prominently featured the story of Jones's commutation on its website. At the same time, it also featured a story on the expected exoneration of the two men who had been convicted of assassinating Malcolm X in 1966.[7] Both stories were top headlines on the *New York Times* home page. We then visited the website of *Fox News*. Here, there were stories about both events, but they were far less prominently displayed and somewhat difficult to find. Rather than featured near the top, the stories were linked near the bottom of the home page, where visitors had to scroll down and actively look to find them. Further, the difference extended beyond the prominence of the stories' placement on the websites (i.e., agenda setting); there also were key differences in how the stories were covered (i.e., framing). The last lines of the *New York Times* story on Jones's commutation featured the words of his mother and left the reader with a sense of injustice and feelings of sympathy for Jones and his family; it was, in short, a story of a wrongful conviction and near execution. The story read,

> Madeline Davis-Jones, Mr. Jones's mother, said she was grateful that her son was not executed for a murder she said he did not commit.
>
> "I still believe that every day Julius spends behind bars is an injustice, and I will never stop speaking out for him or fighting to free him," she said in a statement. "But today is a good day, and I am thankful to Governor Stitt for that."[8]

By contrast, the last lines of the *Fox News* story featured the words of the murder victim's sister and left the reader with a different sense of injustice—one in which the legal system erroneously overturned a well-deserved death sentence. This story read,

> Paul Howell's sister, Megan Tobey, testified before the board that she distinctly remembers seeing Jones shoot her brother in front of his two young daughters.
>
> "He is the same person today as he was 22 years ago. He's still getting into trouble. He's still in a gang. He's still lying. And he still feels no shame, guilt or remorse for his action," Tobey said. "We need Julius Jones to be held responsible."[9]

If someone only visited the *Fox News* website and did not scroll down to the bottom of the home page, they probably would have missed these stories altogether. For those who got their news from the *New York Times* home page, the stories were difficult to miss. Beyond this, however, even for those who did see the stories, the experiences of reading them and their key takeaways were drastically different. That is, for those who actually read the stories, the events were depicted in two sharply distinct ways. Of course, we recognize that this represents only two cases that were covered in a single moment in time, but we suspect that it may reflect broader patterns in news coverage of wrongful convictions and, potentially, other errors in the legal system. The news bubbles in which liberals and conservatives live probably result in very different pictures of systemic flaws, both their nature and their pervasiveness. Although we view it as outside the scope of our current endeavor, a systematic content analysis of multiple media outlets' coverage (or lack thereof) and framing of wrongful convictions may yield important insights about differences in media coverage across outlets and help us further understand differences in public awareness and responsiveness to such information.

The fact that wrongful conviction is a political issue does not mean that it cannot gain traction. As we have shown, there is a rich record of policy reform in this area. Still, understanding the nuances in how ideology shapes people's views is an important consideration, as public opinion influences policy in some contexts. As such, it is vital to consider communication strategies that hold broad appeal and have the potential to garner support across the ideological spectrum.

How, then, might innocence advocates and activists go about building a support network among the public? Many involved in the movement may be intuitively aware of some of the patterns we have discussed, but our findings both provide empirical evidence of the nuances involved and point to specific messaging strategies. In particular, they suggest that innocence advocates should think carefully about both *who* their target audience is and *what* they are trying to accomplish when considering how to craft the most effective messages.

Targeted Messaging

One approach to building a support network may be for innocence advocates to tailor their messages to the potential audience. To explore such a possibility, we might consider some of the findings we presented earlier.

In chapter 4, we found that conservatives were more responsive to an informational message that included numeric information about exonerations when coupled with a public-safety frame. For instance, our numbers message prompted a greater reduction in support for the death penalty among conservatives compared to liberals who were provided the same information. Why might there be such a difference in response to basic factual information?

One possibility lies in our results from chapter 3, where we found that, overall, conservatives were less aware of wrongful convictions and believed that they occurred less often than liberals did. Perhaps, then, the reason that the numeric information was more persuasive for conservatives was because it provided more novel information and, in turn, was more impactful.

Another important consideration is the content of the message. We found the numeric information to be more persuasive for conservatives only when it included a related public-safety consideration. In addition to the exoneration numbers, the message stated (emphasis added), "An official from the National Institute of Justice said, 'These numbers show that not only have thousands of people been wrongfully jailed, but that *just as many criminals remain free*, roaming the streets. Every year a person spent wrongfully incarcerated also represents *a year in which the actual perpetrator remained at-large*.'" We noted in chapter 1 that historical wrongful conviction scholarship reveals ideological differences in how people think about wrongful convictions and that these differences may reflect competing crime control or due process priorities. Perhaps this difference extends to the public at large. Indeed, it seems that encouraging people to reflect on public-safety considerations or "the criminal costs of wrongful convictions" is particularly persuasive for conservatives, who may be more likely to emphasize crime control perspectives and support law-and-order politics.[10] Of course, there may be reasons why those who are engaged in innocence advocacy efforts wish to avoid such rhetoric—it is essentially a fear-based tactic that plays on public anxieties about crime and all that comes with them, often including negative racialized and class-based notions. From a pragmatic perspective, however, the crime control element of wrongful convictions may be the one that resonates with the audience that tends to be less aware of the problem and least supportive of policy reforms, and thus emphasizing it may be an avenue toward expanding the support base.

We are unaware of empirical evidence that suggests innocence organizations engage in these forms of targeted messaging, at least with regard to public outreach. Advocates, though, certainly are aware of this issue when it comes to policy makers. As one advocate said, "Different policy makers respond to different arguments. For some, a wrongful conviction represents the ultimate government overreach. For other people, equity and fairness will carry the day. . . . We pay attention to who we're talking to and what arguments are going to resonate. That said, people can rarely be placed in boxes, and ultimately each discussion with a lawmaker or stakeholder will air different issues and responses."[11] Given the clear ideological element to wrongful conviction advocacy, tailored or targeted messaging is one approach to building a support base among the public. However, there may be ways to reach across party lines and bridge the political divide. And, in fact, we found that certain strategies do just that.

Bridging Gaps and Crafting Persuasive Messages

While tailoring a message to target a particular person or group is important for persuasion, our evidence suggests that, for the most part, the effect of information about wrongful convictions on public opinion is *not* contingent on political ideology. In fact, that ideology moderates the effect of numeric information for capital punishment preferences is the exception rather than the rule. We did not find evidence that the effects of our various framing and priming messages depended on respondents' ideology for trust in police (chapter 4), trust in the justice system (chapter 4), or support for policy reform (chapter 5). Rather, when a message significantly affected these attitudes, it tended to do so equally for liberals and conservatives.

To be clear, we are not suggesting that political ideology does not matter for these opinions—we consistently found that political ideology affects all of them, in fact—but it does not appear to color how people *respond* to the innocence information as we have presented it.[12] In other words, the overall patterns suggest that when wrongful conviction information shifts opinions, it does so for liberals and conservatives alike. This is encouraging insofar that it reveals that wrongful conviction information is broadly appealing and persuasive.

Beyond considering who is (or is not) persuaded by wrongful conviction information, we also must consider what types of attitudes are (or are not) changed by a particular message. As we argued in our discussion of framing theory, different presentations of information cue different considerations and therefore have different effects on various attitudes. For the most part, our findings were consistent with this theoretical argument. For instance, we found that numeric information about the numbers of wrongful convictions and exonerations in the United States (a thematic frame likely to trigger broad, system-level considerations) eroded people's trust in the justice system (a broad, general attitude). The narrative or episodic frame (a single case about a wrongful conviction) had no effect on trust in the system. On the other hand, the narrative increased people's concerns that they or someone they know might be wrongly convicted—potentially prompted by transportation into the story—while the numbers had no effect.

One exception to our argument concerns people's trust in police. We did not find consistent evidence that information about wrongful convictions, whether presented in the form of numbers or a narrative, reduced trust in police. This was true even when the information explicitly attributed blame for such errors to police. We do not have the necessary data to examine why, exactly, this is the case. However, the finding that attitudes toward law enforcement may be well entrenched is not entirely out of line with previous research, including our own.[13] Perhaps this speaks to the highly politicized nature of public opinion about police, especially given the volatile, ideological, and racialized nature of policing and its surrounding discourse in recent years, and the crisis of legitimacy that some people have suggested police are facing in the United States.[14] All is not lost, however. As we discussed earlier, studies have found that particular messages and/or types of information may affect people's views of police, their judgments of particular situations, and their policy preferences.[15] Thus, our limited findings regarding the ability to alter trust in police may simply mean that in this space, criminal justice reformers—whether tied to the innocence movement, specifically, or other areas—must be even more careful and vigilant in their efforts to spark change.

Beyond public trust in the system and in police, for our purposes (and perhaps for the innocence movement), the potential power of wrongful conviction information to shift public opinion is in regard to *policy preferences*. Here, we found that both numeric information and narratives have an effect, though one was clearly more influential than the other. Specifically, we found that information about the number of exonerees in the United States reduced support for capital punishment but did nothing to increase support for innocence-related investigative reforms. The narrative, on the other hand, had a substantial effect on both death penalty preferences and support for policy reform. Perhaps this is unsurprising, but it speaks to the immense power of wrongful conviction stories, and the vital role of exonerees themselves, in building support among the public for improving the criminal legal system.

The Power of Narratives

Generally speaking, this last point about the power of stories to change people's policy attitudes may be the greatest takeaway. This is no surprise. Narratives are a core element of communication, a "dominant form of written discourse" that stretches across people of different ages and races and genders. The psychologist Tom Trabasso has written that "the narrative is powerful because it spans the realm of human mental and social existence"; it "make[s] human experience meaningful and coherent."[16] Stories help us understand the world around us and make sense of our experiences within it.

Unlike statistical information, which is useful and helps contextualize issues, stories help us understand problems in a more visceral and realistic way. We can transport ourselves and the people around us into narratives and better understand our relationships with otherwise-abstract issues and with one another. For instance, while many people do not directly experience use of force by law enforcement, reading a news report about or, even more powerfully, viewing a video of a single controversial instance of use of force prompts strong emotional reactions and alters attitudes toward police.[17] A narrative can thus trigger emotional reactions in ways that numbers may not. In chapter 4, we briefly discussed one of our studies, which revealed that a wrongful conviction narrative made people feel more personally concerned that they or someone they know would be wrongfully convicted; by contrast, wrongful conviction statistics had no impact on this personal concern. We are reminded of a quotation sometimes attributed to Joseph Stalin, who reportedly said that one death is a tragedy, while a million deaths is a statistic. This crude (and possibly misattributed) point raises an important truth: individual stories may be more powerful than more broadly focused factual information for shifting public opinion in many areas.[18]

This point about the power of stories is not lost on innocence advocates, who strategically use various forms of media to share stories of the wrongly convicted and advocate for change. As noted earlier, Barry Scheck has discussed the "power of the press" and the importance of highlighting each individual wrongful conviction as "a learning moment" for the criminal legal system. He has spoken of the tradition of campaigning for reform using stories told through the media, as they allow for "people [to] understand and identify with the innocents who are wrongly convicted. There's an emotional power in it. It's the individual story."[19] Our data support Scheck's point. If innocence advocates want to spark change and encourage people to support policy reforms, individual case stories appear to be the most effective way to do so.

Our findings about the persuasive power of narratives also speak to the important role played by exonerees themselves in wrongful conviction reform. Certainly, the burden for undoing an injustice and preventing future ones should not be placed on victims of such injustices. However, exonerees are not merely passive victims of injustice either. They are the driving force behind the innocence movement and are increasingly involved directly in public education and policy reform campaigns. Not all exonerees engage in public advocacy, of course, but many use various platforms to raise awareness and fight for change. Some exonerees do so through public speaking events, while others share their experiences through artistic expression or contribute to the campaigns of the Innocence Project or other organizations.[20] Some exonerees have even started and/or staff their own organizations.[21] Consider, for example, Witness to Innocence, a nonprofit organization cofounded in 2003 by the anti-death-penalty advocate and author Sister Helen Prejean and Ray Krone, the one hundredth person to be exonerated from death row in the United States.[22] The organization, staffed in part by death-row exonerees, fights for the abolition of capital punishment in the United States through public engagement events, direct lobbying efforts with lawmakers, and partnering with other organizations that share a similar goal.[23] The group was instrumental in the abolition of the death penalty in a number of states, including New Jersey, New Mexico, and Illinois.[24] Witness to Innocence does not stand alone as an exoneree-led organization; other examples include the Deskovic Foundation (founded by the New York exoneree Jeffrey Deskovic) and Exonerated Nation (founded by the California exoneree Obie Anthony).[25]

There is other practical evidence to support this point about the power of exonerees and their stories to spark policy reform. Consider the case of Timothy Cole, which we discussed in chapter 2.[26] After he died in prison and was posthumously exonerated in Texas in 2009, Cole's case became a driving force in the campaign to reform Texas's exoneree compensation statute. His family's direct involvement in the legislative process "provid[ed] a clear link between a policy idea and its real-world implications."[27] The statute, known as the Timothy Cole Act, increased the amount of financial compensation for exonerees, expanded other postrelease services available to exonerees, and allowed for posthumous compensation for the families of exonerees who had already passed.

Cole is far from the only example of wrongful conviction stories serving as direct catalysts for change or of exonerees and their supporters being directly involved in policy reform. Kirk Bloodsworth, whose case was discussed in chapter 4, has been heavily involved in wrongful conviction and related legislation. At the federal level, he influenced the passage of the 2004 Innocence Protection Act, a portion of which was named after him—the Kirk Bloodsworth Post-Conviction DNA Testing Grant Program—and was involved in Maryland's abolition of the death penalty in 2013.[28] Michael Morton's case served as the catalyst for the Texas law named after him that was passed in 2013, which required open-file discovery to reduce prosecutors' suppression of evidence.[29] The Indiana exoneree Kristine Bunch, who cofounded (with fellow exoneree Juan Rivera) a nonprofit organization to assist exonerees in the reentry process, was instrumental in compensation reform in Indiana.[30] And in 2020, New York passed the "Central Park Five" Law, which requires police to record the interrogations of juvenile suspects.[31]

These are only a few of the many examples we can find, and all speak to the immense importance of exonerees and their stories in the innocence movement, which cannot be overstated. Our survey results empirically demonstrate the power of exoneration stories to shift public opinion, suggesting that sharing of these stories may be the most influential path toward achieving support for wrongful conviction policy reforms more broadly. However, we did not test or experimentally manipulate the source of those stories to identify the most impactful message sources. That said, it is likely that exoneree-advocates can be a powerful force for change. If reading a simple narrative can alter people's opinions, hearing the story told straight from the victim of the injustice would probably be even more impactful. Exonerees put human faces on issues that may otherwise seem distant or abstract; their stories of struggle, loss, and redemption connect with people emotionally and, in turn, help generate attitudinal change. In short, the most powerful resource in the fight for justice is the very people at the heart of the movement.[32]

Of course, these findings about the power of narratives and the stories of people with lived experiences to change people's minds are probably not restricted to issues around wrongful convictions. We do not wish to exaggerate the generalizability of our findings, but we suspect that this point, like many of the arguments we have presented throughout this book, extend to other policy domains and criminal justice reforms. If a story transports the message recipient into the narrative and makes them concerned about how an issue might affect them or people close to them, there are opportunities for persuasion, and this probably applies to a number of topics. Take, for example, contemporary issues around policing. Over the past decade, the public has been more exposed to stories and images of excessive police use of force. Recent research has shown that such exposure—in the form of both written news stories and videos—elicits emotional reactions, increases concern about excessive force, and increases support for police reforms.[33] Here, too, the message source may matter; if a news story or a video circulated on social media can change the public's attitudes, then perhaps hearing from someone who was the victim of excessive force or lost a family member to it would generate even stronger support for change.

In short, for those who are engaged in advocacy and fighting for change in the criminal legal system—related to wrongful convictions, police practices, and beyond—narratives may be among the most powerful weapons at their disposal. Narrative framing is not, however, the only fruitful path forward, nor must it be used alone. There are opportunities to wield other types of framing and priming strategies to elicit support for various causes. Although the specific approach would differ by issue domain and other considerations (such as what goal activists seek to accomplish within a given domain), there is no reason to think that the effects of these political communication strategies are confined to issues of innocence.

Looking Ahead: Innocence 2.0

Our discussion throughout this book has been about what *was* and *is*. Our analyses of issues related to policy reforms, in particular, have necessarily focused on reforms that have long been on the radar of researchers and a part of the innocence movement's agenda—policies such as eyewitness identification reform and recording of custodial interrogations. However, these policies, while important to continue implementing and evaluating and improving, are not necessarily representative of the policy reality for innocence advocates, and it seems pertinent to consider what *may be*—that is, where the innocence movement might be headed.

In a conversation with the Innocence Project's director of policy, Rebecca Brown, she noted that the policy issues that we examined and that are most often discussed publicly and in academic circles—eyewitness reform, recording interrogations, DNA access laws, preservation of biological evidence, and compensation statutes—do not fully capture the breadth and scope of the organization's current policy work. She described those as their "Innocence 101 reforms," the "early innocence work [that] really focused on reliability and accuracy." Those issues were and are important, but it is also important for the organization (and, presumably, the innocence movement at large) to pivot to broader issues. Indeed, the Innocence Project has increasingly become involved in more "structural, transformational work." To offer just a few examples, Brown said the Innocence Project has been heavily involved in work around the United States related to police accountability, in particular, making police disciplinary records public and eliminating the legal doctrine of qualified immunity. It has also been involved in pretrial justice reform—discovery, bail, and speedy trial work, in particular—and reform on issues around parole and probation.

> We also very much are working on the intersection of suspect development, innocence, race, and blanket surveillance technologies, like predictive policing and facial recognition technology, and investigative systems, like gang databases. [We're] also looking at incentives baked into the system, which are really more systemic—quota-based policing, the fact that [many] state crime labs . . . are paid by conviction and not by forensic test, so you see a baked-in incentive to get more convictions. And that runs all the way through the system. Prosecutors are incentivized to upcharge. The innocent are incentivized to self-incriminate through coerced pleas.[34]

None of this is to suggest that innocence advocates are moving away from wrongful convictions as a primary focus. It does, however, suggest that the innocence movement is evolving to consider broader issues that go beyond the tangible and fairly simplistic contributors to wrongful convictions—eyewitness errors and false confessions, for instance—and considering more fundamental, systemic issues that influence negative outcomes. For instance, while the Innocence Project continues to work on issues around the validation of forensic science techniques, expanding into issues related to how law enforcement uses surveillance technologies represents something of a next step in wrongful conviction work, as "the innocent are necessarily going to be ensnared by those kinds of policies and technologies."[35] It is not, then, that wrongful conviction work is going away but that it is evolving and expanding.

Such expansion of the innocence movement into broader advocacy has not been entirely without discussion. In an earlier book on the movement, one of the authors discussed "the skepticism toward calling innocence a social movement" and, more specifically, a civil rights movement.[36] While innocence cases certainly touch on civil rights issues, several people interviewed for that project disagreed with the characterization of innocence as a civil rights movement, as did the author: "While wrongful conviction cases touch on issues that go far beyond the criminal justice system—race and class but, even more broadly, culture and power—the innocence movement's agenda does not appear poised to address such big issues. The innocence reform agenda has been focused on vitally important but relatively narrow criminal justice factors that lead to wrongful convictions, . . . but innocence advocates are far less involved in sweeping discussions about race, class, and gender."[37] The sentiment was perhaps best captured by Steve Drizin, a law professor at who has been heavily involved in Northwestern University's Center on Wrongful Convictions, who said, "The simple fact of the matter is that the innocence movement, for it to become a civil rights movement, is going to have to broaden its scope to have an impact on the entire criminal justice system, and as of now, innocence is a very small piece of the criminal justice pie."[38]

This appears to be exactly the type of shift of which Brown spoke. "Some of the framing that I'm really trying to do here," she said, "you know, early innocence work really focused on reliability and accuracy.

And, to me, it has to advance more broadly and intentionally into issues of fairness, equity, and addressing human factors that enable wrongful conviction, like implicit—and explicit—racism."[39]

But what, if anything, are the potential costs of such a shift in framing? Does, for example, highlighting racial disparities throughout the criminal legal system—which are related to wrongful convictions but also reach far beyond them—have the potential to racialize the innocence issue in ways that make some audiences more resistant to the message? Or can involvement in issues such as bail reform potentially distract from the more easily palatable issue of wrongful convictions? These are empirical questions to which we do not yet have answers. However, Brown spoke about the politicization of wrongful conviction reform and some people's resistance to it in ways that might be instructive here. In talking about the challenges of reaching lawmakers and the public, she said, "There's no question that innocence is going to resonate more than 'What do we do for somebody who committed a crime?' That said, some see our movement as a stalking horse for larger issues." For example, she mentioned the massive plea problem in the US legal system and how a critical conversation about it speaks directly to issues of decriminalization. "I think, in many ways, the more that these things light up for the public, it's a credible threat to the criminal legal system as we know it. And I think a lot of our reforms are all about injecting reasonable doubt, and to many, that sort of becomes innocence as an entry point into dismantling the system from a lawmaker perspective and sometimes from a public perspective."[40]

It is also possible that linking wrongful convictions to fundamental flaws in the criminal legal system might trigger defensiveness or backlash in response; that is, if innocence advocates are seen as seeking to fundamentally alter or dismantle the system, lawmakers, practitioners, and the public might immediately shift into defending it at all costs. We found that information about wrongful convictions can shift some relevant political attitudes for liberals and conservatives alike, but if innocence advocates broaden their agenda to challenging the fundamentals of the criminal legal system, the issue may become increasingly politicized and polarized. It is certainly possible that, if politicized to a greater extent, the messages that we found to be persuasive across the ideological spectrum could become less effective over time. Still, that does not mean that shifting the innocence movement in the direction of more fundamental issues is misguided. "I really believe that if we're doing our job well, it's not just about innocence," Brown said. "It's about really questioning the fault lines in the criminal legal system broadly and really scrutinizing them. And I think that really is a threat to people who want to maintain the system." Of course, the existing criminal legal system is deeply embedded in our wider sociopolitical culture, and as Brown said, "You can never legislate a culture."[41]

A key issue for policy advocates, then, is about finding the right "balance" and understanding where and how far to push the boundaries, as Brown indicated: "Sometimes, we don't dream big enough. We're kind of thinking, 'Okay, what's achievable in this environment?' And being a policy person, you're always trying to say, 'How far can I push? But if I push this far, are they gonna just not listen at all?' We're really always calibrating how far you can go and that's really just trying to assess the landscape."[42] Certainly, in the fight for change, innocence advocates do not have to blindly guess about how to strike the right balance, and they certainly do not have to work alone. Through careful research designs, social scientists can isolate the types of messages and communication strategies that resonate with different audiences. The survey-experimental methods we employed throughout this book provide one example of how this can be done, and there are alternative research designs that may be used and other topics to explore. Rather than assume how any particular audience might respond to a certain message, policy advocates can work together with social scientists to empirically test various strategies and types of rhetoric, which can then be developed and adapted based on both policy experience and empirical evidence. And, importantly, this work is ongoing and ever changing; the messages that work today may not work tomorrow. This book has repeatedly emphasized the impact of political ideology for awareness of and opinions about wrongful convictions, but we cannot assume that these ideological divisions are fixed. News media coverage may change. Heightened attention to innocence in entertainment media may ultimately diminish the gap in awareness between liberals and conservatives. Repeated exposure to narratives might desensitize the public such that these stories lose some of their persuasive power. It is also possible that wrongful convictions—like so many other issues—become politicized and the ideological cleavage in the public is accentuated. New evidence-based political communication strategies may need to be identified. Thus, continuing to develop our understanding of how various communication strategies influence public opinion is, in our view, an important future avenue for partnerships between social scientists and practitioners and, potentially, a fruitful area of inquiry for interested scholar-activists. Together, researchers and policy advocates can work together in assessing the boundaries of the policy landscape.

Only time will tell if and where those boundaries are established. Regardless, it is incumbent on innocence advocates to reach the mass public. As we demonstrated in chapter 2, public opinion is consequential for policy adoption, a fact not lost on Brown, who noted that many constituents, even when relatively progressive, "are not progressive on criminal justice": "And all lawmakers are doing is responding to what their constituents want and thinking about the next election. We can't legislate culture change. We have to do the hard work of changing hearts and minds." Many lawmakers might support innocence reforms in the abstract but, when pressed, will counterargue and resist them on the basis of minor quibbles. It is, in a sense, performative and might remain so "until there's a mass education piece": "We're only as successful as the level of knowledge of voters and the pressure they're willing to put on their lawmakers."[43]

To the point of "changing hearts and minds" and increasing voter knowledge, our survey results show that there is much room for growth with regard to basic awareness of wrongful convictions, and despite not exploring directly the potential issues related to broadening the scope of innocence advocacy, they suggest that there may be approaches to message construction that are effective in cutting across political lines and generating meaningful change in public opinion. Further, a secondary benefit of broadening innocence advocacy efforts is expanding the network of potential supporters and reaching new audiences, some of whom may already be sympathetic to the cause. Indeed, Brown said, working in the "transformational, structural space . . . is always done in coalition. Like, we're never going to change the bail system without working with impacted people, community groups, racial justice groups, data scientists."[44]

Perhaps, then, this is the future of the innocence movement: a broader coalition of advocates fighting for change not only in the wrongful conviction space but also in other areas of the criminal legal system. There are undoubtedly political implications to such a shift—future researchers have plenty of fodder with which to work—but moving in this direction may help solidify the innocence movement as a true force for progressive change in the criminal legal system. "Innocence should be a wedge into the larger system," Brown said. "If we're not using it as wedge into the larger system, it's a real squandered opportunity because it is true that innocence will get you in the door."[45] Let us hope that that door remains open for some time to come.

ACKNOWLEDGMENTS

This book was a long time in the making, more than six years, in fact. Like many things worth pursuing, it began over pizza (shout-out to Lost Province Brewing Company in Boone, North Carolina). A lunch conversation between colleagues turned to the first season of the podcast *Serial*, which covered the questionable murder conviction of Adnan Syed in Maryland. One of us—we will not say which one, but those who know us may well make an educated guess—expressed the feeling of insecurity that arose from hearing such stories. *If it happened to him, could it happen to me?* From that meeting came the question of how people respond to such stories of injustice. That conversation happened in 2016, and from there, the ideas developed and expanded until we eventually realized we had a book on our hands. Now, years later, here we are.

As with any project of this nature, it would not have gotten to this point without the kindness and support of many others whose names are not listed on the cover. First and foremost, we are grateful to the wonderful people at New York University Press who have helped us develop this from proposal to book. We are particularly indebted to our editor, Ilene Kalish, who has offered support and enthusiasm for this project from the outset, and to Yasemin Torfilli, Alexia Traganas, Andrew Katz, and everyone else who helped get this book across the finish line.

We also thank the many friends, colleagues, and scholars who have contributed to this work in some way. Whether it was feedback after a conference presentation, critiques of earlier manuscripts, or ideas shared through informal conversations, the questions and comments we have received throughout the process have undoubtedly made this a better product.

Perhaps more than anyone, we collectively must thank the many exonerees, advocates, and activists who are on the front lines of the innocence movement, working in the trenches to improve criminal legal systems across the United States and around the world. Your work is important and inspiring, and we hope that the research we share in this book can be a resource as you continue to fight against injustice.

Finally, we each have some personal thanks to share.

Rob would like to thank Caitlyn O'Donnell and the rest of his family for their constant support. He would also like to thank his colleagues, students, and friends, both at his former (Appalachian State University) and current (George Mason University) employers and within the innocence advocacy community, for their ideas, constructive feedback, and encouragement. There are too many to name, but you know who you are. Finally, he supposes he should thank his coauthors, Will and Kevin, for putting up with him, at least. He is very proud to call them both collaborators and friends, even if Will is wrong about Tootsie-Pops being better than Blow-Pops (they are not) and despite Kevin's false claims about having the skills of a professional gamer (he does not).

Will would like to thank his wife, Allison Fredette. She is an incredible partner. Her willingness not just to listen but to also debate his research makes him a much, much stronger scholar. He would also like to thank his children, Henry and Walter, who remind him every day that we can and should strive to make the world better by solving one problem at a time, even if that means first completing a drawing of a Quetzalcoatlus. He would like to thank his colleagues in the Government and Justice Studies Department at Appalachian State, which includes scholars of political science and criminal justice. The unique mixture of fields provides an amazing environment that both fuels and improves his research. Last, but certainly not least, he would like to thank Kevin and Rob, both of whom made the experience of writing this book an incredibly exciting and rewarding experience.

Kevin thanks his best friend, Kelly Mullinix. Her love, kindness, and patience are everything to him. He sincerely appreciates all the hours she pretended to listen as he discussed his research. He also thanks his children, Kinsley and Kyser, who are his greatest sources of joy. He is indebted to his friends and colleagues at Appalachian State University and the University of Kansas for their support and feedback on this project. He owes a special thanks to Jamie Druckman and Dennis Chong—the scholars who never cease to mentor and inspire him.

Finally, he is thankful that this was a book written by friends. He discussed chapter ideas with Will during their kids' birthday parties and refined study designs with Rob while playing online video games. He counts himself lucky to learn from and work alongside these fantastic individuals.

APPENDIX

Data and Analyses

DATA OVERVIEW

The analyses we have presented throughout this book drew on a wide range of data. For the sake of brevity and readability, we sought to present our key findings clearly and in visual form in the main text. Here, we provide more details about our data and analytical methods, both overall and broken down by each individual chapter.

In chapter 2—our analysis of state-level policy adoption from 1989 to 2018—we relied on an original data set we compiled using state-level criminal justice and political data. The data were described in the main text, and more detailed information is included in the chapter 2 section of this appendix. Here, suffice it to say that the data set included information from the National Registry of Exonerations, the Innocence Project, the Innocence Network, the FBI's Uniform Crime Report, the US Census, and independent academics.

Chapters 3, 4, and 5—our examinations of public opinion in the realm of wrongful convictions—relied on original survey data. Specifically, we conducted six different surveys. For the sake of simplicity, we numbered them in the order they are discussed throughout the book, rather than chronological order based on date of implementation. In chapter 3, we relied on Surveys 1 and 2. In chapter 4, we relied on Surveys 3, 4, and 5. And in chapter 5, we relied on Surveys 1, 4, 5, and 6. All six surveys were conducted online. The following tables provide more detailed information about dates of implementation and the companies through which they were administered.

All of our surveys drew on national samples collected online. The companies with which we contracted to collect our data use opt-in panels of respondents with samples drawn to match particular characteristics of the US adult population. Although the specific subject

TABLE A.1. Survey Implementation and Sample Sizes

Survey label	Date of implementation	Survey administrator	Sample size
Survey 1	January 2020	Dynata	717
Survey 2	April 2021	Lucid	712
Survey 3	Oct.–Dec. 2016	CCES (YouGov)	1,000
Survey 4	March 2017	SSI	1,824
Survey 5	March 2018	SSI	1,092
Survey 6	Sept.–Oct. 2018	SSI	2,116

recruitment and sampling methodology vary by survey firm, they all first build a large pool of potential respondents. This larger pool of respondents is not a probability-based sample, nor is it statistically "representative" of the target population (e.g., US adults). However, the survey firms draw a sample from this pool such that it is representative of particular demographic variables in the target population. As such, the broader pool of potential respondents may not be representative, but the sample is designed such that it should reflect the known distribution of many demographic characteristics of the target population. Table A.2 shows the basic descriptive statistics from all six surveys. Importantly, this table features basic information about variables we use in our statistical models. We discuss our specific variables in more detail in the chapter-by-chapter breakdowns that follow. Many of our covariates took the form of binary/dummy variables, and those measuring respondents' education, age, interest in politics, trust in police, and level of political knowledge were measured with discrete qualitative categories. It is important to note that the specific number of respondents (i.e., the N) may differ slightly by variable because some respondents may have chosen not to respond to a particular item or to provide a "don't know" type of response. As a result, the N in our regression models throughout the book, particularly when they incorporate many control variables, will vary slightly.

CHAPTER 2

Our goal in this chapter was to identify the conditions that underlie the adoption of specific wrongful-conviction-related reforms. As such, we developed several complementary statistical models. Our

TABLE A.2. Descriptive Statistics of Key Covariates

Variable	Statistic	Survey 1 2020	Survey 2 2021	Survey 3 2016	Survey 4 2017	Survey 5 2018	Survey 6 2018
Liberal	Proportion	0.34	0.3552	0.2973	0.326	0.360	0.367
	min., max.	[0,1]	[0,1]	[0,1]	[0,1]	[0,1]	[0,1]
Moderate	Proportion	0.356	0.3147	0.3994	0.278	0.269	0.32
	min., max.	[0,1]	[0,1]	[0,1]	[0,1]	[0,1]	[0,1]
Conservative	Proportion	0.304	0.3301	0.303	0.396	0.371	0.313
	min., max.	[0,1]	[0,1]	[0,1]	[0,1]	[0,1]	[0,1]
Education	Mean	2.991	3.084	2.672	3.002	2.772	2.593
	min., max.	[0,5]	[0,5]	[0,5]	[0,5]	[0,5]	[0,5]
Male	Proportion	0.464	0.4747	0.475	0.482	0.484	0.483
	min., max.	[0,1]	[0,1]	[0,1]	[0,1]	[0,1]	[0,1]
Female	Proportion	0.536	0.5253	0.525	0.518	0.516	0.517
	min., max.	[0,1]	[0,1]	[0,1]	[0,1]	[0,1]	[0,1]
White	Proportion	0.635	0.7338	0.735	0.712	0.622	0.695
	min., max.	[0,1]	[0,1]	[0,1]	[0,1]	[0,1]	[0,1]
Black	Proportion	0.153	0.0775	0.12	0.104	0.126	0.118
	min., max.	[0,1]	[0,1]	[0,1]	[0,1]	[0,1]	[0,1]
Hispanic	Proportion	0.105	0.1028	0.075	0.132	0.176	0.109
	min., max.	[0,1]	[0,1]	[0,1]	[0,1]	[0,1]	[0,1]
Race other	Proportion	0.107	0.0859	0.07	0.0521	0.0762	0.0779
	min., max.	[0,1]	[0,1]	[0,1]	[0,1]	[0,1]	[0,1]
Age	Mean	2.157	2.31	2.31	2.177	2.252	2.126
	min., max.	[0,4]	[0,4]	[0,4]	[0,4]	[0,4]	[0,4]
Political interest	Mean	1.594	1.668	2.171	1.674		
	min., max.	[0,3]	[0,3]	[0,3]	[0,3]		
Trust police	Mean	3.418	3.319		2.237	2.023	
	min., max.	[0,6]	[0,6]		[0,4]	[0,4]	
Political knowledge	Mean					1.555	1.471
	min., max.					[0,3]	[0,3]
N		717	712	1,000	1,824	1,092	2,116

Note: Age categories include the following: 18–24, 25–34, 35–50, 51–65, and over 65. Education includes the following categories: less than high school, high school, some college, associate's degree, bachelor's degree, bachelor's plus postgrad degree. Trust police varies from "none at all" to "a great deal." Surveys 1 and 2 include the same question, but answer choices vary from "almost none" to "almost complete trust." Political interest varies from "not at all interested" to "very interested." Political knowledge, based on three questions, varies from minimum knowledge to maximum knowledge. N represents the sample size as the number of respondents with valid responses. It varies to a small degree with missing values.

dependent variable represents a count, in each year and state, of the number of reforms the government has adopted (0–5). Clustered, time-varying data such as these are complicated to model. We used growth curve models to analyze the data; these provided flexibility in how we account for serial correlation. For example, we fit a random intercept to each state (i.e., years are nested within states) and model temporal dependence directly with polynomials for time (measured as a yearly counter). We also used lagged versions of our independent variables, where appropriate, to ensure that their values temporally preceded those of the dependent variable.

Although we only present our findings from multilevel models, we also explored many alternatives. For example, we experimented with some duration/survival models. Our exploration of survival models took us down two paths. First, we disaggregated our dependent variable and analyzed discrete survival models fit to each of our five policy reforms. Here, we investigated the probability that a state adopts a *specific* policy, provided it has not already done so. While we found mixed results with these models, our biggest concern with their use is conceptual in nature.[1] We think that state adoptions of a single reform fail to capture governments' *commitment* to wrongful conviction reform more broadly. In other words, we think that a count of all the laws captures something more than a series of binary logits would otherwise indicate.

For this reason, we explored survival models that allow for repeated, multiple, or competing events. One example is Andersen and Gill's counting process estimator.[2] This model allowed us to evaluate the number of events that occurred, in no particular order, over a specified period of time. We preferred such a model conceptually to alternatives like so-called marginal or conditional models, which concern the likelihood that an event or events occur in certain sequences or in light of other events. All of the models we used for repeated, multiple, or competing events allow very limited capabilities for including time-varying covariates. Although we found some support for our expectations with these models, their failure to flexibly allow for time-varying covariates made them problematic for our purposes.

A final issue we faced in our estimation strategy was deciding the most appropriate method to estimate the residual error-covariance matrix. We assumed that our data were correlated over time, for example, that South Carolina's residuals in time t are related to South Carolina's residuals in time $t-1$. However, the nature of this correlation forced us to choose between alternatives with a focus on efficiency. One alternative to a simple varying intercepts model with fixed effects for time was to also fit an AR1 (autoregressive error structure to the order of 1 year) error-covariance matrix.[3] This approach allowed us to capture the correlation between the outcome in year t and its value in $t-1$. A second alternative was a random coefficients model that allowed the effect of time to vary between the states randomly. Is the rate of change faster or slower randomly from state to state? Most importantly for our purposes, are our findings subject to one set of assumptions or another?

The findings revealed that the value of the outcome for state i in year t was correlated with its value in $t-1$ given the estimate of the rho parameter (0.866). The random coefficients model similarly revealed evidence that the effect of time was probably not uniform across the states. Furthermore, standard likelihood ratio tests revealed the same conclusions comparing the AR1 model ($p < 0.01$) and random coefficients model ($p < 0.01$) to the basic varying intercepts model.

All of that said, these more complicated alternatives did not change our conclusions regarding public opinion, electoral competition, innocence group advocacy, and the number of exonerations. Our findings were robust to these alternative specifications.

Table A.3 presents our core findings with respect to states' commitment to wrongful conviction reforms. Figures 2.2 through 2.6 are based on the findings reported in the first column of coefficients. The first model is the basic growth curve model we described earlier: a multilevel (i.e., mixed effects) regression with a random intercept fit to each state and a polynomial fit to time. It is also the model we used to produce the plots in the main text of chapter 2.

We compared this model to the two alternatives presented in table A.3. The second model includes an autoregressive error-covariance matrix (order of 1), and the third includes a random coefficient fit to the effect of time. These findings—particularly with respect to variables measuring public opinion, electoral competitiveness, innocence group presence, and the number of exonerations—remained substantively similar regardless of specification.

While we described in chapter 2 how we measured the key variables of public opinion liberalism, electoral competitiveness, the number of innocence organizations, and the number of exonerations, we did not describe in detail how we measured other control variables in the models or why we included them. Our models included two additional political characteristics about the states: citizens' party identification and

TABLE A.3. Exploring the Sources of Wrongful Conviction Reforms in the States

Variable	Mixed effects		AR 1 residual		Random coefficient	
L1 Public opinion lib.	−0.9874***	(0.2680)	−0.6274***	(0.2346)	−1.0515***	(0.2644)
Electoral competitiveness	−0.004	(0.0055)	−0.0006	(0.0046)	0.0005	(0.0049)
Elect. comp. X L1 Pub. op.	0.0185***	(0.0047)	0.0116***	(0.0042)	0.0161***	(0.0048)
L1 # Innocence orgs.	0.1650***	(0.0458)	0.1477**	(0.0578)	0.1667***	(0.0556)
L1 # of exonerations	0.0296***	(0.0091)	0.0210*	(0.0110)	0.0206**	(0.0101)
L1 Violent Crime rate	−0.0006**	(0.0002)	−0.0005*	(0.0003)	0.0001	(0.0003)
Democratic Margin House	−0.0038**	(0.0017)	0.0021	(0.0016)	0.0040**	(0.0016)
Democratic Margin Senate	0.0045***	(0.0016)	−0.0015	(0.0015)	−0.0029*	(0.0015)
Democratic governor	0.1692***	(0.0449)	0.0344	(0.0428)	0.1985***	(0.0389)
L1 % Democrats	1.4877	(0.9550)	0.8239	(0.9522)	0.0029	(0.8309)
L1 % Black	0.3245	(0.9920)	1.1945	(0.9500)	−0.9462	(0.8439)
L1 % Hispanic	−0.367	(0.9590)	0.1056	(0.9424)	−1.4157	(0.8746)
L1 Median HH income	0.0271***	(0.0056)	0.0178***	(0.0061)	0.0092	(0.0064)
Legislative professionalism	0.1429	(0.4485)	0.6828	(0.4525)	0.8910**	(0.4041)
L1 Term limits	0.1241	(0.0862)	−0.0033	(0.1030)	−0.0438	(0.0976)
Yearly counter	−0.1757***	(0.0481)	−0.1533**	(0.0630)	−0.0900**	(0.0429)
Yearly counter squared	0.0199***	(0.0030)	0.0190***	(0.0042)	0.0171***	(0.0026)
Year counter cubed	−0.0004***	(0.0001)	−0.0004***	(0.0001)	−0.0004***	(0.0001)
Constant	−0.5367	(0.5334)	−0.3643	(0.5294)	−0.2999	(0.4708)
Var(State)	0.3554	(0.0782)	0.0951	(0.0899)	0.4344	(0.1027)
Var(Residual)	0.4162	(0.0168)	0.6443	(0.0964)	0.2696	(0.0112)
Rho			0.8636	(0.0205)		
Var(Yearly counter)					0.0029	(0.0006)
Cov(Yearly counter, State)					−0.0252	(0.0070)
N	1,274		1,274		1,274	

Note: Dependent variable represents count (0,5) of wrongful conviction reforms adopted in each state 1989–2018. First column represents a mixed effects model with variance component fit to states; second represents a mixed effects model with an autoregressive structure to the order of 1 year (AR1) fit to the residual error matrix; and the third column represents a mixed effects model with a random coefficient fit to the effect of time. "L1" represents variables whose values are lagged 1 year. Electoral competitiveness is most recent, prior election. "Var" stands for "variance," "Cov" stands for "covariance." Standard errors in parentheses.
*p < 0.1; **p < 0.05; ***p < 0.01

the partisan control of governments. For the former, we used Caughey and Warshaw's estimates for the share of each state's population that identifies with the Democratic Party, in each year from 1988 to 2017.[4] For the latter, we included three variables: Democratic margin of control in state houses (i.e., the percentage of Democrats minus the percentage of Republicans), Democratic margin of control in state senates, and a dummy variable indicating state/years with Democratic governors.[5] Our rationale to include these variables was that among both citizens and elites, wrongful conviction reforms may operate like a wedge issue. Most Democrats support their passage, but Republicans are cross-pressured given the fact that such reforms by their nature are critical of the criminal legal system and law enforcement.

As is common in studies of state policy adoption, our models also accounted for institutional differences between state legislatures. We used variables for legislative professionalism and whether legislators are subject to term limits. To measure legislative professionalism, we used the Squire index.[6] Because professional legislatures may have larger capacities to discover, manage, and reform policy problems, we suspected that legislative professionalism may impact the likelihood that legislatures adopt wrongful conviction reforms.[7] We measured term limits with a simple binary variable, coded 1 for a state legislature that has adopted *and implemented* term limits and coded 0 otherwise. By increasing turnover, term limits may enhance the power of governors, bureaucratic agencies, and interest groups over the legislature.[8] These changes may make it easier for external actors like these to push reforms through the policy-making branch, thereby enhancing legislative efficiency.[9]

Our models also included one additional characteristic about states' criminal justice system. We included a measure for states' violent crime rate using estimates from the FBI's Uniform Crime Report.[10] We suspected that the violent crime rate might have a negative effect on wrongful conviction reforms, whereby higher violent crime rates could motivate lawmakers to prefer a more punitive set of criminal justice policies, other things being equal, while lower violent crime rates could make wrongful conviction reforms more attractive.

Finally, we included a set of variables that capture states' racial composition and citizens' economic situation. We derived our data from US Census estimates via IPUMS USA.[11] Our Census data include decennial estimates from 1980, 1990, 2000, and 2010. We added additional yearly variation between 2000 and 2010 and, after 2010, using the Census Bureau's American Community Survey. State values are constant between 1990 and 2000, however, and 1988–1989. Our findings did not change when using interpolated values during the 1990s. The variables we included were the percentages of states' population that are Black and Hispanic and states' median household income (adjusted to 2016 dollars).

CHAPTER 3

Table A.4 provides our findings with respect to wrongful conviction awareness. Figures 3.1 and 3.2 are based on these models. These data were derived from Survey 1, which was administered by Dynata in January 2020. Table A.4 presents the results of three logit models. All three outcomes were measured as binary: respondents who had heard of the Innocence Project (1) versus respondents who had not (0); respondents who had heard a true story of a wrongful conviction (1) versus those who had not (0); and respondents who had heard a fictional story of a wrongful conviction (1) versus those who had not (0).

We measured ideology by creating mutually exclusive and exhaustive dummy variables based on respondents' self-reported ideology. Respondents who identified as "liberal" or "very liberal" were categorized as liberal, and respondents who identified as "conservative" or "very conservative" were categorized as conservatives. Respondents who identified as "moderates" were categorized as moderates. We also measured political interest with the following common survey item: "In general, how interested are you in politics and public affairs?" With this question, we grouped respondents from "not at all interested" (0) to "very Interested" (4).

Our models controlled for respondents' education, sex/gender, race, and age. We measured education by asking respondents, "What is the highest level of education you have completed?" Respondents had the following options: "less than a high school degree" (0), "high school degree or equivalent" (1), "some college but no degree" (2), "associate's degree" (3), "bachelor's degree" (4), and "graduate degree" (5). We measured sex/gender with a binary variable that grouped respondents as "female" or "male." We used dummy variables to group respondents on the basis of their racial and ethnic identity as "white," "Black," "Hispanic/Latino," and

TABLE A.4. Who Hears about Wrongful Convictions?

Variable	Heard of IP	Heard true	Heard fictional
Moderates	−0.209	−0.347	0.11
	(0.199)	(0.220)	(0.199)
Conservatives	−0.888**	−0.604**	0.252
	(0.212)	(0.226)	(0.207)
Educational attainment	0.143*	0.029	0.035
	(0.063)	(0.066)	(0.061)
Woman	−0.147	−0.262	−0.466**
	(0.174)	(0.185)	(0.173)
Black	0.512*	0.981**	0.401+
	(0.237)	(0.292)	(0.238)
Hispanic/Latino	0.195	0.107	0.18
	(0.271)	(0.288)	(0.270)
Other	−0.405	−0.035	0.246
	(0.285)	(0.278)	(0.270)
Age	−0.018	0.057	−0.453**
	(0.072)	(0.078)	(0.074)
Political interest	0.426**	0.446**	0.194*
	(0.091)	(0.098)	(0.089)
Trust police	0.074	−0.052	0.002
	(0.058)	(0.062)	(0.056)
Constant	−1.272**	0.409	0.376
	(0.381)	(0.404)	(0.372)
N	689	689	689

Note: Estimates based on logit models. Outcome for the first model is whether or not (1 for "yes," 0 for "no") respondents have heard of the Innocence Project; the second is whether or not respondents have heard a true story about a wrongful conviction; and the third is whether or not respondents have heard a fictional story about a wrongful conviction. Standard errors are in parentheses. Omitted category for race is "white," for ideology it is "Liberal," and for woman, it is "man." These data are derived from Survey 1.
+ $p < 0.10$, * $p < 0.05$, ** $p < 0.01$

"other." We made these categories mutually exclusive and exhaustive. The "other" category represents both respondents who identified as something other than those categories and those who identified with multiple categories. Finally, we grouped citizens by age using the following categories: less than twenty-five (0), twenty-five to thirty-four (1), thirty-five to fifty (2), fifty-one to sixty-four (3), sixty-five and over (4).

Using the same set of independent variables just described, table A.5 presents our findings with respect to respondents' perceptions about the frequency of wrongful convictions. We base figure 3.4 on the third model presented in this table. The first two models were based on ordinary least squares estimates, and the final model was a logit. The outcome for the first model was based on respondents' answer to the question, "Overall in the United States, of all the people who are convicted of felonies (serious crimes that lead to a prison sentence), what percent do you think are wrongfully convicted?" As we plotted in the text of chapter 3, the seven answer choices ranged from "less than 1%" (0) to "more than 25%" (7). The second outcome was similar but asked about "misdemeanors (less serious crimes that lead to short sentences or fines)" rather than felonies.

TABLE A.5. How Common Are Wrongful Convictions/Executions?

Variables	Felonies	Misdemeanors	Executions
Moderates	0.173	0.12	−0.125
	(0.185)	(0.197)	(0.210)
Conservatives	−0.539**	−0.542**	−0.984**
	(0.195)	(0.208)	(0.220)
Educational attainment	0.021	0.105+	−0.054
	(0.057)	(0.061)	(0.065)
Woman	0.389*	0.153	−0.23
	(0.160)	(0.170)	(0.185)
Black	1.067**	0.471*	1.071**
	(0.220)	(0.234)	(0.278)
Hispanic/Latino	0.104	−0.106	−0.233
	(0.250)	(0.267)	(0.279)
Other	−0.119	−0.183	0.008
	(0.253)	(0.270)	(0.283)
Age	−0.296**	−0.166*	−0.480**
	(0.066)	(0.070)	(0.080)
Political interest	0.219**	0.209*	0.241*
	(0.084)	(0.089)	(0.096)
Trust police	−0.178**	−0.261**	−0.126*
	(0.052)	(0.056)	(0.061)
Heard of Innocence Project	0.295+	0.290+	0.608**
	(0.157)	(0.168)	(0.181)
Constant	4.051**	4.076**	1.458**
	(0.347)	(0.371)	(0.406)
N	689	689	689

Note: The first two columns of coefficients are derived from ordinary least squares models, with the outcome ranging from 0 to 7, or "less than 1%" to "more than 25%." See figure 3.4. The third column of coefficients is derived from a logit model whose outcome represents people who think a person has been wrongfully convicted and executed in the past five years (1) and people who do not (0). Standard errors are in parentheses. These data are derived from Survey 1.
+ $p < 0.10$, * $p < 0.05$, ** $p < 0.01$

Finally, the third outcome grouped people according to whether they think "a person has been executed under the death penalty in the past five years who was, in fact, innocent of the crime he or she was charged with."

Table A.6 presents our findings with respect to a follow-up survey, Survey 2, administered by Lucid in the spring of 2021. This survey included a set of experimental conditions that exposed respondents to one of five (not including a control group) different fictional stories about a wrongful conviction. The details of these conditions should be irrelevant for this analysis on wrongful conviction awareness aside from priming respondents to think about the criminal justice system. However, to ensure that our findings regarding wrongful conviction awareness were not contaminated by these experimental conditions, we included them as control variables in our analysis. The omitted category in this analysis included respondents randomly slotted into the control group. If any of the coefficients we report with respect to these experimental conditions reached conventional levels of statistical significance, it would reveal that our conditions systematically shaped respondents' awareness. We found no evidence that respondents exposed to these experimental conditions had systematically different levels of awareness than our control group.

All the other covariates we included in these models were measured with identical questions to the findings from the other survey discussed earlier. Similar to our previous analysis, we found strong evidence that respondents' ideology and their political interest affect wrongful conviction awareness by way of having heard a true story about a wrongful conviction or having heard of the Innocence Project. We also continued to find that ideology does not seem to affect the likelihood that respondents have heard a fictional wrongful conviction story.

CHAPTER 4

Table A.7 provides results from the effect of our numbers frame (described in the text of chapter 4) on respondents' opinion about the death penalty. We present the critical findings regarding the effect of this experiment in figure 4.1. These data were derived from Survey 3, which was a module included on the 2016 Cooperative Congressional Election Survey (CCES). To determine the effect of the experimental frame, we fit an ordinary least squares regression model to death penalty support.

TABLE A.6. Who Hears about Wrongful Convictions? Follow-Up Survey 2

Variables	Heard of IP	Heard true	Heard fictional
Moderates	−0.470*	−0.27	−0.104
	(0.207)	(0.210)	(0.208)
Conservatives	−0.790**	−0.716**	−0.078
	(0.213)	(0.214)	(0.212)
Educational attainment	0.257**	0.143*	0.171**
	(0.059)	(0.059)	(0.059)
Woman	−0.08	−0.247	−0.206
	(0.174)	(0.175)	(0.173)
Black	0.228	0.155	−0.08
	(0.319)	(0.326)	(0.324)
Hispanic/Latino	0.108	0.777*	0.634*
	(0.278)	(0.313)	(0.284)
Other	−0.796*	−0.083	−0.356
	(0.324)	(0.300)	(0.307)
Age	−0.055	−0.252**	−0.397**
	(0.069)	(0.070)	(0.070)
Political interest	0.367**	0.615**	0.316**
	(0.094)	(0.099)	(0.094)
Trust police	0.137**	−0.107*	0.129*
	(0.052)	(0.053)	(0.052)
Narrative	0.275	−0.165	0.364
	(0.284)	(0.286)	(0.282)
Narrative + Safety	0.314	−0.38	0.061
	(0.283)	(0.289)	(0.285)
Safety	−0.044	−0.186	−0.179
	(0.284)	(0.285)	(0.283)
Wrongful liberty narrative	0.165	0.006	−0.044
	(0.282)	(0.290)	(0.284)
Wrongful liberty narrative + Safety	0.111	−0.256	0.235
	(0.285)	(0.288)	(0.283)
Constant	−1.667**	0.203	−0.804*
	(0.409)	(0.401)	(0.396)
N	703	702	702

Note: These estimates are based on logit models. The outcome for the first model is whether or not (1 for "yes," 0 for "no") respondents have heard of the Innocence Project; the second is whether or not respondents have heard a true story about a wrongful conviction; and the third is whether or not respondents have heard a fictional story about a wrongful conviction. Standard errors are in parentheses. Omitted category for race is "white," for ideology it is "liberal," and for woman, it is "man." The coefficients associated with the last five covariates, Narrative through Wrongful liberty narrative + Safety, represent experimental conditions, and the control group represents the baseline. These data are derived from Survey 2.

+ $p < 0.10$, * $p < 0.05$, ** $p < 0.01$

TABLE A.7. Numbers Frame and Attitudes toward the Death Penalty in the 2016 CCES

Variable	b/(se)
Numbers frame	−0.422** (0.117)
Moderate	0.812** (0.146)
Conservative	1.552** (0.163)
Educational attainment	−0.127** (0.042)
Female	−0.124 (0.120)
Black	−0.553** (0.181)
Hispanic/Latino	−0.169 (0.223)
Other	−0.365 (0.235)
Age	−0.012 (0.053)
Political interest	−0.163* (0.070)
N	999

Note: Death penalty attitudes measured (0) strongly opposed, (1) somewhat opposed, (2) somewhat support, (3) strongly support. These quantities are based on an ordered logit fit to this outcome. We suppressed the cut point estimates for efficiency. These data are derived from Survey 3.
+ $p < 0.10$, * $p < 0.05$, ** $p < 0.01$

We used a dummy variable to separate respondents who were exposed to the numbers frame from respondents who were not.

We also used dummy variables to separate respondents on the basis of their ideology (the CCES asks respondents, "In general, how would you describe your own political viewpoint?"). The model omits people who identified as "liberal" or "very liberal" as the baseline category. Conservative, of course, includes people who identified as "conservative" or "very conservative," while moderate includes people who identified as "moderate" or "not sure." We measured respondents' educational attainment using an ordinal variable with categories ranging from 0 to 5, including "no high school," "high school graduate," "some college," "two-year/associate's," "four-year/bachelor's," and "postgrad." We controlled for respondents' sex/gender via a dummy variable that separates women from men. We controlled for respondents' race and ethnicity by separating them into four mutually exclusive and exhaustive groups, including "white non-Hispanic," "Black non-Hispanic," "Hispanic," and "Other." In this model, "white" served as our reference or omitted category. We captured respondents' age with an ordinal variable grouping respondents into one of five groups: eighteen to twenty-four, twenty-five to thirty-four, thirty-five to fifty, fifty-one to sixty-five, and over sixty-five. Finally, we measured respondents' political interest using the CCES question, "Some people seem to follow what's going on in government and public affairs most of the time, whether there's an election going on or not. Others aren't that interested. Would you say you follow what's going on in government and public affairs?" Answer choices included "hardly at all" (0), "only now and then" (1), "some of the time" (2), and "most of the time" (3).

Table A.8 provides our findings with respect to the influence of our experimental frames on support for the death penalty, based on Survey 4, a survey administered by Survey Sampling International (SSI) in 2017. We present our core findings, based on the first column of coefficients, in figure 4.2 in chapter 4. This first column presents the results of a regression model fit to the seven-point measure of respondents' support for the death penalty that we described in chapter 4. The next two columns present the results from a multinomial logit model that separated respondents into one of three mutually exclusive groups: those who support capital punishment for persons convicted of murder, those who support life without the possibility of parole for persons convicted of murder, and those who support life with the possibility of parole for persons convicted of murder. Multinomial logit requires that one group be omitted to serve as the model's reference. We chose to omit (or use as the base) persons who support life with the option of parole, given that this arguably represents the most progressive attitude among the options given.

Consistent with our other analyses, we used dummy variables to separate respondents according to their ideology, using those who identified as "liberal" or "very liberal" as the reference category. We measured educational attainment using an ordinal variable that included the exact

TABLE A.8. Numbers, Narrative, and Numbers Plus Narrative Frames and Attitudes toward the Death Penalty

	7-point support	Life without parole	Capital punishment
Moderate	0.888***	0.495**	1.016***
	(0.115)	(0.184)	(0.190)
Conservative	1.427***	0.740***	1.749***
	(0.106)	(0.191)	(0.191)
Educational attainment	−0.081*	−0.048	−0.084
	(0.032)	(0.055)	(0.055)
Female	−0.282**	0.433**	−0.136
	(0.090)	(0.155)	(0.156)
Black	−0.318*	−0.094	−0.761**
	(0.149)	(0.217)	(0.244)
Hispanic/Latino	−0.159	0.307	−0.115
	(0.135)	(0.230)	(0.239)
Other	0.373	−0.37	−0.138
	(0.200)	(0.328)	(0.314)
Age	0.03	0.143*	0.102
	(0.037)	(0.063)	(0.064)
Political interest	−0.140**	0.067	−0.012
	(0.048)	(0.084)	(0.085)
Numbers	−0.251*	0.001	−0.378
	(0.123)	(0.226)	(0.225)
Narrative	−0.471***	−0.129	−0.597**
	(0.123)	(0.220)	(0.220)
Numbers + Narrative	−0.556***	−0.282	−0.822***
	(0.122)	(0.214)	(0.215)
Constant	3.807***	0.26	0.912**
	(0.199)	(0.338)	(0.338)
N	1748	1748	1748

Note: First model is a regression whose dependent variable represents respondents' death penalty support via a seven-point scale. Second model (presented in the final two columns) is a multinomial logit whose dependent variable separates respondents into three categories: prefer life with option for parole (base outcome), prefer life without option for parole, and prefer capital punishment. These data are derived from Survey 4. + $p < 0.10$, * $p < 0.05$, ** $p < 0.01$

same categories as the ones described earlier in the CCES sample. We also used a dummy variable to separate respondents on the basis of sex/gender (women versus men). We separated respondents on the basis of their racial and ethnic identity using the same four groups as earlier. We measured age using the same ordinal categories as those in the CCES sample, ranging from eighteen to twenty-four to over sixty-five. Finally,

TABLE A.9. Experimental Frames and Trust in
Criminal Justice System and Police

Variable	CJ	Police
Moderate	0.132*	0.270***
	(0.058)	(0.063)
Conservative	0.505***	0.767***
	(0.053)	(0.058)
Educational attainment	0.058***	0.057**
	(0.016)	(0.017)
Female	−0.002	0.005
	(0.045)	(0.050)
Black	−0.511***	−0.665***
	(0.075)	(0.082)
Hispanic/Latino	−0.134*	−0.317***
	(0.068)	(0.074)
Other	−0.013	−0.213
	(0.100)	(0.110)
Age	0.065***	0.070***
	(0.018)	(0.020)
Political interest	0.051*	0.034
	(0.024)	(0.027)
Numbers	−0.147*	−0.135*
	(0.061)	(0.067)
Narrative	−0.084	−0.065
	(0.062)	(0.068)
Numbers + Narrative	−0.132*	−0.121
	(0.061)	(0.067)
Constant	1.436***	1.676***
	(0.100)	(0.109)
N	1731	1745

Note: First model is a regression whose dependent variable represents respondents' trust in the criminal justice system on a five-point scale. Second model is a regression whose dependent measures respondents' trust in police. These data are derived from Survey 4.
$+ p < 0.10$, $* p < 0.05$, $** p < 0.01$

we captured respondents' political interest using a question that asked them, "In general, how interested are you in politics and public affairs?" Respondents were given four options ranging from "not at all interested" to "very interested."

Table A.9 presents our findings with respect to trust in the criminal justice system and trust in police. We present the findings from the first model in figure 4.3 and the findings from the second in figure 4.4. These data were also derived from Survey 4. The first column presents coefficients and standard errors based on an ordinary least squares regression whose outcome was measured with a five-point scale of respondents' trust in the criminal justice system. The second column is also based on a regression model, but the outcome is respondents' trust in police. Other variables were measured in the same way as we described with respect to table A.8.

Table A.10 presents our findings based on data derived from Survey 5, an SSI sample administered in 2018. This table presents the results of three ordinary least squares regression models fit to three different measures of respondents' trust in law enforcement. We described these variables in the chapter text, as well as the three different experimental frames to which we randomly exposed respondents (here labeled "Numbers," "Police cue," and "Numbers + Police cue"). Respondents in the control group served as the omitted or reference category in each model. We measured all other independent variables using the same questions and strategies as we described earlier with respect to Survey 4. The model in the first column (Measure 1) is the basis for figure 4.5.

In table A.11, we explore the idea that the effects of the experimental treatments depend on respondents' political ideology; these are the basis for figure 4.6. Here, we replicated our findings from table A.8 and added interaction effects between respondents' ideology and the experimental stimuli. We found one interaction effect that met conventional levels of statistical significance ($p < 0.05$). Specifically, it was the coefficient for Conservative × Numbers in the second model, based on respondents support for capital punishment versus life without parole and life with the option of parole. Importantly, the p-value associated with Conservative x Numbers in the first model was just above the conventional threshold for statistical significance ($p \approx 0.051$). Also, the p-value associated with Conservative x Numbers + Narrative in the second model was slightly higher, too ($p \approx 0.06$). We replicated our findings with other outcomes and incorporated interaction effects, but none of these reached conventional levels of significance.

CHAPTER 5

Table A.12 presents the findings of OLS models fit to survey respondents' support for wrongful conviction reforms (presented in figure 5.1 in the

TABLE A.10. Experimental Frames and Multiple Measures of Trust in Law Enforcement

Variable	Measure 1	Measure 2	Measure 3
Moderate	0.350*** (0.083)	0.441*** (0.120)	0.474*** (0.127)
Conservative	0.616*** (0.078)	0.913*** (0.112)	0.877*** (0.119)
Educational attainment	0.04 (0.024)	0.064 (0.034)	0.112** (0.036)
Female	−0.05 (0.068)	−0.006 (0.098)	−0.057 (0.103)
Black	−0.472*** (0.109)	−0.731*** (0.158)	−0.743*** (0.166)
Hispanic/Latino	−0.117 (0.102)	−0.432** (0.146)	−0.395* (0.155)
Other	−0.012 (0.134)	−0.016 (0.192)	0.088 (0.203)
Age	0.073* (0.030)	0.071 (0.043)	0.06 (0.046)
Political knowledge	0.01 (0.034)	0.086 (0.049)	0.034 (0.051)
Numbers	0.084 (0.092)	0.059 (0.133)	−0.045 (0.141)
Police cue	0.097 (0.092)	0.185 (0.133)	0.037 (0.141)
Numbers + Police cue	0.01 (0.092)	0.069 (0.132)	0.014 (0.140)
Constant	1.472*** (0.141)	2.707*** (0.202)	2.626*** (0.214)
N	1054	1054	1054

Note: First model is an ordinary least squares regression that uses respondents' trust that police treat people fairly as the dependent variable; the second model uses respondents' trust that police make decisions that are right for their communities; the third model uses respondents' trust that police protect people's basic rights as the dependent variable. All measures of trust allow respondents seven answer choices, from strongly disagree to strongly agree. These data are derived from Survey 5.
+ $p < 0.10$, * $p < 0.05$, ** $p < 0.01$.

main text of the chapter). We measured support for wrongful conviction reforms on a scale from 0 (strongly opposed) to 6 (strongly support). Each column presents the results of an equivalent model fit to a different survey sample. We checked our models against ordered logistic regression. Our results were equivalent, so we present OLS, which is more

TABLE A.11. Exploring the Conditional Effects of Frames Depending on Ideology

Variable	7-point support	Life without parole	Capital punishment
Moderate	0.687**	0.382	0.875*
	(0.229)	(0.384)	(0.387)
Conservative	1.588***	0.996*	2.382***
	(0.204)	(0.468)	(0.457)
Numbers	0.016	0.076	−0.059
	(0.219)	(0.323)	(0.345)
Narrative	−0.551*	−0.365	−0.62
	(0.217)	(0.303)	(0.332)
Numbers + Narrative	−0.656**	−0.16	−0.529
	(0.212)	(0.300)	(0.331)
Moderate x Numbers	−0.102	0.24	0.107
	(0.322)	(0.549)	(0.559)
Moderate x Narrative	0.445	0.427	0.362
	(0.317)	(0.510)	(0.525)
Moderate x Numbers + Narrative	0.412	−0.233	0.078
	(0.318)	(0.507)	(0.518)
Conservative x Numbers	−0.563	−0.681	−1.139*
	(0.289)	(0.587)	(0.579)
Conservative x Narrative	−0.103	0.436	−0.058
	(0.292)	(0.623)	(0.619)
Conservative x Numbers + Narrative	−0.008	−0.469	−1.061
	(0.287)	(0.569)	(0.568)
Constant	3.788***	0.269	0.774*
	(0.226)	(0.362)	(0.369)
N	1748	1748	1748

Note: The first model is a regression whose dependent variable represents respondents' death penalty support via a seven-point scale. Second model (presented in the final two columns) is a multinomial logit whose dependent variable separates respondents into three categories: prefer life with option for parole (base outcome), prefer life without option for parole, and prefer capital punishment. These data are derived from Survey 4. These models included control variables measuring respondents' race and ethnicity, age, educational attainment, sex/gender, and political interest. Our findings with respect to these variables is suppressed for space; see table A.8.
+ $p < 0.10$, * $p < 0.05$, ** $p < 0.01$.

efficient with regard to both statistical computation and our interpretation of the findings.

We measured ideology with a series of dummy variables that separated respondents according to their self-reported ideology. Liberals included all respondents who placed themselves as extremely liberal, liberal, or somewhat liberal, and the same vis-à-vis conservatives. In the

TABLE A.12. Wrongful Conviction Reform Attitudes

Variable	Survey 1	Survey 4	Survey 5	Survey 6
Moderate	0.015	−0.250**	−0.116	−0.034
	−0.117	−0.082	−0.129	−0.080
Conservative	−0.352**	−0.492**	−0.372**	−0.195*
	−0.121	−0.079	−0.123	−0.083
Educational attainment	0.067+	0.053*	0.035	0.080**
	−0.036	−0.023	−0.036	−0.025
Female	0.018	0.036	0.363**	0.037
	−0.101	−0.064	−0.104	−0.068
Black	0.023	0.032	−0.342*	−0.109
	−0.139	−0.108	−0.169	−0.106
Hispanic/Latino	−0.431**	−0.099	−0.372*	−0.195+
	−0.158	−0.097	−0.156	−0.112
Other	−0.359*	−0.089	0.049	−0.170
	−0.160	−0.144	−0.205	−0.126
Age	−0.030	0.040	0.098*	−0.007
	−0.042	−0.026	−0.046	−0.030
Political interest	0.219**	0.165**		
	−0.052	−0.034		
Trust police	0.072*	−0.055+	−0.055	
	−0.033	−0.031	−0.048	
Political knowledge			0.156**	0.179**
			−0.052	−0.034
Constant	3.042**	3.710**	3.136**	3.178**
	−0.219	−0.137	−0.211	−0.115
N	689	1743	1054	1939
R²	0.073	0.053	0.050	0.034

Note: Dependent variable represents support for wrongful conviction reforms, 0 to 6. Reference/omitted categories for nominal variables include liberal, male, and white. We estimate coefficients with ordinary least squares.
+ $p < 0.10$, * $p < 0.05$, ** $p < 0.01$

models we present, self-classified liberals serve as the reference or omitted category. Thus, the coefficients for "moderate" and "conservative" represent the average difference between these two groups and liberals, other things being equal.

We also measured and accounted for respondents' race and ethnicity with a series of dummy variables. We separated respondents into four racial/ethnic groups according to their self-expressed identity: white, Black, Hispanic/Latino, and other. Importantly, in the models we present, respondents who identified as white serve as the omitted category; each coefficient thus measures the conditional difference between each other racial group and white respondents on average. We also controlled for respondents' educational attainment and sex/gender. Educational attainment was measured with an ordinal variable (0 to 5) that included the following categories: less than high school, high school, some college, associate's degree, bachelor's degree, and bachelor's plus (which includes PhDs, JDs, and other professional degrees beyond a bachelor's). Sex/gender was measured via a dummy variable that separated respondents who identified as women (female =1) from respondents who identified as men (female = 0). We also measured age with an ordinal variable that grouped respondents into the following age groups: eighteen to twenty-four (0), twenty-five to thirty-four (1), thirty-five to fifty (2), fifty-one to sixty-five (3), and over sixty-five (4).

We also controlled for respondents' political interest or political knowledge. Political interest was measured by asking respondents how interested they are in politics, from 0 (not interested at all) to 3 (very interested). Political knowledge represents respondents' factual knowledge on a few questions about the federal government and its personnel. In Survey 5, we asked respondents the size of majority required to overcome a presidential veto in Congress, to identify the Senate majority leader, and to identify the chief justice of the Supreme Court with closed-ended questions. We classified respondents' answer to each item as either correct (1) or incorrect (0) and then added them together to make an index ranging from 0 (minimal knowledge) to 3 (maximum knowledge). Survey 6 measured knowledge in the exact same way, but with different items. On this survey, we asked respondents if they could identify which party holds a majority in Congress, to identify the secretary of state, and to identify the Senate majority leader.

Finally, three of our models controlled for respondents' trust in police. Survey 4 asked respondents, "How much trust do you have in police to treat people fairly?" Answer choices ranged from 0 ("none at all") to 4 ("a great deal"). Survey 5 asked the exact same question, with the same answers. Survey 1 asked a slightly different question: "To what extent do you agree or disagree that the police can be trusted to make decisions that are right for the people in their communities?" The response set varied from 0 ("strongly disagree") to 6 ("strongly agree"). We expected

TABLE A.13. Awareness of Innocence Project and Opinions on Wrongful Conviction Reforms

Variable	Survey 1
Moderate	0.033
	(0.116)
Conservative	−0.278*
	(0.122)
Educational attainment	0.055
	(0.036)
Female	0.031
	(0.100)
Black	−0.02
	(0.138)
Hispanic/Latino	−0.448**
	(0.157)
Other	−0.326*
	(0.158)
Age	−0.029
	(0.041)
Political interest	0.183**
	(0.053)
Trust police	0.066*
	(0.033)
Heard of Innocence Project	0.370**
	(0.099)
Constant	2.964**
	(0.218)
N	689
R^2	0.092

Note: Dependent variable represents support for wrongful conviction reforms, 0 to 6. Reference/omitted categories for nominal variables include liberal, male, white, and have not heard of Innocence Project. We estimate coefficients with ordinary least squares.
+ $p < 0.10$, * $p < 0.05$, ** $p < 0.01$

people with lower levels of trust in police to be more supportive of wrongful conviction reforms.

Table A.13 represents a nearly identical model to the one presented in the fourth column of coefficients in table A.12 but with one key difference. We added to this model a new variable that represented respondents' awareness of the Innocence Project. This model revealed, controlling for other things, that respondents who had heard of the

Innocence Project were significantly and substantively more likely to support wrongful conviction reforms. This finding was shown in chapter 5 in figure 5.2.

Table A.14 presents OLS models fit to respondents' support for wrongful conviction reforms using the same variables described earlier, but we added to the set of covariates the experimental frames to which we exposed random groups in each survey (see figures 5.3 and 5.4 in the main text). For brevity, we suppress coefficients associated with the control variables from these tables, leaving only findings regarding the effect of our experimental frames. In both models, the reference or omitted category includes respondents who were not exposed to any frame (i.e., the control group), and then we separate the remaining respondents with dummy variables according to which frame they received. The wording of each frame is outlined in chapter 5. Each coefficient, then, represents the average difference with regard to respondents' support for wrongful

TABLE A.14. Experimental Frames and Opinion on Wrongful Conviction Reforms

Variable	Survey 4	Survey 5
Numbers cue	0.084 (0.088)	
Narrative cue	0.225* (0.088)	
Numbers + Narrative	0.225* (0.087)	
Numbers cue		0.083 (0.142)
Police cue		0.082 (0.142)
Numbers + Police cue		−0.002 (0.141)
Constant	3.556** (0.151)	3.100** (0.228)
N	1743	1054
R^2	0.059	0.051

Note: Dependent variable represents support for wrongful conviction reforms, 0 to 6. Reference/omitted categories for nominal variables include liberal, male, and white. We estimate coefficients with ordinary least squares. We suppress coefficients for other covariates, age, education, ideology, sex/gender, political knowledge/interest, race, and trust in police for convenience
$+ p < 0.10$, $* p < 0.05$, $** p < 0.01$

TABLE A.15. Experimental Primes and Opinion on Wrongful Conviction Reforms

Variable	Survey 6
Police prime	0.164*
	(0.081)
Police + Compensation prime	0.345**
	(0.080)
Constant	3.014**
	(0.122)
N	1939
R^2	0.044

Note: Dependent variable represents support for wrongful conviction reforms, 0 to 6. Reference/omitted categories for nominal variables include liberal, male, and white. We estimate coefficients with ordinary least squares. We suppress coefficients for other covariates, age, education, ideology, sex/gender, political knowledge/interest, race, and trust in police for convenience

$+ p < 0.10$, $* p < 0.05$, $** p < 0.01$

conviction reform between their experimental group and the baseline of respondents who did not receive any treatment message.

Table A.15 presents a final OLS model that includes the priming experiment we described in the chapter (see figure 5.5 in the main text). This model also included the control variables we outlined earlier, but we suppress those findings for brevity as well. This table presents the differences between respondents who received the police prime, the compensation prime, or the baseline group of respondents who did not receive any prime (or, more specifically, they did not receive it *before* they were asked about their level of support for wrongful convictions). This final group serves as the omitted category in the table.

NOTES

INTRODUCTION

1. Unless otherwise specified, information about the case comes from the National Registry of Exonerations case profiles. See Possley, "Henry McCollum"; Possley, "Leon Brown."
2. On virtually every IQ rating system, 51 is near the lowest end of the spectrum.
3. The other three boys implicated by McCollum (two of whom were also implicated by Brown) were not charged. Two had verified alibis, and no evidence linked the third to the events.
4. The Innocence Inquiry Commission was established by the North Carolina General Assembly in 2006, the first of its kind in the United States. Its website reports that, as of January 4, 2022, the agency received 3,155 claims, including 268 claims in 2021 alone. The claims ultimately led to eighteen hearings, and the commission's investigations led to fifteen exonerations. See North Carolina Innocence Inquiry Commission, "About."
5. For more on the civil rights lawsuit, see Associated Press, "$9M Settlement for 2 Men"; Carter, "Jury Awards Wrongfully Convicted NC Brothers."
6. Gross, O'Brien, et al., "Rate of False Conviction," 7230.
7. For examples of rate estimates in the 3–6 percent range, see Gross, O'Brien, et al., "Rate of False Conviction"; Loeffler, Hyatt, and Ridgeway, "Measuring Self-Reported Wrongful Convictions"; Risinger, "Innocents Convicted." For a general discussion of the rate issue and critique of all published attempts at estimating such a rate, see Zalman and Norris, "Measuring Innocence." We discuss these estimates again in chapter 1.
8. As of midsummer 2022, the National Registry of Exonerations database includes 3,180 cases. The NRE database is not an exact measure of actual innocence, which is often impossible to determine with absolute certainty, nor is it a full enumeration of wrongful convictions. Rather, it is a database of exonerations, for which it uses the following definition: "A person has been exonerated if he or she was convicted of a crime and, following a post-conviction re-examination of the evidence in the case, was either: (1) declared to be factually innocent by a government official or agency with the authority to make that declaration; or (2) relieved of all the consequences of the criminal conviction by a government official or body with the authority to take that action. The official action may be: (i) a complete pardon by a governor or other competent authority, whether or not the pardon is

designated as based on innocence; (ii) an acquittal of all charges factually related to the crime for which the person was originally convicted; or (iii) a dismissal of all charges related to the crime for which the person was originally convicted, by a court or by a prosecutor with the authority to enter that dismissal. The pardon, acquittal, or dismissal must have been the result, at least in part, of evidence of innocence that either (i) was not presented at the trial at which the person was convicted; or (ii) if the person pled guilty, was not known to the defendant and the defense attorney, and to the court, at the time the plea was entered. The evidence of innocence need not be an explicit basis for the official action that exonerated the person. A person who otherwise qualifies has not been exonerated if there is unexplained physical evidence of that person's guilt." National Registry of Exonerations, "Glossary."

9. Feld, *Kids, Cops, and Confessions*, 244. The "tip of the iceberg" metaphor has been used by several other prominent innocence scholars. See Acker, "Flipside Injustice of Wrongful Convictions," 1629n1.

10. Westervelt and Cook, *Life after Death Row*, 83–90.

11. Westervelt, quoted in Lopez, "Authors Discuss Wrongful Convictions."

12. Thompson and Baumgartner, "American Epidemic."

13. We discuss the innocence movement in more detail in chapter 2. For more on the movement, see, generally, Norris, *Exonerated*; Baumgartner, De Boef, and Boydstun, *Decline of the Death Penalty*; Zalman, "Integrated Justice Model."

14. See, generally, Baumgartner, De Boef, and Boydstun, *Decline of the Death Penalty*; Fan, Keltner, and Wyatt, "Matter of Guilt or Innocence"; Sarat et al., "Rhetoric of Abolition."

15. For instance, the popular author John Grisham has written at least one nonfiction and two fiction best-sellers dealing with wrongful convictions. See Grisham, *Innocent Man*; Grisham, *Confession*; Grisham, *Guardians*. Elsewhere in popular culture, wrongful or questionable convictions have been the subject of a number of popular movies, shows, documentaries, and podcasts, including *Serial, Making a Murderer, When They See Us, The Staircase*, and many more. For a discussion of the popularity of some of these, see Norris, *Exonerated*, 4–5, 109–111.

16. See, generally, Norris, Bonventre, et al., "Than That One Innocent Suffer"; Norris, Bonventre, et al., "Preventing Wrongful Convictions"; Kent and Carmichael, "Legislative Responses."

17. Marshall, "Innocence Revolution"; Findley, "Innocence Found," 3.

18. This sentiment has been echoed by legal scholars, most notably Daniel Medwed, who wrote, "It may not be farfetched to suggest, as others have done, that the effort to free the innocent has become the civil rights movement of the twenty-first century" ("Innocentrism," 1550). Medwed began a later article by saying, "Efforts to rectify wrongful convictions in the United States arguably represent a new civil rights movement for the twenty-first century" ("Emotionally Charged," 2187). In these statements, Medwed echoes a sentiment shared by some innocence movement participants, including Innocence Project cofounders Barry Scheck and Peter

Neufeld. However, not all within the movement agree with this particular framing. For more on these perspectives among movement participants and a critical discussion of civil rights discourse in regard to the innocence movement, see Norris, *Exonerated*, 167–177. We also discuss this issue in the conclusion of this book.

19. Norris has suggested that we consider the innocence movement a *revelation* rather than a *revolution* and that it may best be viewed as a piece of the larger fight for civil rights and social justice, rather than as its own civil rights movement. We discuss some of these matters in the conclusion. For more, see Norris, *Exonerated*, 164–177.

20. Zalman, "Integrated Justice Model," 1468.

21. We say that the true perpetrator *usually* remains free because there have been a number of cases in which the actual offender was also arrested. Furthermore, about one-third of known exonerations involved "no-crime" wrongful convictions, in which someone was erroneously convicted of a crime that never happened, and thus there was no true perpetrator to remain free. For more on true perpetrators, see Norris, Weintraub, et al., "Criminal Costs of Wrongful Convictions"; Baumgartner et al., "Mayhem of Wrongful Liberty"; Conroy and Warden, *Special Investigation*. For more on no-crime wrongful convictions, see, generally, Henry, *Smoke but No Fire*.

22. Findley, "Toward a New Paradigm," 134.

23. The research presented in this book draws on some of our previously published work. However, the data presented here have been greatly expanded. The data set used in chapter 2 was updated and includes new variables compared to our previous publication on state policy adoption. See Hicks, Mullinix, and Norris, "Politics of Wrongful Conviction Legislation." In addition, our public opinion data for this book were drawn from six unique and original surveys, rather than the two used in our previous publication on the topic. See Norris and Mullinix, "Framing Innocence." Beyond updating and expanding our data, we expanded our analyses, tested new theoretical perspectives, and explored new issues that we were unable to in our earlier work, such as a deeper examination of interest group influence on state policy, public awareness of wrongful convictions, and the role of political interest in shaping people's views.

24. Norris, Acker, et al., "Thirty Years of Innocence."

25. Rebecca Brown, interview with Robert Norris, February 10, 2021.

CHAPTER 1. THE INNOCENCE MOVEMENT IN THE UNITED STATES

1. Information about the Dotson case was derived from Warden, "First DNA Exoneration"; Innocence Project, "Gary Dotson"; Kennedy, "Gary Dotson."

2. Dotson's parole was revoked in 1987 when his wife accused him of assault. On Christmas Eve, he was granted parole again, but it was revoked two days later after he was involved in a bar fight. See Innocence Project, "Gary Dotson."

3. Information about the Vasquez case was derived from Horwitz and Warden, "David Vasquez."

4. An *Alford* plea largely functions like a *nolo contendere*, or no contest, plea but allows the defendant to explicitly maintain their innocence. Its name comes from the case *North Carolina v. Alford*, 400 U.S. 25 (1970).

5. Horwitz and Warden, "David Vasquez."

6. For more on the Boorn case, see Warden, "First Wrongful Conviction." There were, of course, other (probably many) miscarriages of justice in the American colonies, most notably, perhaps, the witchcraft trials in Salem, Massachusetts. For more on the Salem Witchcraft Trials, see Norton, *In the Devil's Snare*; Boyer and Nissenbaum, *Salem Possessed*. And for more on early wrongful convictions generally, see Yant, "Media's Muddled Message." The "DNA fingerprint," as it was sometimes called, was discovered in 1984. For more on the history of forensic DNA testing, see, generally, Aronson, *Genetic Witness*; Norris, *Exonerated*, 30–71.

7. There also were several prominent miscarriages of justice outside the United States. For a discussion of some of these, see, generally, Yant, "Media's Muddled Message"; Norris, *Exonerated*, 13–17, 227n4.

8. For more on the Sacco and Vanzetti case, see Watson, *Sacco & Vanzetti*. For more on the Gardner's work, see Gardner, *Court of Last Resort*; Yant, "Media's Muddled Message." For more on the case of Rubin "Hurricane" Carter, see Carter and Klonsky, *Eye of the Hurricane*; Hirsch, *Hurricane*. For a general discussion about these events in light of the modern innocence movement, see Norris, *Exonerated*, 13–17.

9. The foundations of the innocence movement are discussed in detail by Norris, *Exonerated*, 115–139; Norris, "Framing DNA."

10. This quotation was attributed to Meese in an October 1985 interview. See "Meese's Miranda Reply."

11. The first use of DNA in a criminal case occurred in England following the murders of Lydia Mann in 1983 and Dawn Ashworth in 1986. Police had mistakenly arrested Richard Buckland, though DNA tests showed he was not the perpetrator and he was released prior to being convicted. Following widespread testing of men in the community, DNA results linked Colin Pitchfork to the murders, and he pled guilty in 1988. For more on the case, see Wambaugh, *Blooding*. For more on the case in relation to the contemporary innocence movement, see Norris, *Exonerated*, 32–33.

12. The Bloodsworth case is discussed in more detail later in this book. Readers are also referred to the full-length book about his case: Junkin, *Bloodsworth*.

13. One particularly telling example was recounted by Bloodsworth, who said that community members would leave newspaper clippings on his work station and write "child killer" in the dirt on the side of his truck. See Neal, "Life after Death Row."

14. For more, see Norris, "Framing DNA."

15. See, generally, Aronson, *Genetic Witness*. For some discussion of the O. J. Simpson case in reference to the innocence movement specifically, see Norris, *Exonerated*, 63–66.

16. Connors et al., *Convicted by Juries*. For more on the development of DNA technology and its growth in the legal system, see, generally, Aronson, *Genetic*

Witness. For more on the development of DNA in relation to the innocence movement, see Norris, "Framing DNA"; Norris, *Exonerated*, 30–71, 121–133. Interestingly, Barry Scheck and Peter Neufeld, who founded the Innocence Project in 1992, were members of O. J. Simpson's defense team as the forensic experts.

17. For more on the background and establishment of the network, see Innocence Network, "Who We Are"; Norris, *Exonerated*, 88–98. As of February 2022, the network has sixty-eight member organizations, including at least twelve outside the US.

18. It is debatable whether the innocence movement should be categorized as a true social movement. At the very least, it can be considered an organized and sustained legal advocacy movement that seeks to change government institutions. For a discussion of innocence as a social movement, see Norris, *Exonerated*, 163–180.

19. For broader discussion of the movement and its meaning, see, generally, Norris, *Exonerated*; Zalman, "Integrated Justice Model."

20. See Breyer et al., *2020 Annual Report*, 56, table 11. See also Gramlich, "Only 2% of Federal Criminal Defendants Go to Trial."

21. Guilty pleas may further restrict defendants from seeking postconviction relief. Although not always the case, guilty pleas often require defendants to waive their right of appeal. See Reimelt, "Unjust Bargain."

22. Brooks, Simpson, and Kaneb, "If Hindsight Is 20/20," 1053.

23. As of midsummer 2022, the NRE includes 3,180 exonerations. For the most current figures, see http://exonerationregistry.org. Importantly, as we discussed in note 8 of the introduction, the NRE is not a complete database of all wrongful convictions or even of all exonerations. Cases must fit its criteria for inclusion, and even some that do may be excluded for other reasons.

24. It is important to note that these numbers change, even for past years, as the NRE research team learns about new cases. These figures were collected on January 24, 2022. At that point, the most exonerations in a single year was 2016, when there were 183 exonerations nationwide.

25. We note that the percentages and language used to describe the racial categories among current exonerees (namely, the use of "Hispanic" and not including the more inclusive "Latino/a/x/e") are those used by the National Registry of Exonerations. Because we are reporting summaries of its data, we are using its terminology. To our knowledge, according to a 2017 NRE report, those who are categorized as "white" or "Black" do not include those who identify as Hispanic or Latino. See Gross, Possley, and Stephens, *Race and Wrongful Convictions*, 1.

26. See National Registry of Exonerations, "Interactive Data Display." These four leading states account for 1,566 of the first 3,180 (49 percent) exonerations. We would, however, caution readers from drawing too much from those figures on their face. There are any number of potential explanations for why certain states have more exonerations than others—perhaps wrongful convictions are more likely or exonerations are more likely or the figures are indicative of other political trends

or legal system factors—and those reasons are not mutually exclusive. To better understand this would require more and better data than is currently available and is beyond the scope of this book.

27. The NRE's full definition of exoneration is included in note 8 of the introduction of this book. All of the NRE's full definitions are available on its website. See National Registry of Exonerations, "Glossary."

28. Anecdotally, one of the authors has a friend who was wrongly convicted and exonerated—they received their bill of innocence from the court after winning a lengthy postconviction battle—but is not included in the database for specific legal reasons. It is impossible to know how many such cases exist.

29. For the full "dark figure" quotation, see Bedau and Radelet, "Miscarriages of Justice," 87.

30. See National Registry of Exonerations, "Longest Incarcerations." As of July 11, 2022, there are 206 exonerees who were incarcerated for twenty-five years or more.

31. According to the National Registry of Exonerations, the first 3,250 exonerees cumulatively lost 28,171 years (current as of November 3, 2022). See National Registry of Exonerations, "Interactive Data Display."

32. For more on no-crime wrongful convictions, see Henry, *Smoke but No Fire*.

33. In chapter 3, we examine the public's awareness and beliefs about these and other contributing factors.

34. Borchard authored several articles related to compensation for the wrongly convicted in addition to his vaunted tome, *Convicting the Innocent*. See Borchard, "European Systems"; Borchard, "State Indemnity." For further discussion of policy work during this era, see Norris, *Exonerated*, 14–15; Zalman, "Edwin Borchard."

35. It is likely that Borchard's proposed preventive measures would not have prevented many wrongful convictions, as they generally included broad, sweeping ideals or changes to criminal procedure, rather than addressing specific contributing factors. See Bedau and Radelet, "Miscarriages of Justice," 86–89. Furthermore, his proposed compensation bill would have excluded some individuals who falsely confessed, which is generally considered a flawed approach given what we now know about interrogations and confessions. See, generally, Norris, "Assessing Compensation Statutes"; Norris, *Exonerated*, 228n12.

36. See Norris, *Exonerated*, 95–103.

37. The Innocence Protection Act was a part of the larger Justice for All Act of 2004. See American Civil Liberties Union, "H.R. 5107." For more on the Wrongful Convictions Tax Relief Act, see Innocence Project, "Innocence Project Applauds Congress."

38. A number of scholars have addressed innocence-related policy reforms in various domains and at various levels. See, for example, Baumgartner, Westervelt, and Cook, "Public Policy Responses"; Bernhard, "Short Overview"; Hicks, Mullinix, and Norris, "Politics of Wrongful Conviction Legislation"; Kent and Carmichael, "Legislative Responses"; Norris, "Assessing Compensation Statutes"; Norris,

Bonventre, et al., "Than That One Innocent Suffer"; Norris, Bonventre, et al., "Preventing Wrongful Convictions"; Owens and Griffiths, "Uneven Reparations"; T. Sullivan, *Police Experiences*; Zalman, "Criminal Justice System Reform."

39. Barry Scheck, quoted in Norris, *Exonerated*, 141–142.

40. There are many examples of books and articles that have examined collections of exoneration cases or individual wrongful convictions. For two prominent examples of analyses of exonerations en masse, see Garrett, *Convicting the Innocent*; Gross, Jacoby, et al., "Exonerations in the United States." For some prominent examples of individual case studies or narratives, see Burns, *Central Park Five*; Hinton and Hardin, *Sun Does Shine*; Wells and Leo, *Wrong Guys*.

41. There are vast bodies of research, mostly developed in psychology, on eyewitness identifications and (false) confessions. For examples, see the following scientific consensus papers on those topics: Wells, Small, et al., "Eyewitness Identification Procedures"; Wells, Kovera, et al., "Policy and Procedure Recommendations"; Kassin et al., "Police-Induced Confessions." For an example of research on forensic science and its relation to wrongful convictions, see S. Cole, "Forensic Science and Wrongful Convictions." For an example of research on the aftermath of wrongful convictions, see Westervelt and Cook, *Life after Death Row*.

42. See Innocence Staff, "What to Expect from 'The Innocence Files.'"

43. See Salazar, "Time Magazine Special Edition."

44. Leo, "Rethinking the Study of Miscarriages of Justice." For Leo's updated impressions on how the field developed in the decade following his initial argument, see Leo, "Criminology of Wrongful Conviction." For additional discussion of Leo's argument and other issues involving theory and methods in the innocence literature, see, generally, Gould and Leo, "One Hundred Years Later"; Leo and Gould, "Studying Wrongful Convictions"; Norris and Bonventre, "Advancing Wrongful Conviction Scholarship."

45. Packer, "Two Models," 11–13.

46. Findley, "Toward a New Paradigm," 146.

47. The phrase "wrongful liberty" comes from Baumgartner et al., "Mayhem of Wrongful Liberty." A couple of studies have sought to determine the harms generated by wrongful liberty. One study identified nine North Carolina cases in which a true perpetrator remained free and was later identified. Six of those nine committed additional crimes during their period of wrongful liberty, committing a total of ninety-nine crimes. See Baumgartner et al., "Mayhem of Wrongful Liberty." Another recent study found more than three hundred additional crimes among true perpetrators identified through DNA testing and suggested that the wrongful convictions that occur in a single year may ultimately generate tens of thousands of additional crimes. See Norris, Weintraub, et al., "Criminal Costs of Wrongful Convictions."

48. This approach was discussed by several innocence advocates when interviewed by one of the authors for another book. See Norris, *Exonerated*, 158–160.

49. Norris, Acker, et al., "Thirty Years of Innocence."

50. Zalman and Norris, "Measuring Innocence," 611 (emphasis in original).

51. For more on the ideological divisions in the innocence rate scholarship, see Zalman and Norris, "Measuring Innocence," 610–614. For the "foundations" quote, see Norris, "Framing DNA," 29.

52. The term "moral accessibility" was used by Norris, *Exonerated*, 158. The quote referring to the innocence movement as being about "just good law enforcement" is from Barry Scheck, quoted in Norris, 159.

53. Christine Mumma, director of the North Carolina Center of Actual Innocence, quoted in Norris, *Exonerated*, 158. Mumma also discussed the challenges of working on innocence reforms in a state in which the death penalty was popular. See Norris, *Exonerated*, 187.

54. Owens and Griffiths, "Uneven Reparations"; Kent and Carmichael, "Legislative Responses."

55. Zalman, Larson, and Smith, "Citizens' Attitudes," 62. While criminal justice rhetoric, opinions, and policy do not always fall neatly along ideological lines, much scholarship suggests that ideology influences public attitudes toward many aspects of the criminal justice system, such as attitudes toward police, punitiveness, and death penalty support, among others. For just a few of the many examples in published literature, see Harkin, "Political Legitimacy"; Gerber and Jackson, "Authority and Punishment"; Gerber and Jackson, "Justifying Violence"; Unnever, Cullen, and Applegate, "Turning the Other Cheek"; Gromet and Darley, "Political Ideology"; Britt, "Race, Religion, and Support"; Soss, Langbein, and Metelko, "Why Do White Americans Support the Death Penalty?"

CHAPTER 2. STATE POLITICS, INNOCENCE ADVOCACY, AND WRONGFUL CONVICTION REFORMS

1. Unless otherwise specified, information about the case comes from the case profiles on the websites of the Innocence Project and National Registry of Exonerations: Innocence Project, "Timothy Cole"; Innocence Project and Possley, "Timothy B. Cole."

2. Being a secretor means that a person's blood type can be determined from other types of bodily fluid. This case predated what we now think of as DNA testing. Early forensic testing sought, generally, to determine blood types and was useful for making generic comparisons or eliminating suspects. However, the "DNA fingerprint" was not available. It was not used in criminal cases in the United States until the late 1980s. See, generally, Aronson, *Genetic Witness*; Norris, *Exonerated*, 30–71.

3. Cole was officially exonerated by a judge. He was later given a gubernatorial pardon by Texas Governor Rick Perry in March 2010.

4. Evidence suggests that the law, limited as it was on the books, was even more frugal in practice. From 1985 to 2001, only two claims were paid, totaling just under $51,000 combined. Norris, "Theoretical Perspectives."

5. Norris, "Theoretical Perspectives."

6. Transcript, Texas House Committee on Criminal Jurisprudence Public Hearing and Testimony, April 1, 2009.

7. According to the Innocence Project, in Texas, "a wrongfully convicted person is entitled to $80,000 per year of wrongful incarceration, an annuity, as well as $25,000 per year spent on parole or as a registered sex offender. The wrongfully convicted person is also entitled to compensation for child support payments, tuition for up to 120 hours at a career center or public institution of higher learning, reentry and reintegration services, and the opportunity to buy into the Texas State Employee Health Plan" ("Texas"). The text of the Texas statutes is available through the Innocence Project's website: www.innocenceproject.org. In addition to compensation reform, the Texas legislature also created the Timothy Cole Exoneration Review Commission to study exonerations in Texas, identify contributors, and make policy recommendations. The commission filed its report in December 2016 and was then dissolved. Its report is available through the Texas Courts website: Timothy Cole Exoneration Review Commission, *Report*.

8. According to the Sentencing Project, as of this writing, Texas has the sixth-highest state imprisonment rate, at 529 per 100,000. Sentencing Project, "Facts." Further, according to data from the Death Penalty Information Center, Texas trails behind only Florida in death sentences given in the past decade and is far and away the leader in executions. Since 1976, Texas has executed 573 individuals through November 2021. The next closest states are Virginia and Oklahoma, each with 113 executions. Death Penalty Information Center, "Death Sentences"; Death Penalty Information Center, "Executions by State and Region."

9. See, generally, Norris, *Exonerated*.

10. As of February 2022, Texas has had four hundred exonerations since 1989. National Registry of Exonerations, "Interactive Data Display."

11. The three current innocence projects in Texas include (1) the Innocence Project of Texas, which appears to be the largest and seemingly most active in the state, (2) the Actual Innocence Clinic at the University of Texas Law School, and (3) the Thurgood Marshall School of Law Innocence Project. Innocence Network, "Network Member Organization." Other organizations have come and gone in Texas. The first project was the Texas Innocence Network at the University of Houston Law Center, established in 2000. Wesleyan School of Law also had an innocence project for a time. Norris, "Theoretical Perspectives."

12. The language of "estimator" and "system" variables comes from the classic work of the psychologist Gary L. Wells. See Wells, "Applied Eyewitness-Testimony Research."

13. A vast literature in psychology has uncovered much more about these issues. For example, scholars have explored the "weapon-focus effect," whereby the presence of a weapon in a crime reduces the accuracy of a witness's description of the suspect and the likelihood of a correct identification. Research also shows that characteristics of the witness, such as their age or race, may affect the accuracy of identifications. One prominent example is the "other-race effect" or "own-race

bias"; numerous studies have found that witness identifications across racial groups are significantly less accurate than those within racial groups and that this is one reason for the major racial disparities in exoneration cases, particularly sexual assaults, in which Black-on-white crimes are highly overrepresented compared to their prevalence among all violent crimes. The body of research on eyewitness issues is so well developed that the American Psychology-Law Society has commissioned two scientific consensus papers (or "white papers") on the topic. See Wells, Small, et al., "Eyewitness Identification Procedures"; Wells, Kovera, et al., "Policy and Procedure Recommendations."

14. For more on some of the suggested reforms, see Norris, Bonventre, et al., "Than That Some Innocent Suffer"; Norris, Bonventre, et al., "Preventing Wrongful Convictions."

15. As with eyewitness identifications, the established body of research was so significant that the AP-LS commissioned a white paper on the topic. See Kassin et al., "Police-Induced Confessions." Many additional studies have further developed and expanded on the ideas presented in the white paper.

16. Kassin et al., "Police-Induced Confessions," 14.

17. In addition to voluntary and compliant false confessions, there is another category of internalized or persuaded confessions. These include those cases in which an innocent suspect actually comes to believe that they committed the crime and confesses to it, often in response to psychologically manipulative tactics used by interrogators. See, generally, Kassin et al., "Police-Induced Confessions"; Leo, *Police Interrogation*.

18. Police in the United States have moved away from the "third-degree" tactics of the past, which were often physical and, in some cases, bordered on or were torture. For more on the historical and contemporary nature of criminal interrogations, see, generally, Leo, *Police Interrogation*.

19. The one study of which we are aware that examined the length of interrogations in false-confession cases found that among known false confessions, the interrogations lasted an average of about sixteen hours. Drizin and Leo, "Problem of False Confessions."

20. Others include minimization and maximization techniques, appealing to suspects' faith or religion, and more. For more on these and other coercive tactics, see Kassin et al., "Police-Induced Confessions." For a study of the "Prisoner's Dilemma" in the context of interrogations and pleas—where cosuspects or defendants are played against one another—see Norris and Redlich, "Seeking Justice, Compromising Truth?"

21. Other characteristics that may increase suspects' vulnerability include suggestibility, risk preferences, and conditions such as ADHD. Kassin et al., "Police-Induced Confessions."

22. Kassin et al., "Police-Induced Confessions," 5.

23. Although support for recording interrogations is nearly ubiquitous among researchers and advocates, the specifics of the policies may differ. For instance,

virtually all reformers support recording the entire proceeding, from the reading of the suspect's rights through the final confession statement, and most support doing so with an "equal focus" perspective, in which the camera captures both the suspect and the interrogator(s). Other issues are less clear-cut, however, such as how situations in which recording is not practical should be handled, how to address equipment failure, and what are the appropriate consequences for failure to record. Despite these questions, recording custodial interrogations only helps in our understanding of interrogations and confessions and is generally regarded as one of the most important investigatory reforms related to wrongful convictions.

24. For more on DNA access laws, see Innocence Project, "Access to Post-Conviction DNA Testing."

25. See Innocence Project, "Preservation of Evidence."

26. Westervelt and Cook, "Foreword," 1224 (quoting Westervelt and Cook, "Framing Innocents," 261). Exonerees face untold numbers of challenges upon reentering their communities. Some are similar to those experienced by most formerly incarcerated people: financial challenges, mental and physical health problems, educational or vocational difficulties, and so forth. However, in other ways, the social and psychological consequences are exacerbated for, or entirely unique to, those who were imprisoned wrongfully. For more, see, generally, Alexander-Bloch et al., "Mental Health Characteristics"; Grounds, "Psychological Consequences"; Westervelt and Cook, *Life after Death Row*.

27. For more on exoneree compensation statutes, see, for example, Bernhard, "When Justice Fails"; Bernhard, "Justice Still Fails"; Norris, "Assessing Compensation Statutes"; Owens and Griffiths, "Uneven Reparations."

28. We derived these data from the Innocence Project, which tracks these specific reforms. More information about the IP's policy work, these specific reforms, and state-by-state information can be accessed through the organization's website: Innocence Project, "Policy Reform."

29. For a review of scholarship on policy responsiveness to public opinion, see, generally, Beyer and Hanni, "Two Sides of the Same Coin?" For more on dynamic representation, see Caughey and Warshaw, "Policy Preferences and Policy Change"; Erikson, MacKuen, and Stimson, *Macro Polity*; Erikson, Wright, and McIver, *Statehouse Democracy*; Stimson, MacKuen, and Erikson, "Dynamic Representation."

30. Stimson, MacKuen, and Erikson, "Dynamic Representation," 559.

31. See Rogers, "Electoral Accountability"; Hogan, "Challenger Emergence."

32. Stimson, MacKuen, and Erikson, "Dynamic Representation," 548. For more on policy mood and public opinion in relation to criminal justice policies, see Pickett, "Public Opinion and Criminal Justice Policy."

33. See Caughey and Warshaw, "Policy Preferences and Policy Change."

34. For more on ideology and attitudes toward law enforcement, see, for example, Brown and Benedict, "Perceptions of the Police"; Gerber and Jackson, "Justifying Violence."

35. See, for example, Rudolph and Evans, "Political Trust."
36. For example, Payne and colleagues found that there are some general demographic patterns in punitive justifications for sentencing but that differences between ideological (and other) groups may depend on the specific situation being evaluated, for example, different types of crimes. See, generally, Payne et al., "What Drives Punitive Beliefs?"
37. For more on the ideological components of criminal justice preferences in general, see, for example, Beckett, *Making Crime Pay*; Gromet and Darley, "Political Ideology"; Miller, "Ideology and Criminal Justice Policy"; Payne et al., "What Drives Punitive Beliefs?"
38. In particular, innocence advocates are often "lumped together with the defense community" (Norris, *Exonerated*, 186).
39. See, for example, Baumgartner, De Boef, and Boydstun, *Decline of the Death Penalty*; Byfield, *Savage Portrayals*; Gross, Possley, and Stephens, *Race and Wrongful Convictions*; Norris, *Exonerated*.
40. See Chong and Mullinix, "Information and Issue Constraints."
41. See, generally, Barrilleaux, Holbrook, and Langer, "Electoral Competition"; Carroll and Eichorst, "Role of Party"; Hicks, "Partisan Competition."
42. For more, see Rogers, "Electoral Accountability."
43. Although social movement organizations and interest groups are not synonymous, there is significant overlap between scholarly conceptualizations of the two concepts. In part, the terminology used is related to academic discipline and substantive area of study. For discussion of innocence organizations as social movements, see, generally, Norris, *Exonerated*. For discussion of innocence organizations as interest groups, see Kent and Carmichael, "Legislative Responses."
44. An earlier version of this section was previously published. See Hicks, Mullinix, and Norris, "Politics of Wrongful Conviction Legislation." Since publication of that article, we expanded our data and updated our analysis. For example, the original analysis relied on the number of death-row exonerations, while the present one includes the total number of exonerations.
45. Hicks et al., "Home Rule Be Damned."
46. The policy department at the Innocence Project works with officials and lawmakers "to pass laws and policies that prevent wrongful convictions and make it easier for the innocent to receive justice." State-by-state information about these and other policies can be found on the IP website: Innocence Project, "Policy Reform."
47. Caughey and Warshaw estimate public-opinion liberalism on social and economic policy using annual group-level (e.g., state, race, urban residence) item response models. Their data include more than a thousand polls, which reveal citizen preferences on hundreds of domestic policy questions. See Caughey and Warshaw, "Policy Preferences and Policy Change." Importantly, because Caughey and Warshaw's measure spans all fifty states in each year until 2014, we had to manage missing values for 2015, 2016, and 2017. Rather than throwing out those years or simply using 2014 values for each of the remaining years, we forecasted

public-opinion values with a longitudinal model. Specifically, we modeled, in each state and year, public-opinion liberalism with a dynamic panel model. We used fixed effects for states and incorporated time with a cubic polynomial for year. The cubic effect of time was statistically significant (p < 0.01), and we used it to forecast values in each state for 2015–2017.

48. Social-policy liberalism exerts a stronger influence on policy making than economic liberalism does because (1) state governments usually have more control over social policies, (2) citizens often have stronger and more stable opinions on social policy, and (3) citizens' attitudes on social policies, given their relatively simpler technical complexity, are easier for politicians to infer. See Caughey and Warshaw, "Policy Preferences and Policy Change," 252.

49. See Klarner, "State Legislative Election Returns." We specifically used an index of electoral competitiveness similar to Holbrook and Van Dunk, "Electoral Competition."

50. To accommodate multimember districts, we used the measure of "margin of victory" from Berry, Berkman, and Schneiderman, "Legislative Professionalism." Their measure, for each seat, subtracts the number of votes earned by the losing candidate with the most votes from the number of votes earned by the winning candidate. This value is then divided by the ratio of the total number of votes to the district magnitude (i.e., the number of seats for each district). We measured each state's average in an election year by only including "contested" seats, which were those in which the margin of victory was smaller than eighty percentage points.

51. See Norris, *Exonerated*, 91–95.

52. Our measurement equation is $Exon = 0.4*Exon+0.3*L1.Exon+0.2*L2.Exon+0.1*L3.Exon$, where Exon is the number of exonerations in year t, and L1 represents year $t-1$, L2 represents year $t-2$, and so forth. Measuring exonerations this way allows us to capture the idea that more recent exonerations probably exert a stronger effect than ones more distant in the past but that past exonerations can also play a role, especially as the number of exonerations from year to year increases. Additionally, exonerations may act like triggering events, and to the extent that that is true, this helps us capture this phenomenon in our empirical model.

53. See Hicks, "Partisan Competition."

CHAPTER 3. PUBLIC AWARENESS OF WRONGFUL CONVICTIONS

1. Larson, "Serial."

2. Hesse, "'Serial' Takes the Stand"; Larson, "Serial."

3. PBS, "What 'Serial'-mania Says." The first season of *Serial* averaged 2.25 million downloads per episode over its first two months. The series spawned three seasons, each with a different focus, which collectively garnered 420 million downloads, making it the most downloaded podcast ever. Quah, "*Serial* Season 3 Is the Podcast's Biggest Ever."

4. As a sign of how quickly and dramatically things happen in the wrongful conviction arena, Syed's release occurred while this book was in production. For more on the case, see Levenson, "Judge Vacates Murder Conviction"; Bailey, "Adnan Syed and Serial."

5. Pierce, "'Serial' Podcast Success." For just a few examples of popular podcasts addressing wrongful convictions and related issues, readers are referred to *Wrongful Conviction with Jason Flom*, *Wrongful Conviction: False Confessions*, and *Undisclosed*.

6. See Waxman, "President Trump Played a Key Role."

7. Bennett, "When They See Us"; Spangler, "Netflix Says."

8. Nededog, "Here's How Popular." See also Tassi, "Why 'Making a Murderer.'"

9. Hinton and Hardin, *Sun Does Shine*.

10. For the nonfiction book, see Grisham, *Innocent Man*; the two novels referenced include *The Confession* and *The Guardians*. The latter features a protagonist based on McCloskey. Interestingly, McCloskey himself recently authored a memoir focusing on his life and his work to free the wrongly convicted, for which Grisham wrote the foreword. McCloskey, *When Truth Is All You Have*.

11. Baumgartner, De Boef, and Boydstun, *Decline of the Death Penalty*, 116.

12. For a nonexhaustive selection of articles from these outlets that address issues related to wrongful convictions, see, generally, Cohen, "Wrongful Convictions"; White, "Taxing the Wrongfully Convicted"; Rose and ProPublica, "Deal Prosecutors Offer"; Grann, "Trial by Fire"; Levy, "Price of a Life"; Cobb, "Central Park Five"; Bazelon, "Innocence Deniers"; Morgan, "I Was Wrongfully Imprisoned"; Salazar, "Time Magazine Special Edition."

13. The search was for the phrase "wrongful conviction" in Google Scholar on July 6, 2021. We did not examine and verify every search result, so it is possible that some results are not indicative of wrongful conviction coverage as we discuss it in this chapter. However, we sampled the results, and all of them were related to wrongful convictions as discussed here. Some articles may discuss wrongful convictions using alternative phrases, such as "actual innocence" or "miscarriages of justice," so these figures are not representative of all innocence scholarship. Rather, they are only presented to emphasize the point about the growth of wrongful convictions as a topic in academic scholarship and higher education.

14. Examples of such books and edited volumes include Acker and Redlich, *Wrongful Conviction*; Covey and Beety, *Wrongful Convictions Reader*; Huff and Killias, *Wrongful Conviction*; Norris, Bonventre, and Acker, *When Justice Fails*; Redlich et al., *Examining Wrongful Convictions*; Westervelt and Humphrey, *Wrongly Convicted*; Zalman and Carrano, *Wrongful Conviction and Criminal Justice Reform*.

15. Norris, *Exonerated*, 5.

16. We surveyed an online sample of US adult respondents. The sample was drawn from a broader pool of potential respondents such that the demographic characteristics of the sample approach particular benchmarks on variables such as sex/gender, age, region, and race. It was not a probability-based random sample of

the national population, and we recognize that researchers should exercise caution when making descriptive inferences in these situations. However, given that the sample demographics match those of the target population, our descriptive inferences about awareness as well as inferences about the predictors of awareness (based on regression models with a robust set of controls) should generalize to the broader population. We encourage future research to examine these topics with different samples to ensure the robustness of the findings, but we also recognize that awareness and its predictors may also change over time.

17. See Krumpal, "Determinants of Social Desirability Bias."

18. Baumgartner, De Boef, and Boydstun, *Decline of the Death Penalty*. See also Fan, Keltner, and Wyatt, "Matter of Guilt or Innocence"; Unnever and Cullen, "Executing the Innocent."

19. This quantity represents an odds ratio that is calculated, first, by dividing the number of Black respondents who said yes by the number of Black respondents who said no. This gives us the *odds* that a Black respondent heard a true story versus had not. We, next, do the same for white respondents to calculate the *odds* that a white respondent heard a true story versus had not. Finally, we divide the *odds* that a Black respondent heard a true story by the *odds* that a white respondent heard a true story to retrieve the *odds ratio.*

20. The name "Innocence Project" is trademarked and may be used only by members of the Innocence Network in good standing. However, it is not associated solely with the New York–based Innocence Project. All of the Innocence Network members are independent organizations, and there is sometimes confusion over the use of the phrase "Innocence Project." For more, see Norris, *Exonerated,* 203–205.

21. We use "sex/gender" throughout for the sake of clarity, but we note that question wording varied between surveys; some asked respondents for self-reported "sex," while others asked for "gender." While we are aware of the important differences between these two terms, our analyses generally report the differences between those who identify as males and those who identify as females.

22. Bennett and Iyengar, "New Era of Minimal Effects?," 720. There is a vast literature on this and related issues, often discussed as "partisan selective exposure." See Rodriguez et al., "Partisan Selective Exposure." Although ideology exerts a strong influence on media consumption, there is also evidence that "citizens often consume a wide variety of political media at any one point in time and the various political media outlets which become part of their routine often vary in ideological orientations." Holbert, Hmielowski, and Weeks, "Clarifying Relationships," 207.

23. Prior, "You've Either Got It or You Don't?," 747.

24. Prior, "You've Either Got It or You Don't?," 747.

25. We derived these quantities by setting other covariates to their sample median values. We also set the experimental condition to the control group.

26. See Zalman, Larson, and Smith, "Citizens' Attitudes," 56–60.

27. As we and others have discussed elsewhere, estimates of wrongful convictions are shaky, at best, and a wide variety of methodologies have devised estimates ranging from virtually zero to well over 10 percent. However, the most empirically sound estimates have suggested error rates in the 3–6 percent range. See, for example, Risinger, "Innocents Convicted"; Gross, O'Brien, et al., "Rate of False Conviction"; Loeffler, Hyatt, and Ridgeway, "Measuring Self-Reported Wrongful Convictions." For a historical overview of the "rate question" and a summary of all published estimates, see Zalman and Norris, "Measuring Innocence."

28. For Gallup poll results pertaining to this and a variety of other questions related to capital punishment, see Gallup, "Death Penalty." For scholarship on the link between wrongful convictions and the death penalty, see, for example, Baumgartner, De Boef, and Boydstun, *Decline of the Death Penalty*; Sarat et al., "Rhetoric of Abolition."

29. See, for example, Peffley and Hurwitz, "Persuasion and Resistance"; Unnever and Cullen, "Executing the Innocent."

30. For more on the relationship between ideology/partisanship and perceptions of science, see, generally, Azevedo and Jost, "Ideological Basis of Antiscientific Attitudes"; Lewandowsky and Oberauer, "Motivated Rejection of Science"; Lewandowsky and Oberauer, "Many Conservatives"; Fridman, Gershon, and Gneezy, "COVID-19 and Vaccine Hesitancy."

31. Bartels, "Beyond the Running Tally."

32. For more, see, generally, Baumgartner and Jones, *Agendas and Instability*; Karch, *Democratic Laboratories*; Kingdon, *Agendas, Alternatives, and Public Policies*.

CHAPTER 4. HOW WRONGFUL CONVICTIONS SHAPE PUBLIC OPINION

1. Information about the Bloodsworth case comes from the National Registry of Exoneration's profile of the case (see Warden, "Kirk Bloodsworth") and from Norris, *Exonerated*, 57–59.

2. Wiggins, "Former Maryland Death Row Inmate."

3. The Innocence Protection Act was part of the 2004 Justice for All Act, which included provisions related not only to wrongful convictions but also to crime victims' rights, DNA testing generally, and defense counsel in capital cases. Among other things, the Innocence Protection Act established the "Kirk Bloodsworth Post-Conviction DNA Testing Grant Program," which authorized $25 million to help states pay for post-conviction DNA testing. For a summary of the Innocence Protection Act, see Death Penalty Information Center, "DPIC Summary." The full Justice for All Act is available at www.govinfo.gov. For more on Maryland's death penalty, see Cassie, "Innocent Man"; and Death Penalty Information Center, "Maryland."

4. See Junkin, *Bloodsworth*; Bayne, *Bloodsworth*.

5. Portions of the research presented in this chapter were previously published. See Norris and Mullinix, "Framing Innocence." In that article, we presented partial

results from two surveys. In this chapter, we present additional results from those surveys, as well as a third, unique one.

6. Grisham, *Innocent Man*; Tweel, *Innocent Man*.

7. Stevenson, *Just Mercy*; Cretton, *Just Mercy*.

8. As discussed throughout this book, Baumgartner and colleagues discovered that innocence became a leading frame in popular media coverage of the death penalty. See Baumgartner, De Boef, and Boydstun, *Decline of the Death Penalty*. For some recent examples of coverage in specific, high-profile, national newspapers, see Feuer, "Falsely Imprisoned for 23 Years"; Bromwich and Closson, "After Key Evidence Was Withheld"; Jackman, "More than Half"; Phillips, "Police Misconduct."

9. Clark, "Floyd Bledsoe Shares What Life Is Like." For more on the Bledsoe case, see the National Registry of Exonerations case profile: Possley, "Floyd Bledsoe."

10. See, for example, Wiggins, "Former Maryland Death Row Inmate"; Beals, "Maryland Awards."

11. For scholarly attention on wrongful convictions and aggregate public opinion, see, generally, Baumgartner, De Boef, and Boydstun, *Decline of the Death Penalty*; Fan, Keltner, and Wyatt, "Matter of Guilt or Innocence"; Unnever and Cullen, "Executing the Innocent."

12. According to the Gallup website, the most recent data for this follow-up question come from October 2014. Among those who indicated that they opposed the death penalty, Gallup asked the open-ended question, "Why do you oppose the death penalty for persons convicted of murder?" The second most common response, given by 17 percent of the sample, was "Persons may be wrongly convicted." See Gallup, "Death Penalty."

13. There are a number of examples of individual-level studies with mixed results. For instance, one survey examined whether a gubernatorial candidate's anti-death-penalty stance based on innocence affected voting decisions and found that effects were small and mostly insignificant; see Bobo and Johnson, "Taste for Punishment." Others have found different responses to an innocence argument based on race; see Peffley and Hurwitz, "Persuasion and Resistance." Finally, some have found a significant level of responsiveness to an innocence argument about the death penalty; see Dardis et al., "Media Framing of Capital Punishment"; Lambert and Clarke, "Impact of Information on an Individual's Support"; Lambert et al., "Impact of Information on Death Penalty Support."

14. Peffley and Hurwitz, "Persuasion and Resistance," 999.

15. The innocence movement and anti-death-penalty movement are distinct advocacy pursuits but are closely tied in some important ways. For more on the important overlaps of these two phenomena, see, generally, Norris, *Exonerated*, 57–63, 72–91, 143–145. For more information on the wrongful convictions and the death penalty in general, see the Death Penalty Information Center, "Innocence." For scholarly writing on innocence and the death penalty, see, for example, Marshall,

"Innocence Revolution"; Warden, "How and Why Illinois Abolished the Death Penalty"; Radelet, "Role of the Innocence Argument."

16. Baumgartner, De Boef, and Boydstun, *Decline of the Death Penalty*. For more on innocence coverage and the death penalty, see, generally, Dardis et al., "Media Framing of Capital Punishment"; Radelet, "Role of the Innocence Argument"; Sarat et al., "Rhetoric of Abolition."

17. For a general overview of framing theory, see Chong and Druckman, "Framing Theory." For research in political science examining framing effects, see, for example, Busby, Flynn, and Druckman, "Studying Framing Effects"; Gamson and Modigliani, "Media Discourse and Public Opinion"; Nelson, Clawson, and Oxley, "Media Framing of Civil Liberties Conflict." For examples of framing theory in criminology, examining topics such as racialized coverage of crime and public punitiveness, among others, see, generally, Park, Holody, and Zhang, "Race in Media Coverage"; Peelo, "Framing Homicide Narratives"; Applegate and Sanborn, "Public Opinion"; Ramirez, "Punitive Sentiment"; Simmons, "Cultivating Support."

18. See, generally, Iyengar, *Is Anyone Responsible?*

19. Aaroe, "Investigating Frame Strength," 209.

20. See, for example, Aaroe, "Investigating Frame Strength"; Chong and Mullinix, "Information and Issue Constraints."

21. See Busby, Flynn, and Druckman, "Studying Framing Effects"; Price and Tewksbury, "News Values and Public Opinion"; Nisbett and Ross, *Human Inference*; Tal-Or et al., "Counterfactual Thinking."

22. See, generally, Cohen, Tal-Or, and Mazor-Tregerman, "Tempering Effect of Transportation"; De Graaf et al., "Identification as a Mechanism"; Green and Brock, "Role of Transportation."

23. Aaroe, "Investigating Frame Strength."

24. For an overview of this theoretical perspective, see Shanahan et al., "Narrative Policy Framework."

25. We focus in this chapter on support for the death penalty in our examination of the effects of these frames on policy preferences, but we extend this argument in chapter 5 to also test their effects on support for policy reforms designed to reduce the likelihood of wrongful convictions. Narratives not only should be more persuasive than thematic frames in reducing support for capital punishment but also should be more effective at increasing support for other innocence-related policy reforms.

26. Busby, Flynn, and Druckman, "Studying Framing Effects," 31. For more, see Iyengar, *Is Anyone Responsible?*; Iyengar, "Framing Responsibility for Political Issues."

27. See, generally, Lord, Ross, and Lepper, "Biased Assimilation and Attitude Polarization."

28. Taber and Lodge, "Motivated Skepticism."

29. Baumgartner, De Boef, and Boydstun, *Decline of the Death Penalty*, 9. For more on morality policies, see Mooney and Schuldt, "Does Morality Policy Exist?"

30. Peffley and Hurwitz, "Persuasion and Resistance."
31. Baumgartner, De Boef, and Boydstun, *Decline of the Death Penalty*, 9.
32. Portions of the results presented in this chapter were published in an earlier article. See Norris and Mullinix, "Framing Innocence." Here, we present an expanded set of results, offer further interpretation and discussion of those findings, and discuss new original studies conducted after the original publication.
33. The content of our treatment text was informed by a small pretest. Prior to the implementation of the main study, a sample of undergraduate students was asked several open- and closed-ended questions to evaluate treatment text options and the credibility of the sources attached to the information.
34. For instance, Peffley and Hurwitz asked, "Do you favor or oppose the death penalty for persons convicted of murder?" ("Persuasion and Resistance"). Gallup polls ask, "Are you in favor of the death penalty for a person convicted of murder?" ("Death Penalty").
35. Some surveys have shown that some people, particularly Republicans, increasingly think that universities have a negative effect on the country. See Pew Research Center, "Since 2015, Sharp Rise."
36. This figure was based on some common estimates of a wrongful conviction rate, which often fall between 1 and 5 percent. See Zalman and Norris, "Measuring Innocence." At the time, there were more than 2.1 million people incarcerated in the United States. See, for example, Kaeble and Cowhig, *Correctional Populations*. Thus, an error rate of 5 percent would equate to more than one hundred thousand innocents incarcerated.
37. For more on the crimes of true perpetrators, see Acker, "Flipside Injustice of Wrongful Convictions"; Baumgartner et al., "Mayhem of Wrongful Liberty"; Conroy and Warden, *Special Investigation*; Norris, Weintraub, et al., "Criminal Costs of Wrongful Convictions."
38. We thought that this rhetoric might resonate with conservatives and death penalty supporters. For an example of this discourse in the media, state senator Joseph Pennacchio of New Jersey (R), a "law-and-order conservative," recently stated, "If we convict somebody wrongfully, that means the person who committed the crime is still out there" (S. Sullivan, "What Happens If You're Wrongfully Convicted in N.J.?").
39. Regarding the use of a racially ambiguous name, data from the Social Security Administration reveals that the name Michael was in the top-fifteen most common names from 1950 to 2017. According to 2010 US Census data, Williams was the third-most-common surname and was almost equally divided between white (45.8 percent) and Black (47.7 percent) individuals. Regarding the certainty of innocence, we pretested variations of the narrative to ensure that it achieved our goal. We pretested our message on a sample of university students, of whom 95 percent reported that they believed the individual was innocent after reading the narrative. The remaining individuals selected "don't know"; no respondent believed that he was "guilty."

40. Gallup, "Death Penalty."
41. We found no evidence of question-order effects.
42. We derive this quantity by dividing the exponentiated coefficient for "Narrative plus Numbers" in table A.8 by 1—i.e., x = 1/exp(coefficient).
43. This literature is voluminous and spans several disciplines. For several examples, readers are referred to Boudreau, MacKenzie, and Simmons, "Police Violence and Public Perceptions"; Brown and Benedict, "Perceptions of the Police"; Mullinix and Norris, "Pulled-Over Rates"; Mullinix, Bolsen, and Norris, "Feedback Effects"; Schafer, Huebner, and Bynum, "Citizen Perceptions of Police Services"; Testa and Dietrich, "Seeing Is Believing"; Weitzer and Tuch, "Determinants of Public Satisfaction with the Police"; Wu, "Race/Ethnicity and Perceptions of the Police."
44. See, for example, Braga, "Better Policing"; Natarajan, "Racial Profiling"; National Institute of Justice, *Race, Trust, and Police Legitimacy*.
45. See Mullinix and Norris, "Pulled-Over Rates."
46. See Mullinix, Bolsen, and Norris, "Feedback Effects."
47. We discussed this in the first article published from these data. See Norris and Mullinix, "Framing Innocence," 325–326.
48. For more on police legitimacy, see, generally, Tankebe, "Viewing Things Differently"; Tyler, "Enhancing Police Legitimacy"; Hinds and Murphy, "Public Satisfaction with Police"; Hawdon, Ryan, and Griffin, "Policing Tactics."
49. These values are based on the second model in table A.11 in the appendix, and all other covariates are held to their median values.
50. Christine Mumma, executive director of the North Carolina Center on Actual Innocence, quoted in Norris, *Exonerated*, 158.

CHAPTER 5. PUBLIC SUPPORT FOR INNOCENCE REFORMS

1. Grisham, foreword to *When Truth Is All You Have*, ix.
2. Norris, *Exonerated*, 192.
3. Paul Caseteleiro, quoted in Norris, *Exonerated*, 192.
4. Jim McCloskey, quoted in Norris, *Exonerated*, 192.
5. Erika Applebaum, quoted in Norris, *Exonerated*, 192–193.
6. In his history of the innocence movement, Norris notes that while the foundations of the modern movement date to the 1980s, innocence did not really resemble a widespread, organized movement until the middle of the first decade of this century. See, generally, Norris, *Exonerated*. For more on state-level reforms related to wrongful convictions, see Kent and Carmichael, "Legislative Responses to Wrongful Conviction"; Norris, Bonventre, et al., "Than That One Innocent Suffer"; Norris, Bonventre, et al., "Preventing Wrongful Convictions."
7. Importantly, while a majority of respondents in Zalman et al.'s sample believed that reform was warranted, there were significant differences between white and nonwhite respondents, such that nonwhite respondents answered yes at a higher rate (Zalman, Larson, and Smith, "Citizens' Attitudes," 59).

8. For more on the crimes of actual offenders, see Baumgartner et al., "Mayhem of Wrongful Liberty"; Norris, Weintraub, et al., "Criminal Costs of Wrongful Convictions"; West and Meterko, "Innocence Project"; Conroy and Warden, *Special Investigation*.

9. See, for example, Brown and Benedict, "Perceptions of the Police." This pattern is also evident in the results of our analyses presented in chapter 4.

10. The fiscal concerns with compensation statutes have often been overcome in the legislative process by recognizing the state's moral obligation to exonerees and/or highlighting the relatively few claims that are awarded. See Norris, "Exoneree Compensation." Related to the latter point, it is also important to recognize that exoneree compensation statutes often may not function well in practice. For research on exonerees' compensation claims and awards, see Gutman, "Empirical Reexamination"; Gutman and Sun, "Why Is Mississippi the Best State?" Finally, even if preventive reforms do cost the government money up front, to the extent that they are effective in reducing wrongful convictions, they may actually *save* money in down-the-line costs associated with additional investigations, court processes, and exoneree awards.

11. See, for example, Jacoby, "Issue Framing"; Jacoby, "Public Attitudes"; Rudolph and Evans, "Political Trust."

12. For some discussion of the link between ideology and punitiveness or punitive policy, see, for example, Beckett, *Making Crime Pay*; Gromet and Darley, "Political Ideology"; Miller, "Ideology and Criminal Justice Policy"; Payne et al., "What Drives Punitive Beliefs?"

13. See, for example, Baumgartner, De Boef, and Boydstun, *Decline of the Death Penalty*; Byfield, *Savage Portrayals*; Gross, Possley, and Stephens, *Race and Wrongful Convictions*.

14. Countless studies have explored racial disparities throughout the criminal legal system. For some examples, see Cole, *No Equal Justice*; Epp, Maynard-Moody, and Haider-Markel, *Pulled Over*; Tonry, *Punishing Race*.

15. Some versions of this question did not include the word "accurate." See the appendix for full details on question wording by survey.

16. Our other measures of awareness—questions about whether people have heard true or fictional stories of wrongful convictions—are revealing but are broader in their target. If someone says that they are aware of the Innocence Project, they are probably part of a smaller subsection of the population that is more familiar than those whose only exposure to wrongful convictions was through a single novel, television show, film, or podcast. Indeed, the results in chapter 3 showed that fewer people said they have heard of the Innocence Project than our other measures of awareness. That said, these alternative measures of awareness are undoubtedly related, as hearing true and fictional accounts of wrongful convictions was a significant predictor of familiarity with the Innocence Project.

17. See Chong and Druckman, "Framing Theory."

18. Iyengar and Kinder, *News That Matters*, 63.

19. Scheufele and Tewksbury, "Framing, Agenda Setting, and Priming," 11.
20. For more on exoneree compensation statutes, see, for example, Bernhard, "When Justice Fails"; Bernhard, "Justice Still Fails"; Campbell, "Exoneration and Compensation"; Griffiths and Owens, "Remedying Wrongful Convictions"; Keith, "Wronged without Recourse"; Madrigal and Norris, "Good, the Bad, and the Uncertain."
21. For more on the costs of compensation statutes in practice, see Gutman, "Empirical Reexamination"; Gutman and Sun, "Why Is Mississippi the Best State?"
22. We recognize that this experimental design does not tell us the effects of priming only the compensation considerations. It tells us the effect of priming attitudes toward police and the effect of priming those attitudes coupled with compensation considerations.
23. In the model without controls, this effect was significant at $p < 0.06$; in the model with controls, it was significant at $p < 0.05$.

CONCLUSION

1. For more on the original survey design, see Norris and Mullinix, "Framing Innocence." As of July 2022, there are 3,180 cases listed on the National Registry of Exonerations. See exonerationregistry.org.
2. For the 2011 polices, see Norris, Bonventre, et al., "Than That One Innocent Suffer." For the most up-to-date information on current policies, see Innocence Project, "Policy Reform," where state-by-state information is easily accessible.
3. For more on the 2011 policies, see Norris, "Assessing Compensation Statutes." For more on current statutes as of early 2022, see Madrigal and Norris, "Good, the Bad, and the Uncertain."
4. For overviews of the relationship between public opinion and policy, see, generally, Burstein, "Impact of Public Opinion"; Beyer and Hanni, "Two Sides of the Same Coin?"
5. Levenson, Cramer, and Romero, "Oklahoma Governor Commutes Inmate's Death Sentence."
6. See, for example, ESPN, "Death Sentence for Julius Jones." For more on the Jones case, see, generally, Innocence Staff, "Gov. Stitt Grants Julius Jones Clemency."
7. Southall and Bromwich, "2 Men Convicted of Killing Malcolm X."
8. Levenson, Cramer, and Romero, "Oklahoma Governor Commutes Inmate's Death Sentence."
9. Conklin, "Julius Jones."
10. For the "criminal costs" language and a discussion of this issue and its implications, see Norris, Weintraub, et al., "Criminal Costs of Wrongful Convictions."
11. Rebecca Brown, interview with Robert Norris, February 10, 2021.
12. We should be cautious about making bold inferences here, as it is possible that in larger samples we might detect significant differences between liberals and conservatives in their responsiveness to these messages.

13. Mullinix and Norris, "Pulled-Over Rates." See also Elkins, "Policing in America"; Gallup, "Confidence in Institutions."
14. See, for example, Braga, "Better Policing"; Khan, "Getting Killed by Police"; National Institute of Justice, *Race, Trust, and Police Legitimacy*; Zimring, "Police Killings."
15. See, for example, Boudreau, MacKenzie, and Simmons, "Police Violence and Public Perceptions"; Mullinix, Bolsen, and Norris, "Feedback Effects"; Testa and Dietrich, "Seeing Is Believing"; Turner et al., "Body Camera Footage."
16. Trabasso, "Power of the Narrative," 187–188.
17. See Mullinix, Bolsen, and Norris, "Feedback Effects."
18. There is debate as to whether Stalin ever actually said this, and there is little evidence that he did. However, it is a useful point for our purpose here. For more, see Norris, *Exonerated*, 142, 251n10.
19. See Norris, *Exonerated*, 142–143.
20. For two fascinating examples of the intersection between wrongful convictions and art, see Morse, "Valentino Dixon"; Smith, "I Have a Responsibility."
21. For more on exonerees and their involvement in the policy reform process, see Konvisser and Werry, "Exoneree Engagement."
22. See Witness to Innocence, "About."
23. At the time of this writing, the executive director of Witness to Innocence is Kirk Bloodsworth, whose case was discussed in detail in chapter 4. Other exoneree staff members include Shujaa Graham (peer organizer), Derrick Jamison (peer specialist), and Randal Padgett (older adult peer specialist). See Witness to Innocence, "Staff." A number of exonerees are also on the organization's board. See Witness to Innocence, "Board."
24. Keine, "Exoneree Initiatives and Innocence Reform," 119.
25. For more on the Deskovic Foundation, see deskovicfoundation.org. For more on Exonerated Nation, see exoneratednation.org. Our discussion only scratches the surface of how exonerees and their stories contribute to innocence organizations. For example, Korey Wise, one of the defendants who was wrongly convicted in the Central Park Jogger case, donated $190,000 to the innocence project at the University of Colorado Law School, and it has been renamed the Korey Wise Innocence Project. Further, immediately after the debut of the immensely popular Netflix miniseries *When They See Us*, which covered the Central Park Jogger case, donations to the Colorado-based group increased tenfold. McGhee, "Korey Wise's Donation." For a more general, academic discussion of exoneree involvement in policy reform, see Konvisser, "Exoneree Engagement."
26. Information about the case comes from the National Registry of Exonerations' case profile: Innocence Project and Maurice Possley, "Timothy B. Cole."
27. Norris, "Exoneree Compensation," 299.
28. The Innocence Protection Act was part of the larger 2004 Justice for All Act, which also included provisions about victims' rights and defense counsel in

capital cases. See American Civil Liberties Union, "H.R. 5107." For more on Maryland, see Cassie, "Innocent Man."

29. See Grissom, "Perry Signs Michael Morton Act."
30. For more on Bunch's compensation battle, see Chapman, "Legal Panel Approves Payouts." For more on Bunch and Rivera's organization, Justis 4 Justus, see its website at justis4justus.org.
31. See Adams, "New 'Central Park Five' Law."
32. For more on the power of narratives as related to innocence advocacy, see Norris and Mullinix, "In Exonerations."
33. See Mullinix, Bolsen, and Norris, "Feedback Effects."
34. Rebecca Brown, interview with Robert Norris, February 10, 2021.
35. Brown, interview Norris.
36. Norris, *Exonerated*, 169.
37. Norris, *Exonerated*, 172.
38. Drizin, quoted in Norris, *Exonerated*, 172.
39. Brown, interview with Norris.
40. Brown, interview with Norris.
41. Brown, interview with Norris.
42. Brown, interview with Norris.
43. Brown, interview with Norris.
44. Brown, interview with Norris.
45. Brown, interview with Norris.

APPENDIX
1. For example, we find evidence that the presence of innocence organizations increases the odds that a state adopts laws addressing the recording of interrogations, evidence preservation, and exoneree compensation. However, we fail to find evidence that organizations are associated with eyewitness procedures or post-conviction DNA testing. On the other hand, we find evidence that public opinion and electoral competition exert a significant effect only on evidence preservation and eyewitness reforms.
2. See Andersen and Gill, "Cox's Regression Model." See also Andersen et al., *Statistical Models*.
3. We also evaluated an AR1 against an AR2 and MA1 (moving average 1), and model fit statistics imply that the AR1 is definitely preferable.
4. See Caughey and Warshaw, "Policy Preferences and Policy Change." Like our measure of public opinion liberalism, we had to forecast the values of state party identification for 2015, 2016, and 2017. We used the same approach: in each state and year, we model the share of the population that identifies with the Democratic Party. Our dynamic panel model uses fixed effects for states and incorporates time with a cubic polynomial for year. The cubic effect of time is statistically significant ($p < 0.01$), and we use it to forecast estimates in each state for 2015–2017.

5. For state-years 2011 and earlier, we derive the data from Klarner, "State Legislative Election Returns." We supplement more recent years with the Council of State Governments' *Book of the States*.

6. We used Squire's legislative professionalism scores in all fifty states for 2015, 2009, 2003, 1996, and 1986. In each state and year, we used the most recent, prior or contemporaneous value of legislative professionalism (i.e., Alabama's professionalism score in 2014 is the same as it was for 2009, but it changes in 2015 marginally). The 2015 and 2009 values were derived from Squire, "Squire Index Update." All prior values were derived from Squire, "Measuring State Legislative Professionalism."

7. See, for example, Epp, *Structure of Policy Change*.

8. See, for example, Carey et al., "Effects of Term Limits."

9. See Hicks, "Partisan Competition."

10. Data for 1988–2014 were accessed using the Federal Bureau of Investigation's "Summary Reporting System: Estimated Crimes"; data from 2015–2017 were accessed using the Federal Bureau of Investigation's *Crime in the United States* 2016 and 2017 annual publications.

11. This resource can be accessed at https://usa.ipums.org.

BIBLIOGRAPHY

Aaroe, Lene. "Investigating Frame Strength: The Case of Episodic and Thematic Frames." *Political Communication* 28, no. 2 (2011): 207–226.

Acker, James R. "The Flipside Injustice of Wrongful Convictions." *Albany Law Review* 76, no. 3 (2012–2013): 1629–1712.

Acker, James R., and Allison D. Redlich. *Wrongful Conviction: Law, Science, and Policy.* Durham, NC: Carolina Academic Press, 2011.

Adams, Rose. "New 'Central Park Five' Law Requires Cops to Videotape Juvenile Interrogations." *Brooklyn Paper*, December 14, 2020. www.brooklynpaper.com.

Alexander-Bloch, Benjamin, Molly A. Miller, Megan M. Zeringue, and Sonia L. Rubens. "Mental Health Characteristics of Exonerees: A Preliminary Exploration." *Psychology, Crime, and Law* 26, no. 8 (2020): 768–775.

American Civil Liberties Union. "H.R. 5107: The Justice for All Act of 2004." Accessed October 6, 2020. www.aclu.org.

Andersen, Per Kragh, Ornulf Borgan, Richard D. Gill, and Niels Keiding. *Statistical Models Based on Counting Processes.* New York: Springer, 2012.

Andersen, Per Kragh, and Richard D. Gill. "Cox's Regression Model for Counting Processes: A Large Sample Study." *Annals of Statistics* 10, no. 4 (1982): 1100–1120.

Applegate, Brandon K., and Joseph B. Sanborn. "Public Opinion on the Harshness of Local Courts: An Experimental Test of Question Wording Effects." *Criminal Justice Review* 36, no. 4 (2011): 487–497.

Aronson, Jay D. *Genetic Witness: Science, Law, and Controversy in the Making of DNA Profiling.* New Brunswick, NJ: Rutgers University Press, 2007.

Associated Press. "$9M Settlement for 2 Men Wrongfully Sent to Death Row." *AP News*, May 14, 2021. https://apnews.com.

Azevedo, Flávio, and John T. Jost. "The Ideological Basis of Antiscientific Attitudes: Effects of Authoritarianism, Conservatism, Religiosity, Social Dominance, and System Justification." *Group Processes and Intergroup Relations* 24, no. 4 (2021): 518–549.

Bailey, Chelsea. "Adnan Syed and Serial: What You Need to Know." *BBC News*, October 11, 2022. www.bbc.com.

Barrilleaux, Charles, Thomas Holbrook, and Laura Langer. "Electoral Competition, Legislative Balance, and American State Welfare Policy." *American Journal of Political Science* 46, no. 2 (2002): 415–427.

Bartels, Larry M. "Beyond the Running Tally: Partisan Bias in Political Perceptions." *Political Behavior* 24, no. 2 (2002): 117–150.

Baumgartner, Frank R., Suzanna L. De Boef, and Amber E. Boydstun. *The Decline of the Death Penalty and the Discovery of Innocence*. New York: Cambridge University Press, 2008.

Baumgartner, Frank R., Amanda Grigg, Rachelle Ramirez, and J. Sawyer Lucy. "The Mayhem of Wrongful Liberty: Documenting the Crimes of True Perpetrators in Cases of Wrongful Incarceration." *Albany Law Review* 81, no. 4 (2017–2018): 1263–1288.

Baumgartner, Frank R., and Bryan D. Jones. *Agendas and Instability in American Politics*. Chicago: University of Chicago Press, 2010.

Baumgartner, Frank R., Saundra D. Westervelt, and Kimberly J. Cook. "Public Policy Responses to Wrongful Convictions." In *Examining Wrongful Convictions: Stepping Back, Moving Forward*, edited by Allison D. Redlich, James R. Acker, Robert J. Norris, and Catherine L. Bonventre, 251–266. Durham, NC: Carolina Academic Press.

Bayne, Gregory, dir. *Bloodsworth: An Innocent Man*. Kino Lorber, 2016.

Bazelon, Lara. "The Innocence Deniers." *Slate*, January 10, 2018. https://slate.com.

Beals, Monique. "Maryland Awards Exonerated Former Death Row Inmate $400k." *The Hill*, October 7, 2021. https://thehill.com.

Beckett, Katherine. *Making Crime Pay: Law and Order in Contemporary American Politics*. New York: Oxford University Press, 1997.

Bedau, Hugo Adam, and Michael L. Radelet. "Miscarriages of Justice in Potentially Capital Cases." *Stanford Law Review* 40, no. 1 (1987): 21–179.

Bennett, Anita. "'When They See Us' Watched by More than 23 Million Netflix Accounts Worldwide." *Deadline*, June 25, 2019. https://deadline.com.

Bennett, W. Lance, and Shanto Iyengar. "A New Era of Minimal Effects? The Changing Foundations of Political Communication." *Journal of Communication* 58, no. 4 (2008): 707–731.

Bernhard, Adele. "Justice Still Fails: A Review of Recent Efforts to Compensate Individuals Who Have Been Unjustly Convicted and Later Exonerated." *Drake Law Review* 52 (2004): 703–738.

———. "A Short Overview of the Statutory Remedies for the Wrongly Convicted: What Works, What Doesn't, and Why." *Boston University Public Interest Law Journal* 18 (2009): 403–425.

———. "When Justice Fails: Indemnification for Unjust Conviction." *University of Chicago Law School Roundtable* 6, no. 1 (1999): 73–112.

Berry, William D., Michael B. Berkman, and Stuart Schneiderman. "Legislative Professionalism and Incumbent Reelection: The Development of Institutional Boundaries." *American Political Science Review* 94, no. 4 (2000): 859–874.

Beyer, Daniela, and Miriam Hanni. "Two Sides of the Same Coin? Congruence and Responsiveness as Representative Democracy's Currencies." *Policy Studies Journal* 46, no. S1 (2018): S13–S47.

Bobo, Lawrence D., and Devon Johnson. "A Taste for Punishment: Black and White Americans' Views on the Death Penalty and the War on Drugs." *Du Bois Review* 1, no. 1 (2004): 151–180.

Borchard, Edwin M. *Convicting the Innocent: Errors of Criminal Justice*. New Haven, CT: Yale University Press, 1932.

———. "European Systems of State Indemnity for Errors of Criminal Justice." *Journal of the American Institute of Criminal Law and Criminology* 3, no. 5 (1913): 684–718.

———. "State Indemnity for Errors of Criminal Justice." *Boston University Law Review* 21, no. 2 (1941): 201–211.

Boudreau, Cheryl, Scott A. MacKenzie, and Daniel J. Simmons. "Police Violence and Public Perceptions: An Experimental Study of How Information and Endorsements Affect Support for Law Enforcement." *Journal of Politics* 81, no. 3 (2019): 1101–1110.

Boyer, Paul, and Stephen Nissenbaum. *Salem Possessed: The Social Origins of Witchcraft*. Cambridge, MA: Harvard University Press, 1974.

Braga, Anthony A. "Better Policing Can Improve Legitimacy and Reduce Mass Incarceration." *Harvard Law Review Forum* 129 (2016): 233–241.

Breyer, Charles R., Danny C. Reeves, Patricia K. Cushwa, and Candice C. Wong. *2020 Annual Report and Sourcebook of Federal Sentencing Statistics*. Washington, DC: United States Sentencing Commission. www.ussc.gov.

Britt, Chester L. "Race, Religion, and Support for the Death Penalty: A Research Note." *Justice Quarterly* 15, no. 1 (1998): 175–191.

Bromwich, Jonah E., and Troy Closson. "After Key Evidence Was Withheld, 2 Men Spent 3 Decades in Prison." *New York Times*, August 9, 2021. www.nytimes.com.

Brooks, Justin, Alexander Simpson, and Paige Kaneb. "If Hindsight Is 20/20, Our Justice System Should Not Be Blind to New Evidence of Innocence: A Survey of Post-Conviction New Evidence Statutes and a Proposed Model." *Albany Law Review* 79, no. 3 (2015–2016): 1045–1090.

Brown, Ben, and Wm. Reed Benedict. "Perceptions of the Police: Past Findings, Methodological Issues, Conceptual Issues and Policy Implications." *Policing: An International Journal* 25, no. 3 (2002): 543–580.

Burns, Sarah. *The Central Park Five: A Chronicle of a City Wilding*. New York: Knopf, 2011.

Burstein, Paul. "The Impact of Public Opinion on Public Policy: A Review and an Agenda." *Political Research Quarterly* 56, no. 1 (2003): 29–40.

Busby, Ethan, D. J. Flynn, and James N. Druckman. "Studying Framing Effects on Political Preferences: Existing Research and Lingering Questions." In *Doing News Framing Analysis II: Empirical and Theoretical Perspectives*, edited by Paul D'Angelo, 27–50. New York: Routledge, 2018.

Byfield, Natalie P. *Savage Portrayals: Race, Media, and the Central Park Jogger Story*. Philadelphia: Temple University Press, 2014.

Campbell, Kathryn M. "Exoneration and Compensation for the Wrongly Convicted: Enhancing Procedural Justice?" *Manitoba Law Journal* 42, no. 3 (2019): 249–279.

Carey, John M., Richard G. Niemi, Lynda W. Powell, and Gary F. Moncrief. "The Effects of Term Limits on State Legislatures: A New Survey of the 50 States." *Legislative Studies Quarterly* 31, no. 1 (2006): 105–134.

Carroll, Royce, and Jason Eichorst. "The Role of Party: The Legislative Consequences of Partisan Competition." *Legislative Studies Quarterly* 38, no. 1 (2013): 83–109.

Carter, Andrew. "Jury Awards Wrongfully Convicted NC Brothers $75 Million in Federal Civil Rights Case." *Charlotte (NC) News & Observer*, May 14, 2021.

Carter, Rubin, and Ken Klonsky. *Eye of the Hurricane: My Path from Darkness to Freedom.* Chicago: Lawrence Hill Books, 2011.

Cassie, Ron. "An Innocent Man." *Baltimore Magazine*, November 2013. www .baltimoremagazine.com.

Caughey, Devin, and Christopher Warshaw. "Policy Preferences and Policy Change: Dynamic Responsiveness in the American States, 1936–2014." *American Political Science Review* 112, no. 2 (2018): 249–266.

Chapman, Sandra. "Legal Panel Approves Payouts for Wrongfully Convicted." *WTHR*, October 19, 2020. www.wthr.com.

Chong, Dennis, and James N. Druckman. "Framing Theory." *Annual Review of Political Science* 10 (2007): 103–126.

Chong, Dennis, and Kevin J. Mullinix. "Information and Issue Constraints on Party Cues." *American Politics Research* 47, no. 6 (2019): 1209–1238.

Clark, Mackenzie. "Floyd Bledsoe Shares What Life Is Like 5 Years after Exoneration." *Lawrence (KS) Journal-World*, December 6, 2020. www2.ljworld.com.

Cobb, Jelani. "The Central Park Five, Criminal Justice, and Donald Trump." *New Yorker*, April 19, 2019. www.newyorker.com.

Cohen, Andrew. "Wrongful Convictions: A New Exoneration Registry Tests Stubborn Judges." *Atlantic*, May 21, 2012. www.theatlantic.com.

Cohen, Jonathan, Nurit Tal-Or, and Maya Mazor-Tregerman. "The Tempering Effect of Transportation: Exploring the Effects of Transportation and Identification during Exposure to Controversial Two-Sided Narratives." *Journal of Communication* 65, no. 2 (2015): 237–258.

Cole, David. *No Equal Justice: Race and Class in the American Criminal Justice System.* New York: New Press, 1999.

Cole, Simon A. "Forensic Science and Wrongful Convictions: From Exposer to Contributor to Corrector." *New England Law Review* 46 (2012): 711–736.

Conklin, Audrey. "Julius Jones: Oklahoma Governor Grants Clemency to DeathRow Inmate Amid Public Pressure." *Fox News*, November 18, 2021. www.foxnews.com.

Connors, Edward, Thomas Lundregan, Neal Miller, and Tom McEwen. *Convicted by Juries, Exonerated by Science: Case Studies in the Use of DNA Evidence to Establish Innocence after Trial.* Washington, DC: National Institute of Justice, June 1996. www .ncjrs.gov.

Conroy, John, and Rob Warden. *Special Investigation: The High Costs of Wrongful Convictions.* Chicago: Better Government Association, June 18, 2011. www.bettergov .org.

Council of State Governments. *Book of the States.* Vols. 43–50 (2011–2018). https://issuu .com.

Covey, Russell D., and Valena E. Beety, eds. *Wrongful Convictions Reader*. Durham, NC: Carolina Academic Press, 2019.

Cretton, Destin Daniel, dir. *Just Mercy*. Warner Brothers, 2019.

Dardis, Frank E., Frank R. Baumgartner, Amber E. Boydstun, Suzanna De Boef, and Fuyuan Shen. "Media Framing of Capital Punishment and Its Impact on Individuals' Cognitive Responses." *Mass Communication and Society* 11 (2008): 115–140.

De Graaf, Anneke, Hans Hoeken, José Sanders, and Johannes W. J. Beentjes. "Identification as a Mechanism of Narrative Persuasion." *Communication Research* 39, no. 6 (2012): 802–823.

Death Penalty Information Center. "Death Sentences in the United States since 1977." Accessed February 6, 2022. https://deathpenaltyinfo.org.

———. "DPIC Summary: The Innocence Protection Act of 2004." Accessed February 6, 2022. https://deathpenaltyinfo.org.

———. "Executions by State and Region since 1976." Accessed February 6, 2022. https://deathpenaltyinfo.org.

———. "Innocence." Accessed February 6, 2022. https://deathpenaltyinfo.org.

———. "Maryland." Accessed February 6, 2022. https://deathpenaltyinfo.org.

Drizin, Steven A., and Richard A. Leo. "The Problem of False Confessions in the Post-DNA World." *North Carolina Law Review* 82, no. 3 (2004): 891–1007.

Elkins, Emily E. "Policing in America: Understanding Public Attitudes toward the Police. Results from a National Survey." Accessed July 12, 2022. https://papers.ssrn.com.

Epp, Charles R., Steven Maynard-Moody, and Donald Haider-Markel. *Pulled Over: How Police Stops Define Race and Citizenship*. Chicago: The University of Chicago Press, 2014.

Epp, Derek A. *The Structure of Policy Change*. Chicago: University of Chicago Press, 2018.

Erikson, Robert S., Michael B. MacKuen, and James A. Stimson. *The Macro Polity*. New York: Cambridge University Press, 2002.

Erikson, Robert S., Gerald C. Wright, and John P. McIver. *Statehouse Democracy: Public Opinion and Policy in the American States*. New York: Cambridge University Press, 1994.

ESPN. "Death Sentence for Julius Jones Reduced to Life in Prison by Oklahoma Governor." November 18, 2021. www.espn.com.

Fan, David P., Kathy A. Keltner, and Robert O. Wyatt. "A Matter of Guilt or Innocence: How News Reports Affect Support for the Death Penalty in the United States." *International Journal of Public Opinion Research*, 14, no. 4 (2002): 439–452.

Federal Bureau of Investigation. "Summary Reporting System: Estimated Crimes." *Crime Data Explorer*. Accessed February 15, 2020. https://crime-data-explorer.fr.cloud.gov.

———. "Table 2: Crime in the United States by Region, Geographic Division, and State, 2015–2016." *Crime in the United States*. Accessed February 15, 2020. https://ucr.fbi.gov.

————. "Table 4: Crime in the United States by Region, Geographic Division, and State, 2016–2017." *Crime in the United States*. Accessed February 15, 2020. https://ucr.fbi .gov.

Feld, Barry C. *Kids, Cops, and Confessions: Inside the Interrogation Room*. New York: New York University Press, 2012.

Feuer, Alan. "Falsely Imprisoned for 23 Years: New He's Received $7 Million." *New York Times*, March 5, 2021. www.nytimes.com.

Findley, Keith A. "Innocence Found: The New Revolution in American Criminal Justice." In *Controversies in Innocence Cases in America*, edited by Sarah Lucy Cooper, 3–20. New York: Routledge, 2014.

————. "Toward a New Paradigm of Criminal Justice: How the Innocence Movement Merges Crime Control and Due Process." *Texas Tech Law Review* 41, no. 1 (2008): 133–173.

Fridman, Ariel, Rachel Gershon, and Ayelet Gneezy. "COVID-19 and Vaccine Hesitancy: A Longitudinal Study." *PLOS One*, 2021. https://journals.plos.org.

Gallup. "Confidence in Institutions." Accessed July 12, 2022. https://news.gallup.com.

————. "Death Penalty." Accessed February 6, 2022. https://news.gallup.com.

Gamson, William A., and Andre Modigliani. "Media Discourse and Public Opinion on Nuclear Power: A Constructionist Approach." *American Journal of Sociology* 95, no. 1 (1989): 1–37.

Gardner, Erle Stanley. *The Court of Last Resort*. New York: William Sloane, 1952.

Garrett, Brandon L. *Convicting the Innocent: Where Criminal Prosecutions Go Wrong*. Cambridge, MA: Harvard University Press, 2012.

Gerber, Monica M., and Jonathan Jackson. "Authority and Punishment: On the Ideological Basis of Punitive Attitudes toward Criminals." *Psychiatry, Psychology, and Law* 23, no. 1 (2016): 113–134.

————. "Justifying Violence: Legitimacy, Ideology, and Public Support for Police Use of Force." *Psychology, Crime, and Law* 23, no. 1 (2017): 79–95.

Gould, Jon B., and Richard A. Leo. "One Hundred Years Later: Wrongful Convictions after a Century of Research." *Journal of Criminal Law and Criminology* 100, no. 3 (2010): 825–868.

Gramlich, John. "Only 2% of Federal Criminal Defendants Go to Trial, and Most Who Do Are Found Guilty." Pew Research Center, June 11, 2019. www.pewresearch.org.

Grann, David. "Trial by Fire." *New Yorker*, August 31, 2009. www.newyorker.com.

Green, Melanie C., and Timothy C. Brock. "The Role of Transportation in the Persuasiveness of Public Narratives." *Journal of Personality and Social Psychology* 79, no. 5 (2000): 701–721.

Griffiths, Elizabeth, and Michael Leo Owens. "Remedying Wrongful Convictions: Societal Obligations to Exonerees." In *Examining Wrongful Convictions: Stepping Back, Moving Forward*, edited by Allison D. Redlich, James R. Acker, Robert J. Norris, and Catherine L. Bonventre, 267–282. Durham, NC: Carolina Academic Press.

Grisham, John. *The Confession*. New York: Doubleday, 2010.

————. Foreword to *When Truth Is All You Have: A Memoir of Faith, Justice and Freedom for the Wrongly Convicted*, by Jim McCloskey with Philip Lerman, ix–xii. New York: Doubleday, 2020.

————. *The Guardians*. New York: Doubleday, 2019.

————. *The Innocent Man*. New York: Doubleday, 2006.

Grissom, Brandi. "Perry Signs Michael Morton Act." *Texas Tribune*, May 16, 2013. www.texastribune.org.

Gromet, Dena M., and John M. Darley. "Political Ideology and Reactions to Crime Victims: Preferences for Restorative and Punitive Responses." *Journal of Empirical Legal Studies* 8, no. 4 (2011): 830–855.

Gross, Samuel R., Kristen Jacoby, Daniel J. Matheson, Nicholas Montgomery, and Sujata Patil. "Exonerations in the United States 1989 through 2003." *Journal of Criminal Law and Criminology* 95, no. 2 (2005): 523–560.

Gross, Samuel R., Barbara O'Brien, Chen Hu, and Edward H. Kennedy. "Rate of False Conviction of Criminal Defendants Who Are Sentenced to Death." *Proceedings of the National Academy of Sciences* 111, no. 20 (2014): 7230–7235.

Gross, Samuel R., Maurice Possley, and Klara Stephens. *Race and Wrongful Convictions*. Irvine, CA: National Registry of Exonerations, March 7, 2017. www.law.umich.edu.

Grounds, Adrian. "Psychological Consequences of Wrongful Conviction and Imprisonment." *Canadian Journal of Criminology and Criminal Justice* 46, no. 2 (2004): 165–182.

Gutman, Jeffrey S. "An Empirical Reexamination of State Statutory Compensation for the Wrongly Convicted." *Missouri Law Review* 82, no. 2 (2017): 369–440.

Gutman, Jeffrey S., and Lingxiao Sun. "Why Is Mississippi the Best State in Which to Be Exonerated? An Empirical Evaluation of State Statutory and Civil Compensation for the Wrongfully Convicted." *Northeastern University Law Review* 11, no. 2 (2019): 694–789.

Harkin, Diarmaid. "Police Legitimacy, Ideology and Qualitative Methods: A Critique of Procedural Justice Theory." *Criminology and Criminal Justice* 15, no. 5 (2015): 594–612.

Hawdon, James E., John Ryan, and Sean P. Griffin. "Policing Tactics and Perceptions of Police Legitimacy." *Police Quarterly* 6, no. 4 (2003): 469–491.

Henry, Jessica S. *Smoke but No Fire: Convicting the Innocent of Crimes That Never Happened*. Oakland: University of California Press, 2020.

Hesse, Monica. "'Serial' Takes the Stand: How a Podcast Became a Character in its Own Narrative." *Washington Post*, February 8, 2016. www.washingtonpost.com.

Hicks, William D. "Partisan Competition and the Efficiency of Lawmaking in American State Legislatures, 1991–2009." *American Politics Research* 43, no. 5 (2015): 743–770.

Hicks, William D., Kevin J. Mullinix, and Robert J. Norris. "The Politics of Wrongful Conviction Legislation." *State Politics and Policy Quarterly* 21, no. 3 (2021): 306–325.

Hicks, William D., Carol Weissert, Jeffrey Swanson, Jessica Bulman-Pozen, Vladimir
   Kogan, Lori Riverstone-Newell, Jaclyn Bunch, Katherine Levine Einstein, David
   Glick, and Dorothy M. Daley. "Home Rule Be Damned: Exploring Policy Con-
   flicts between the Statehouse and City Hall." *PS: Political Science & Politics* 51, no. 1
   (2018): 26–38.
Hinds, Lyn, and Kristina Murphy. "Public Satisfaction with Police: Using Procedural
   Justice to Improve Police Legitimacy." *Australian & New Zealand Journal of Crimi-
   nology* 40, no. 1 (2007): 27–42.
Hinton, Anthony Ray, and Lara Love Hardin. *The Sun Does Shine: How I Found Life
   and Freedom on Death Row*. New York: St. Martin's, 2018.
Hirsch, James S. *Hurricane: The Miraculous Journey of Rubin Carter*. New York:
   Houghton Mifflin, 2000.
Hogan, Robert E. "Challenger Emergence, Incumbent Success, and Electoral Account-
   ability in State Legislative Elections." *Journal of Politics* 66, no. 4 (2004): 1283–1303.
Holbert, R. Lance, Jay D. Hmielowski, and Brian E. Weeks. "Clarifying Relationships
   between Ideology and Ideologically Oriented Cable TV News Use: A Case of Sup-
   pression." *Communication Research* 39, no. 2 (2012): 194–216.
Holbrook, Thomas M., and Emily Van Dunk. "Electoral Competition in the American
   States." *American Political Science Review* 87, no. 4 (1993): 955–962.
Horwitz, Jonah, and Rob Warden. "David Vasquez." National Registry of Exonerations.
   Last updated March 11, 2014. www.law.umich.edu.
Huff, C. Ronald, and Martin Killias, eds. *Wrongful Conviction: International Perspec-
   tives on Miscarriages of Justice*. Philadelphia: Temple University Press, 2009.
Innocence Network. "Network Member Organization Locator and Directory." Ac-
   cessed February 5, 2022. https://innocencenetwork.org.
———. "Who We Are." Accessed February 5, 2022. https://innocencenetwork.org.
Innocence Project. "Access to Post-Conviction DNA Testing." Accessed February 5,
   2022. https://innocenceproject.org.
———. "Gary Dotson." Accessed October 5, 2020. www.innocenceproject.org.
———. "Innocence Project Applauds Congress for Passage of the Wrongful Convic-
   tions Tax Relief Act of 2015." December 18, 2015. www.innocenceproject.org.
———. "Policy Reform." Accessed February 5, 2022. www.innocenceproject.org.
———. "Preservation of Evidence." Accessed February 5, 2022. https://innocenceproject
   .org.
———. "Texas." Accessed November 3, 2022. https://innocenceproject.org.
———. "Timothy Cole." Accessed November 3, 2022. https://innocenceproject.org.
Innocence Project, and Maurice Possley. "Timothy B. Cole." National Registry of Exon-
   erations. Last updated March 10, 2015. www.law.umich.edu.
Innocence Staff. "Gov. Stitt Grants Julius Jones Clemency—8 Facts You Need to Know
   about His Case." Innocence Project, September 1, 2021. https://innocenceproject
   .org.
———. "What to Expect from 'The Innocence Files,' Netflix's New Documentary Series." Innocence Project, April 15, 2020. www.innocenceproject.org.

Iyengar, Shanto. "Framing Responsibility for Political Issues." *Annals of the American Academy of Political and Social Science* 546 (1996): 59–70.

———. *Is Anyone Responsible? How Television Frames Political Issues.* Chicago: University of Chicago Press, 1991.

Iyengar, Shanto, and Donald R. Kinder. *News That Matters: Television and American Opinion, Updated Edition.* Chicago: University of Chicago Press, 2010.

Jackman, Tom. "More than Half of All Wrongful Criminal Convictions Are Caused by Government Misconduct, Study Finds." *Washington Post*, September 16, 2020. www.washingtonpost.com.

Jacoby, William G. "Issue Framing and Public Opinion on Government Spending." *American Journal of Political Science* 44, no. 4 (2000): 750–767.

———. "Public Attitudes toward Government Spending." *American Journal of Political Science* 38, no. 2 (1994): 336–361.

Jones, Tayari. *An American Marriage.* Chapel Hill, NC: Algonquin Books.

Junkin, Tim. *Bloodsworth.* Chapel Hill, NC: Algonquin Books, 2004.

Kaeble, Danielle, and Mary Cowhig. *Correctional Populations in the United States, 2016.* Washington, DC: US Department of Justice, April 2018. www.bjs.gov.

Karch, Andrew. *Democratic Laboratories: Policy Diffusion among the American States.* Ann Arbor: University of Michigan Press, 2007.

Kassin, Saul M., Steven A. Drizin, Thomas Grisso, Gisli H. Gudjonsson, Richard A. Leo, and Allison D. Redlich. "Police-Induced Confessions: Risk Factors and Recommendations." *Law and Human Behavior* 34, no. 1 (2010): 3–38.

Keine, Ronald. "Exoneree Initiatives and Innocence Reform: Witness to Innocence." In *Wrongful Conviction and Criminal Justice Reform: Making Justice*, edited by Marvin Zalman and Julia Carrano, 111–123. New York: Routledge.

Keith, Erin Y. H. "Wronged without Recourse: Examining Shortcomings of Compensation Statutes for Black Exonerees." *Georgetown Journal of Law and Modern Critical Race Perspectives* 8 (2016): 335–352.

Kennedy, Dolores. "Gary Dotson." National Registry of Exonerations. Accessed March 12, 2020. www.law.umich.edu.

Kent, Stephanie L., and Jason T. Carmichael. "Legislative Responses to Wrongful Conviction: Do Partisan Principals and Advocacy Efforts Influence State-Level Criminal Justice Policy?" *Social Science Research* 52 (2015): 147–160.

Khan, A. "Getting Killed by Police Is a Leading Cause of Death for Young Black Men in America." *Los Angeles Times*, August 16, 2019. www.latimes.com.

Kingdon, John W. *Agendas, Alternatives, and Public Policies.* New York: Longman, 2010.

Klarner, Carl. "State Legislative Election Returns, 1967–2016." *Harvard Dataverse*, 2018. https://doi.org/10.7910/DVN/3WZFK9.

Konvisser, Zieva, and Ashley Werry. "Exoneree Engagement in Policy Reform Work: An Exploratory Study of the Innocence Movement Policy Reform Process." *Journal of Contemporary Criminal Justice* 33, no. 1 (2017): 43–60.

Krumpal, Ivar. "Determinants of Social Desirability Bias in Sensitive Surveys: A Literature Review." *Quality and Quantity* 47 (2013): 2025–2047.

Lambert, Eric G., Scott D. Camp, Alan Clarke, and Shanhe Jiang. "The Impact of Information on Death Penalty Support, Revisited." *Crime & Delinquency* 57, no. 4 (2011): 572–599.

Lambert, Eric G., and Alan Clarke. "The Impact of Information on an Individual's Support of the Death Penalty: A Partial Test of the Marshall Hypothesis among College Students." *Criminal Justice Policy Review* 12, no. 3 (2001): 215–234.

Larson, Sarah. "'Serial': The Podcast We've Been Waiting For." *New Yorker*, October 9, 2014. www.newyorker.com.

Leo, Richard A. "The Criminology of Wrongful Conviction: A Decade Later." *Journal of Contemporary Criminal Justice* 33, no. 1 (2017): 82–106.

———. *Police Interrogation and American Justice*. Cambridge, MA: Harvard University Press, 2009.

———. "Rethinking the Study of Miscarriages of Justice: Developing a Criminology of Wrongful Conviction." *Journal of Contemporary Criminal Justice* 21, no. 3 (2005): 201–223.

Leo, Richard A., and Jon B. Gould. "Studying Wrongful Convictions: Learning from Social Science." *Ohio State Journal of Criminal Law* 7 (2009): 7–30.

Levenson, Michael. "Judge Vacates Murder Conviction of Adnan Syed of 'Serial.'" *New York Times*, October 11, 2022. www.nytimes.com.

Levenson, Michael, Maria Cramer, and Simon Romero. "Oklahoma Governor Commutes Inmate's Death Sentence Hours Before Execution." *New York Times*, November 18, 2021. www.nytimes.com.

Levy, Ariel. "The Price of a Life." *New Yorker*, April 6, 2015. www.newyorker.com.

Lewandowsky, Stephan, and Klaus Oberauer. "Many Conservatives Have a Difficult Relationship with Science—We Wanted to Find Out Why." *The Conversation*, August 9, 2021. https://theconversation.com.

———. "Motivated Rejection of Science." *Current Directions in Psychological Science* 25, no. 4 (2016): 217–222.

Loeffler, Charles E., Jordan Hyatt, and Greg Ridgeway. "Measuring Self-Reported Wrongful Convictions among Prisoners." *Journal of Quantitative Criminology* 5, no. 2 (2018): 259–286.

Lopez, Robert. "Authors Discuss Wrongful Convictions, Death Penalty." *Greensboro News and Record*, July 31, 2014. www.greensboro.com.

Lord, Charles G., Lee Ross, and Mark R. Lepper. "Biased Assimilation and Attitude Polarization: The Effects of Prior Theories on Subsequently Considered Evidence." *Journal of Personality and Social Psychology* 37, no. 11 (1979): 2098–2109.

Madrigal, Andrew J., and Robert J. Norris. "The Good, the Bad, and the Uncertain: Wrongful Convictions, State Harm, and the Aftermath of Exoneration." Unpublished manuscript on file with author.

Marshall, Lawrence C. "The Innocence Revolution and the Death Penalty." *Ohio State Journal of Criminal Law* 1 (2004): 1573–1584.

McCloskey, Jim, with Philip Lerman. *When Truth Is All You Have: A Memoir of Faith, Justice and Freedom for the Wrongly Convicted*. New York: Doubleday, 2020.

McGhee, Tom. "Korey Wise's Donation Gave CU's Innocence Project Real Power: A Netflix Series on the Central Park 5 Is Making It Even Stronger." *Colorado Sun*, July 4, 2019. https://coloradosun.com.

Medwed, Daniel S. "Emotionally Charged: The Prosecutorial Charging Decision and the Innocence Revolution." *Cardozo Law Review* 31, no. 6 (2010): 2187–2213.

———. "Innocentrism." *University of Illinois Law Review* 2008 (2008): 1549–1572.

"Meese's Miranda Reply Shocking to Law Experts." *Chicago Tribune*, October 10, 1985.

Miller, Walter B. "Ideology and Criminal Justice Policy: Some Current Issues." *Journal of Criminal Law and Criminology* 64, no. 2 (1973): 141–162.

Mooney, Christopher Z., and Richard G. Schuldt. "Does Morality Policy Exist? Testing a Basic Assumption." *Policy Studies Journal* 36, no. 2 (2008): 199–218.

Morgan, Jerome. "I Was Wrongfully Imprisoned by a Nonunanimous Jury." *Slate*, December 10, 2020. https://slate.com.

Morse, Ben. "Valentino Dixon: He Was Convicted for a Crime He Didn't Commit: Now He's Selling Art to the Obamas." *CNN*, April 23, 2021. www.cnn.com.

Mullinix, Kevin J., Toby Bolsen, and Robert J. Norris. "The Feedback Effects of Controversial Police Use of Force." *Political Behavior* 43 (2021): 881–898.

Mullinix, Kevin J., and Robert J. Norris. "Pulled-Over Rates, Causal Attributions, and Trust in Police." *Political Research Quarterly* 72, no. 2 (2019): 420–434.

Natarajan, Ranjana. "Racial Profiling Has Destroyed Public Trust in Police: Cops Are Exploiting Our Weak Laws against It." *Washington Post*, December 15, 2014. www.washingtonpost.com.

National Institute of Justice. *Race, Trust, and Police Legitimacy*. January 9, 2013. https://nij.ojp.gov.

National Registry of Exonerations. "Glossary." Accessed January 21, 2022. www.law.umich.edu.

———. "Interactive Data Display." Accessed November 3, 2022. www.law.umich.edu.

———. "Longest Incarcerations." Accessed February 6, 2022. www.law.umich.edu.

Neal, Rome. "Life after Death Row." *CBS News*, March 5, 2001. www.cbsnews.com.

Nededog, Jethro. "Here's How Popular Netflix's 'Making a Murderer' Really Was According to a Research Company." *Yahoo Entertainment*, February 12, 2016. www.yahoo.com.

Nelson, Thomas E., Rosalee A. Clawson, and Zoe M. Oxley. "Media Framing of Civil Liberties Conflict and Its Effect on Tolerance." *American Political Science Review* 91, no. 3 (1997): 567–583.

Nisbett, Richard E., and Lee Ross. *Human Inference: Strategies and Shortcoming in Social Judgment*. Englewood Cliffs, NJ: Prentice-Hall, 1980.

Norris, Robert J. "Assessing Compensation Statutes for the Wrongly Convicted." *Criminal Justice Policy Review* 23, no. 3 (2012): 352–374.

———. *Exonerated: A History of the Innocence Movement*. New York: New York University Press, 2017.

———. "Exoneree Compensation: Current Policies and Future Outlook." In *Wrongful Conviction and Criminal Justice Reform: Making Justice*, edited by Marvin Zalman and Julia Carrano, 289–303. New York: Routledge.

———. "Framing DNA: Social Movement Theory and the Foundations of the Innocence Movement." *Journal of Contemporary Criminal Justice* 33, no. 1 (2017): 26–42.

———. "Theoretical Perspectives on Lawmaking and the Development of Wrongful
Conviction Policies: An Integrative Conflict Approach." Unpublished manuscript
on file with author, May 29, 2011.

Norris, Robert J., James R. Acker, Catherine L. Bonventre, and James R. Acker. "Thirty
Years of Innocence: Wrongful Convictions and Exonerations in the United States,
1989–2018." *Wrongful Convictions Law Review* 1, no. 1 (2020): 2–58.

Norris, Robert J., and Catherine L. Bonventre. "Advancing Wrongful Conviction Scholarship: Toward New Conceptual Frameworks." *Justice Quarterly* 32, no. 6 (2015): 929–949.

Norris, Robert J., Catherine L. Bonventre, and James R. Acker. *When Justice Fails:
Causes and Consequences of Wrongful Convictions*. Durham, NC: Carolina Academic Press, 2018.

Norris, Robert J., Catherine L. Bonventre, Allison D. Redlich, and James R. Acker.
"'Than That One Innocent Suffer': Evaluating State Safeguards against Wrongful
Convictions." *Albany Law Review* 74, no. 3 (2010–2011): 1301–1364.

Norris, Robert J., Catherine L. Bonventre, Allison D. Redlich, James R. Acker, and Car-
men Lowe. "Preventing Wrongful Convictions: An Analysis of State Investigation
Reforms." *Criminal Justice Policy Review* 30, no. 4 (2019): 597–626.

Norris, Robert J., and Kevin J. Mullinix. "Framing Innocence: An Experimental Test of
the Effects of Wrongful Convictions on Public Opinion." *Journal of Experimental
Criminology* 16 (2020): 311–334.

———. "In Exonerations, How You Communicate Matters." *Crime Report*, July 17, 2019.
https://thecrimereport.org.

Norris, Robert J., and Allison D. Redlich. "Seeking Justice, Compromising Truth?
Criminal Admissions and the Prisoner's Dilemma." *Albany Law Review* 77, no. 3
(2013–2014): 1005–1038.

Norris, Robert J., Jennifer N. Weintraub, James R. Acker, Allison D. Redlich, and Catherine L. Bonventre. "The Criminal Costs of Wrongful Convictions: Can We Reduce
Crime by Protecting the Innocent?" *Criminology and Public Policy* 19, no. 2 (2020):
367–388.

North Carolina Innocence Inquiry Commission. "About." Accessed January 4, 2022.
https://innocencecommission-nc.gov.

Norton, Mary Beth. *In the Devil's Snare: The Salem Witchcraft Crisis of 1692*. New York:
Vintage, 2002.

Owens, Michael Leo, and Elizabeth Griffiths. "Uneven Reparations for Wrongful
Convictions: Examining the State Politics of Statutory Compensation Legislation."
Albany Law Review 75, no. 3 (2011–2012): 1283–1327.

Packer, Herbert L. "Two Models of the Criminal Process." *University of Pennsylvania
Law Review* 113, no. 1 (1964): 1–68.

Park, Sung-Yeon, Kyle J. Holody, and Xiaoqun Zhang. "Race in Media Coverage of
School Shootings: A Parallel Application of Framing Theory and Attribute Agenda
Setting." *Journalism and Mass Communication Quarterly* 89, no. 3 (2012): 475–494.

Payne, Brian K., Randy R. Gainey, Ruth A. Triplett, and Mona J. E. Danner. "What Drives Punitive Beliefs? Demographic Characteristics and Justifications for Sentencing." *Journal of Criminal Justice* 32, no. 3 (2004): 195–206.

PBS. "What 'Serial'-mania Says about the Growing Popularity of Podcasts." *PBS News Hour*, December 11, 2014. www.pbs.org.

Peelo, Moira. "Framing Homicide Narratives in Newspapers: Mediated Witness and the Construction of Virtual Victimhood." *Crime, Media, Culture* 2, no. 2 (2006): 159–175.

Peffley, Mark, and Jon Hurwitz. "Persuasion and Resistance: Race and the Death Penalty in America." *American Journal of Political Science* 51, no. 4 (2007): 996–1012.

Pew Research Center. "Since 2015, Sharp Rise in Share of Republicans Saying Colleges Have a Negative Effect on the Country." July 19, 2017. www.pewresearch.org.

Phillips, Kristine. "Police Misconduct, Such as Falsifying Evidence, Is a Leading Cause of Wrongful Convictions, Study Finds." *USA Today*, September 15, 2020. www.usatoday.com.

Pickett, Justin T. "Public Opinion and Criminal Justice Policy: Theory and Research." *Annual Review of Criminology* 2 (2019): 405–428.

Pierce, Scott D. "'Serial' Podcast Success Shocked Even Its Creators." *Salt Lake Tribune*, March 30, 2017. https://archive.sltrib.com.

Possley, Maurice. "Floyd Bledsoe." National Registry of Exonerations. Last updated May 24, 2019. www.law.umich.edu.

———. "Henry McCollum." National Registry of Exonerations. Last updated September 2, 2015. www.law.umich.edu.

———. "Leon Brown." National Registry of Exonerations. Last updated September 2, 2015. www.law.umich.edu.

Price, Vincent, and David Tewksbury. "News Values and Public Opinion: A Theoretical Account of Media Priming and Framing." In *Progress in the Communication Sciences*, edited by George A. Barnett and Franklin J. Boster, 173–212. Greenwich, CT: Ablex, 1997.

Prior, Markus. "You've Either Got It or You Don't? The Stability of Political Interest over the Life Cycle." *Journal of Politics* 72, no. 3 (2010): 747–766.

Quah, Nicholas. "*Serial* Season 3 Is the Podcast's Biggest Ever." *Vulture*, December 3, 2018. www.vulture.com.

Radelet, Michael L. "The Role of the Innocence Argument in Contemporary Death Penalty Debates." *Texas Tech Law Review* 41 (2008–2009): 199–220.

Ramirez, Mark D. "Punitive Sentiment." *Criminology* 51, no. 2 (2013): 329–364.

Redlich, Allison D., James R. Acker, Robert J. Norris, and Catherine L. Bonventre, eds. *Examining Wrongful Convictions: Stepping Back, Moving Forward*. Durham, NC: Carolina Academic Press, 2014.

Reimelt, Alexandra W. "An Unjust Bargain: Plea Bargains and Waiver of the Right to Appeal." *Boston College Law Review* 51, no. 3 (2010): 871–904.

Risinger, D. Michael. "Innocents Convicted: An Empirically Justified Factual Wrongful Conviction Rate." *Journal of Criminal Law and Criminology* 97, no. 3 (2007): 761–806.

Rodriguez, Cristian G., Jake P. Moskowitz, Rammy M. Salem, and Peter H. Ditto. "Partisan Selective Exposure: The Role of Party, Ideology, and Ideological Extremity over Time." *Translational Issues in Psychological Science* 3, no. 3 (2017): 254–271.

Rogers, Steven. "Electoral Accountability for State Legislative Roll Calls and Ideological Representation." *American Political Science Review* 111, no. 3 (2017): 555–571.

Rose, Megan, and ProPublica. "The Deal Prosecutors Offer When They Have No Cards Left to Play." *Atlantic*, September 7, 2017. www.theatlantic.com.

Rudolph, Thomas J., and Jillian Evans. "Political Trust, Ideology, and Public Support for Government Spending." *American Journal of Political Science* 49, no. 3 (2005): 660–671.

Salazar, Carlita. "Time Magazine Special Edition: Commemorating 25 Years of the Innocence Project." Innocence Project, February 13, 2017. https://innocenceproject .org.

Sarat, Austin, Robert Kermes, Haley Cambra, Adelyn Curran, Margaret Kiley, and Keshav Pant. "The Rhetoric of Abolition: Continuity and Change in the Struggle against America's Death Penalty, 1900–2010." *Journal of Criminal Law and Criminology*, 107, no. 4 (2017): 757–780.

Schafer, Joseph A., Beth M. Huebner, and Timothy S. Bynum. "Citizen Perceptions of Police Services: Race, Neighborhood Context, and Community Policing." *Police Quarterly* 6, no. 4 (2003): 440–468.

Scheufele, Dietram A., and David Tewksbury. "Framing, Agenda Setting, and Priming: The Evolution of Three Media Effects Models." *Journal of Communication* 57, no. 1 (2007): 9–20.

Sentencing Project. "The Facts: Criminal Justice Facts." Accessed February 7, 2022. www.sentencingproject.org.

Shanahan, Elizabeth A., Michael D. Jones, Mark K. McBeth, and Claudio M. Radaelli. "The Narrative Policy Framework." In *Theories of the Policy Process*, 4th ed., edited by Christopher M. Weible and Paul A. Sabatier, 173–213. New York: Westview, 2018.

Simmons, Alicia D. "Cultivating Support for Punitive Criminal Justice Policies: News Sectors and the Moderating Effects of Audience Characteristics." *Social Forces* 96, no. 1 (2017): 299–328.

Smith, David. "'I Have a Responsibility to Speak about It': A Wrongfully Imprisoned Artist Making Art from His Ordeal." *Guardian*, January 20, 2022. www.theguardian .com.

Soss, Joe, Laura Langbein, and Alan R. Metelko. "Why Do White Americans Support the Death Penalty?" *Journal of Politics* 65, no. 2 (2003): 397–421.

Southall, Ashley, and Jonah E. Bromwich. "2 Men Convicted of Killing Malcolm X Will Be Exonerated after Decades." *New York Times*, November 17, 2021. www.nytimes .com.

Spangler, Todd. "Netflix Says 'When They See Us' Has Been Most-Watched Show in U.S. since Premiere." *Variety*, June 12, 2019. https://variety.com.

Squire, Peverill. "Measuring State Legislative Professionalism: The Squire Index Revisited." *State Politics and Policy Quarterly* 7, no. 2 (2007): 211–227.

———. "A Squire Index Update." *State Politics and Policy Quarterly* 17, no. 4 (2017): 361–371.

Stevenson, Bryan. *Just Mercy: A Story of Justice and Redemption.* New York: Spiegel and Grau, 2014.

Stimson, James A., Michael B. MacKuen, and Robert S. Erikson. "Dynamic Representation." *American Political Science Review* 89, no. 3 (1995): 543–565.

Sullivan, S. P. "What Happens If You're Wrongfully Convicted in N.J.?" *NJ.com,* March 11, 2017. www.nj.com.

Sullivan, Thomas P. *Police Experiences with Recording Custodial Interrogations.* Chicago: Northwestern University School of Law Center on Wrongful Convictions, 2004. https://mcadams.posc.mu.edu.

Taber, Charles S., and Milton Lodge. "Motivated Skepticism in the Evaluation of Political Beliefs." *American Journal of Political Science* 50, no. 3 (2006): 755–769.

Tal-Or, Nurit, David S. Boninger, Amir Poran, and Faith Gleicher. "Counterfactual Thinking as a Mechanism in Narrative Persuasion." *Human Communication Research* 30, no. 3 (2004): 301–328.

Tankebe, Justice. "Viewing Things Differently: The Dimensions of Public Perceptions of Police Legitimacy." *Criminology* 51, no. 1 (2013): 103–135.

Tassi, Paul. "Why 'Making a Murderer' Is Netflix's Most Significant Show Ever." *Forbes,* January 3, 2016. www.forbes.com.

Testa, Paul, and Bryce J. Dietrich. "Seeing Is Believing: How Video of Police Action Affects Criminal Justice Beliefs." Unpublished manuscript, August 24, 2017. www.brycejdietrich.com.

Thompson, Jennifer E., and Frank R. Baumgartner. "An American Epidemic: Crimes of Wrongful Liberty." Injustice Watch, April 3, 2018. www.injusticewatch .org.

Timothy Cole Exoneration Review Commission. *Report to Texas Governor Gregg Abbott, Texas Legislature, Texas Judicial Council.* December 2016. www.txcourts.gov.

Tonry, Michael. *Punishing Race: A Continuing American Dilemma.* New York: Oxford University Press, 2011.

Trabasso, Tom. "The Power of the Narrative." In *Reading, Language, and Literacy: Instruction for the Twenty-First Century,* edited by Frank Lehr and Jean Osborn, 187–200. New York: Routledge, 2009.

Turner, Broderick L., Eugene M. Caruso, Mike A. Dilich, and Neal J. Roese. "Body Camera Footage Leads to Lower Judgments of Intent than Dash Camera Footage." *Proceedings of the National Academy of Science of the United States of America* 116, no. 4 (2019): 1201–1206.

Tweel, Clay, dir. *The Innocent Man.* Parkside Films.

Tyler, Tom R. "Enhancing Police Legitimacy." *Annals of the American Academy of Political and Social Science* 593, no. 1 (2004): 84–99.

Unnever, James D., and Francis T. Cullen. "Executing the Innocent and Support for Capital Punishment: Implications for Public Policy." *Criminology and Public Policy* 4, no. 1 (2005): 3–38.

Unnever, James D., Francis T. Cullen, and Brandon K. Applegate. "Turning the Other Cheek: Reassessing the Impact of Religion on Punitive Ideology." *Justice Quarterly* 22, no. 3 (2005): 304–339.

Wambaugh, Joseph. *The Blooding: The Dramatic True Story of the First Murder Case Solved by Genetic "Fingerprinting."* New York: Bantam Books, 1989.

Warden, Rob. "First DNA Exoneration: Gary Dotson." Northwestern Center on Wrongful Convictions. Accessed March 12, 2020. www.law.northwestern.edu.

———. "First Wrongful Conviction: Jesse Boorn and Stephen Boorn." Northwestern Center on Wrongful Convictions. Accessed March 12, 2020. www.law.northwestern .edu.

———. "How and Why Illinois Abolished the Death Penalty." *Minnesota Journal of Law & Inequality* 30, no. 2 (2012): 245–286.

———. "Kirk Bloodsworth." National Registry of Exonerations. Last updated October 6, 2021. www.law.umich.edu.

Watson, Bruce. *Sacco and Vanzetti: The Men, the Murders, and the Judgment of Mankind.* New York: Viking, 2007.

Waxman, Olivia B. "President Trump Played a Key Role in the Central Park Five Case: Here's the Real History behind When They See Us." *Time*, May 31, 2019. https://time .com.

Weitzer, Ronald, and Steven A. Tuch. "Determinants of Public Satisfaction with the Police." *Police Quarterly* 8, no. 3 (2005): 279–297.

Wells, Gary L. "Applied Eyewitness-Testimony Research: System Variables and Estimator Variables." *Journal of Personality and Social Psychology* 36, no. 12 (1978): 1546–1557.

Wells, Gary L., Margaret Bull Kovera, Amy Bradfield Douglass, Neil Brewer, Christian A. Meissner, and John T. Wixted. "Policy and Procedure Recommendations for the Collection and Preservation of Eyewitness Identification Evidence." *Law and Human Behavior* 44, no. 1 (2020): 3–36.

Wells, Gary L., Mark Small, Steven Penrod, Roy S. Malpass, Solomon M. Fulero, and C. A. E. Brimacombe. "Eyewitness Identification Procedures: Recommendations for Lineups and Photospreads." *Law and Human Behavior* 22, no. 1 (1998): 1–39.

Wells, Tom, and Richard A. Leo. *The Wrong Guys: Murder, False Confessions, and the Norfolk Four.* New York: New Press, 2008.

West, Emily, and Vanessa Meterko. "Innocence Project: DNA Exonerations, 1989–2014: Review of Data and Findings from the First 25 Years." *Albany Law Review* 79, no. 3 (2015–2016): 717–795.

Westervelt, Saundra D., and Kimberly J. Cook. "Foreword." *Albany Law Review* 75, no. 3 (2011–2012): 1223–1227.

———. "Framing Innocents: The Wrongly Convicted as Victims of State Harm." *Crime, Law, and Social Change* 53 (2010): 259–275.

———. *Life after Death Row: Exonerees' Search for Community and Identity.* New Brunswick, NJ: Rutgers University Press, 2012.

Westervelt, Saundra D., and John A. Humphrey, eds. *Wrongly Convicted: Perspectives on Failed Justice.* New Brunswick, NJ: Rutgers University Press, 2001.

White, Gillian B. "Taxing the Wrongfully Convicted." *Atlantic*, February 22, 2016. www
.theatlantic.com.

Wiggins, Ovetta. "Former Maryland Death Row Inmate Receives $400,000 for His
Wrongful Imprisonment." *Washington Post*, October 6, 2021. www.washingtonpost
.com.

Witness to Innocence. "About." Accessed February 6, 2022. www.witnesstoinnocence
.org.

———. "Board." Accessed February 6, 2022. www.witnesstoinnocence.org.

Wu, Yuning. "Race/Ethnicity and Perceptions of the Police: A Comparison of White,
Black, Asian, and Hispanic Americans." *Policing & Society* 24, no. 2 (2014): 135–157.

Yant, Martin. "The Media's Muddled Message on Wrongful Convictions." In *Examining
Wrongful Convictions: Stepping Back, Moving Forward*, edited by Allison D. Redlich,
James R. Acker, Robert J. Norris, and Catherine L. Bonventre, 71–89. Durham, NC:
Carolina Academic Press, 2014.

Zalman, Marvin. "Criminal Justice System Reform and Wrongful Conviction: A Research Agenda." *Criminal Justice Policy Review* 17, no. 4 (2006): 468–492.

———. "Edwin Borchard and the Limits of Innocence Reform." In *Wrongful Convictions and Miscarriages of Justice: Causes and Remedies in North American and
European Criminal Justice Systems*, edited by C. Ronald Huff and Martin Killias,
329–356. New York: Routledge, 2013.

———. "An Integrated Justice Model of Wrongful Convictions." *Albany Law Review* 74,
no. 3 (2010–2011): 1465–1524.

Zalman, Marvin, and Julia Carrano. *Wrongful Conviction and Criminal Justice Reform:
Making Justice*. New York: Routledge, 2014.

Zalman, Marvin, Matthew J. Larson, and Brad Smith. "Citizens' Attitudes toward
Wrongful Convictions." *Criminal Justice Review* 37, no. 1 (2012): 15–69.

Zalman, Marvin, and Robert J. Norris. "Measuring Innocence: How to Think about the
Rate of Wrongful Convictions." *New Criminal Law Review* 24, no. 4 (2021): 601–654.

Zimring, Franklin E. "Police Killings as a Problem of Governance." *Annals of the
American Academy of Political and Social Science* 687, no. 1 (2020): 114–123.

INDEX

ABOUT THE AUTHORS

ROBERT J. NORRIS is Associate Professor in the Department of Criminology, Law and Society at George Mason University. He is the author of *Exonerated: A History of the Innocence Movement* and coauthor of *When Justice Fails: Causes and Consequences of Wrongful Convictions.*

WILLIAM D. HICKS is Associate Professor of Political Science at Appalachian State University. His research focuses on US political institutions, elections and election laws, criminal justice policy, and quantitative methodology.

KEVIN J. MULLINIX is Associate Professor of Political Science at the University of Kansas. His research concentrates on public opinion, political behavior, and public policy.

www.ingramcontent.com/pod-product-compliance
Lightning Source LLC
Chambersburg PA
CBHW020536030426
42337CB00013B/869